'Nothing can fully prepare us for death, but tl[...] get. More than any other book I've read on t[...] gives you directions and permission to have tl[...] or for someone you love. The shared stories o[...] sometimes funny, and the expert commentaries offer excellent advice without being too prescriptive. Of course, we may not get the death we imagined – it can be a messy and unpredictable business. But this book gave me the sense of joining in and contributing to the most important conversation we may ever have. We are all going to die, but how we do it really matters. So let's start listening and talking…'
Phil Hammond, NHS doctor, broadcaster, writer and comedian

'*Outside the Box* is just that – an entirely different sort of book about dying, death and bereavement. From editor Liz Rothschild's exquisitely written introduction, through the cornucopia of stories, both disquieting and inspirational, to the lucid and eye-opening contributions of death workers and grief counsellors, I found myself caught ineluctably into a healthy reflection on my own mortality. I exhort all those who are avoidant, bereaved or simply curious in the face of death to avail themselves of *Outside the Box* – before they or their loved ones are placed inside it.'
Robert A. Neimeyer, Director of the Portland Institute for Loss and Transition, editor of *Death Studies*

'Telling stories is fundamental to enabling people to find meaning in life and its losses. By bringing together so many people's first-hand experiences of death and dying with the wisdom and knowledge of those who work in the "death industry", this excellent book enables us to prepare better for the end of our own life's journey and make our own "departures" as good as possible – for us and for those we love and who care for us. It is a book not just for the bereaved and dying but, as the title rightly says, for the living too.'
Julia Samuel, psychotherapist, speaker and author of *Grief Works* and *This Too Shall Pass*

'Speaking as one getting ready to go (cancer), I find this book is tailor-made for me. And, unless you're banking on ducking under the Reaper's radar – which (sorry) you very definitely won't – this book is tailor-made for you too. We live in a culture that has a dysfunctional relationship with mortality. Liz Rothschild gently shows how, by taking practical steps to get ready to go, we can dispel much of our terror and do the right thing by our nearest and dearest, who would otherwise inherit a mess. And there's more. *Outside the Box* touches on myriad aspects of death, grief and funerals. Further, Liz has recruited excellent experts, and – here the book's crowning glory – she has gathered stories from all manner of ordinary folk like us. It is difficult to find a readership for books about death. I suspect this one is going to be a breakthrough.'
Charles Cowling, founder of *The Good Funeral Guide*

'This brave and practical book provides a unique and valuable resource for anyone with an interest in care for the dying. These pages will encourage and enable people so they do not find themselves, as Liz Rothschild says, saying 'I wish I'd known that…' when it is too late. *Outside the Box* is compassionate, down to earth and relevant to all who deal with people's journeys towards death and its aftermath. It is that paradox – a life-affirming book on death and dying – a universal topic that many of us find difficult to talk about due to our often-unspoken fears. This book may give you the courage to start a conversation that will make a real difference.
Dr Jo Withers, GP and founder of Finity

'This is a moving, enlightening book. What we want to read about is "lived" experience in so many spheres of our lives – what did it feel like, what might it feel like – and this book achieves this about death – a subject none of us like to think about until we have to – in all its complex psychological impacts on the heart and mind. I loved this book and will keep going back to it often.'
Juliet Rosenfeld, writer and psychotherapist

'This book is a treasure. Personal, poetic and practical, it is a remarkable and beautifully conceived handbook for anyone wishing to learn about, reflect upon and understand more deeply the universal experiences of death and dying, losing and grieving and honouring and remembering. So many of the personal stories and glimpses that Liz Rothschild has tenderly collected are extraordinarily touching, offering insights into the intimate particularities of love and loss with an immediacy and vulnerability that slow one down, move and sensitise the heart, and steadily bring one into the midst of what it is to be human. The whole offering is pervaded by down-to-earth usefulness, contemplative depth, and a generous, courageous compassion. Highly recommended.'
Chris Cullen, Buddhist teacher and psychotherapist

'I utterly loved this book. Moving between expert advice and what real people have to say is a brilliant idea. I did have to take a lot of breaks reading it. Some of the things people wrote I wanted to just sit with and digest for a while. A few times I was crying with laughter, and other stories just brought me to tears. Not one of the accounts was exactly the same as another, and that is pretty much the point. We aren't the same in life; we aren't the same in death; we aren't the same as the person we were before someone left us. As I reflect back on the book as a whole, three things really stick with me: you need to have a conversation about what you want to happen with you when you are gone; you have to give people permission to do anything or everything that you would like, or to do nothing, and how much you spend on their funeral does not equate to how much you love someone.'
Lucy Coulbert, The Individual Funeral Company and Coulbert Family Funerals

OUTSIDE THE BOX

EVERYDAY STORIES OF DEATH, BEREAVEMENT AND LIFE

EDITED BY
LIZ ROTHSCHILD

PCCS BOOKS

First published 2020

PCCS Books Ltd
Wyastone Business Park
Wyastone Leys
Monmouth
NP25 3SR
United Kingdom

contact@pccs-books.co.uk
www.pccs-books.co.uk

This collection © Liz Rothschild, 2020
The individual chapters © the contributors, 2020
The illustrations © the artists, 2020

All rights reserved.
No part of this publication may be reproduced, stored in a retrieval system, transmitted or utilised in any form by any means, electronic, mechanical, photocopying or recording or otherwise, without permission in writing from the publishers.

The authors have asserted their right to be identified as the authors
of this work in accordance with the Copyright, Designs and Patents Act 1988.

Outside the Box: everyday stories of death, bereavement and life

British Library Cataloguing in Publication data: a catalogue record for this book is available from the British Library.

ISBN paperback – 978 1 910919 63 7
          epub – 978 1 910919 74 3

Cover design by Jason Anscomb
Typeset using Minion Pro and Myriad Pro
Printed in the UK by Severnprint, Gloucester

Contents

	Introduction Liz Rothschild	*1*
1	Getting ready	*7*
	Commentaries	
	Making a death plan – Jane Duncan Rogers	*13*
	Your digital legacy – James Norris	*21*
2	The departure lounge	*25*
	Commentaries	
	Preparing for death – Bob Whorton	*32*
	Counselling at death's door – Helen Kewell	*37*
3	Far too soon	*47*
	Commentary	
	The death of a child: stillbirth, neonatal and postnatal deaths – Jen Coates, Helen Pepler	*51*
4	The wisdom of children	*65*
	Commentaries	
	Helping children and young people through bereavement – Sarah Harris	*72*
	Deaths in military families – Helen Fisher	*78*
5	Out of the blue	*85*
	Commentaries	
	Sudden death and disappearance – Debbie Collins	*97*
	The shock of death – Dr Pat Johnson	*102*
6	Dementia	*111*
	Commentary	
	Living and dying with dementia – Hazel May	*114*
7	It's not all about humans	*123*
	Commentaries	
	When a pet dies – Diane James	*132*
	When it's time: euthanasia – Sophie Stainer	*136*
8	What is dying like?	*141*
	Commentaries	
	Dying in hospital – Dr Andrew Jenks	*151*
	What happens at death – Deb Wilkes	*155*
9	Now what?	*163*
	Commentary	
	After the death – Liz Rothschild	*172*

10	The funeral	*183*
	Commentaries	
	A good funeral – Fran Hall	*194*
	Funeral poverty – Rosie Inman-Cook	*198*
11	Grieving and remembering	*207*
	Commentary	
	Life after a death – Dr Marilyn Relf	*223*
12	Death as a teacher	*235*
	Commentary	
	What death teaches us about life – Liz Rothschild	*247*
13	The wider view *– Liz Rothschild*	*255*
	Postscript: Covid-19 *– Liz Rothschild*	*273*
	The storytellers	*279*
	The artists	*281*

Illustrations

Bird on a diving board (pen drawing) Wren Hughes	vii
Sprouting bulbs (pen and watercolour) Julia Ball	ix
Gestalt (collage) Hugh Cowling	x
Way through the woods (fine pen drawing) Sarah Woolfenden	6
Threshold (ink) Wren Hughes	24
Cherry blossom (papercut) Rowan Twine	46
My family (felt pen) Louis Debonnaire Ward	64
Whitfield tabernacle (lithograph) Jemma Gunning	84
Tangle (pen and ink) Clare Davis	110
Jacob (line drawing) Cathy Turbinskyj	122
Skeleton leaf (monoprint) Hugh Cowling	140
Cyrraedd Enlli (lino cut) Thomas Williams	162
Pattern (ink and crayon on black paper) Halima Cassell	182
In the wilds (woodcut) Thomas Williams	206
A winter Eden (lithograph/print) Meg Buick	234
Starling murmuration (detail) (willow charcoal) Kate Lynch	254
River under A64 (etching) Jake Attree	272
Townscape (linocut) Rowan Twine	278
The nest (handprinted from ink drawing) Carol Honess	286

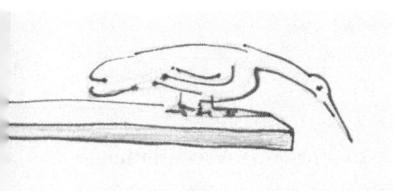

Dedication

Every single one of us has a story to share about death. Many remain untold. We are all the poorer for that. With huge gratitude to all those brave enough to share their stories with me.

About the editor

Liz Rothschild is a writer, actor and founding director of Westmill Woodland Burial Ground in Wiltshire. She has been a funeral celebrant for more than 25 years and has run numerous death cafés and a course on preparing for end of life. In 2012 she launched, and continues to curate, the biennial Kicking the Bucket festival in Oxford. She also wrote and performs a one-woman show, *Outside the Box – a live show about death*, which premiered in 2016 and has toured the UK and US. Many of the stories in this book come from her audiences.

Acknowledgements

Thank you to: All my amazing storytellers, my audiences, the Friends and Family group and staff at Westmill and my expert commentators. You have all taught me so much. Adam Twine, my partner, and my daughter Rowan and son Laurie, for bearing with my prevailing obsession with mortality. Catherine Jackson and the rest of the team at PCCS Books, for backing the idea of a book about death by an unknown author and guiding me through the process with patience, humour and skill. Deb Wilkes, for picking up and running with any question I threw at her. Edie Campbell, for her support of my work and generosity with her resources and contacts. Lucy Coulbert, for research support. Rose-Anne O'Hare, for seeking out dementia stories.

Eleanor Brown, Meredith Debonnaire and Pat Johnson, for taking on jobs my brain could not manage and thus keeping me nominally sane. Jo Bousfield, for directing my show that led to this book and then giving feedback on an early draft. Margaret Robbins, for her constructive suggestions on a later version, and Witney Book group, for reading some of the chapters and giving me their comments. Razia Aziz, for helping me improve the lack of diverse content through her networks. The HandsOn and Phoenix Rising groups, for letting me visit them and sharing their stories for the same purpose. Rosie Inman-Cook of the Natural Death Centre, for her unfailing willingness to answer any question and always at breakneck speed.

And everyone who I have forgotten at this crucial moment, with my apologies. I could not have done this without any of you.

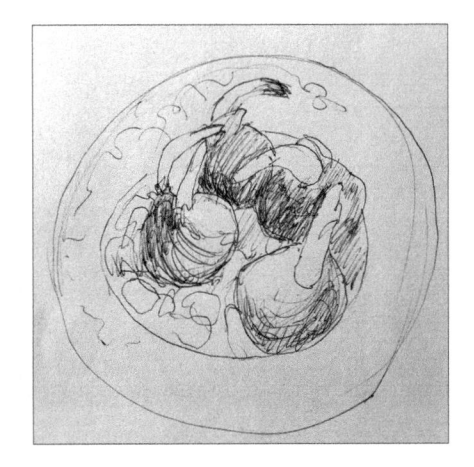

x

Introduction

Stories are how I have always navigated the world. They have taught me how to live. The stories in this book come from my own life, from the people I work with and from my audiences during the performances of my one-person show, *Outside the Box – a live show about death,* which has been on tour since 2016. This is a collective, contradictory cornucopia of wisdom concerning a subject many of us never talk about.

Whenever I receive an email headed 'I thought this might interest you' or 'I saw this and thought of you,' I know what it is going to be about. I am the go-to person in my circle of friends and local community for all matters relating to death. How did this happen? I like a good laugh, flamboyant dancing, delicious food and cheerful arguments. I like life. So how did death become my bag?

Like most of us, I remember the first time death featured in my life. My cat was knocked down and killed while I was at school. When I walked in the door of our home, my mother was there, waiting to tell me. She was crying. I have to be honest and say that I was more disturbed by her tears than by the loss of the cat. Don't think badly of me; it felt as though a tremor passed through my sense of reality; I had never seen my mother cry. The world felt less stable. My own tears came later. When my gran died – rather invisibly – I remember my mother coming to tell me in the middle of the night. I did not go to the funeral. I felt sad but not overwhelmed. I did start to think about the fact that life seemed to have an end and, when I wrote the long version of my address into my schoolbooks, I began to wonder if the Universe or Outer Space was where everyone ended up. But how?

The death that really shocked and upset me was that of one of my contemporaries. I was in my early 30s. It was a sudden and unexpected death (page 169). She fell ill and, within 24 hours, she was dead. No compromises, no second chances. She was gone and we had to deal with it. The received sense of how things should be done did not match our thoughts and feelings about what was appropriate. As her daughter and our circle of close friends worked out how to create her funeral, we drew closer together, pushed back on assumptions and took events into our own hands. I found myself thrust forward as the mistress of ceremonies. It was a tender and joyous day. I turned out to have the right skill-set (writing, public speaking, events management and a profound curiosity about people). I started to get asked to conduct weddings (not the legal bit), namings and other significant life passages. It came very naturally. I became a celebrant as well as a theatre practitioner. Through this work I was allowed into people's lives at some of the most raw, joyous and intimate times. I realised the profound quality of connection that is possible at these times. I found the work around death to be both the most challenging and the most rewarding.

Fast forward a few years and, in 2000, I set up Westmill Woodland Burial Ground in Oxfordshire, on my partner's organic farm. I wanted the flexibility my own site could offer everyone and the chance to build a community out of the families and friends associated with the place. This began to happen. Some funerals took all afternoon and turned into picnics, with people playing music; others lasted barely 20 minutes. Some were entirely managed by the family and friends, including bearing and lowering; others involved a vicar or Buddhist monk and the local undertakers. Coffins arrived in gleaming hearses, in white vans or, on one occasion, on a specially converted motorcycle sidecar, so the dead person could have one last burn down the M4. People met one another at the regular events we held at the burial ground and some struck up friendships, walking alongside one another for a while.

However, by the time many people came to us, it felt as if they were already being whisked along on the death travelator. Often the death occurred without any clear guidance as to their wishes from the person who had died. The bereaved were upset and feeling under pressure to get everything organised – not a good place from which to try to think carefully about the best course of action. This began to trouble me. Why do 70% of people in Britain die without writing a will or letter of wishes? Why do perfectly kind people cross the road to avoid talking to a recently bereaved friend? Why aren't we supposed to talk about any of this stuff? I have always enjoyed giving taboos a good poke, and here was another chance.

I decided to organise a fortnight-long festival of living and dying, in Oxford. I wanted to call it *Kicking the Bucket – a festival of living and dying.* There was a lot of nervousness about the title: 'You can't call it that.' I did. I wanted to signal that we can be humourous about death. Events to do with death can be beautiful, informative, surprising and fun. We might shed a few tears, but that's appropriate.

People came to performances, workshops and discussions. They decorated a coffin and we held a Day of the Dead ceilidh. People talked over coffee, made some end-of-life plans and picked up free resources. One woman said it had been the best two weeks of her life. For a brief moment, we put down our masks of immortality and felt a bit less lonely. We realised we weren't the only ones nursing a range of hopes and fears about our lives and how they might end, and that made us all feel safer.

Then it was over, leaving some valuable ripples in a fairly small geographic area. What next? I decided it was time to climb back on stage and tour a show based on the stories I had gathered over the years and to seek out more stories from around the country. *Outside the Box – a live show about death* has been performed in theatres, arts centres, conference centres, pubs, hospices, hospitals, village halls, houses, festivals and muddy fields. And everywhere I go, I have the same experience. It is as if the whole audience relaxes and breathes out as the stories unfold – because there is so much we want to say and ask but feel we can't. We worry that we might upset someone, that we might get upset ourselves. At the end, in the post-show discussions, invariably the audience starts telling each other their stories, giving advice and getting outraged, informed and moved. This can last as long as the show, and once it went on for two hours. We were in a pub; I think that helped. Some people write their stories down and we share them on our website; some email them afterwards. You can read every story we have received at *www.fullcircleproductions.org.uk*

I wanted the stories to travel further and reach more people – people who might not look at a website or are unable to do so; people who prefer to hold words in their hands – and so, with the skill and support of the PCCS Books team, this book came into being.

My hope is that the book will attract a general readership and also be of benefit to professionals looking to expand their understanding of death, dying and bereavement. Thank you for picking it up. That may have required some courage. I hope you will find yourself at home among this community of storytellers. There are voices here I am sure you will chime with, and others that I hope will surprise or even provoke you. It is a rare chance to hear such a wide variety of people talking so openly about their experiences of death, bereavement and life in 20th and 21st century Britain. It is also confirmation of my belief that, despite received attitudes, we do want to talk about death, if we can only find the right way to begin the conversation. Maybe this book will help you do just that, with yourself or others.

Some stories included here are very short indeed, scribbled on a small index card after a performance or emailed to me later. Others are much longer – these tend to be the ones I sought out to ensure we covered certain important themes. The families I work with at Westmill Woodland Burial Ground are predominantly, but not exclusively, white. So too are my audiences, to my regret. They have also been largely female and middle class, although this is not the case in my role as a celebrant and burial ground manager. Many, although not all, by any means, are non-religious. All these factors have shaped the collection. I have actively worked to restore the balance, but it is still not as diverse as I would have hoped. Some stories come from other countries. This does not offer a comprehensive overview of wider practices, but each glimpse into another approach shines a light on our own and invites questions about what we might learn or what we have lost. All the stories are presented anonymously to protect the identities of those who wish to be anonymous. However, the names of the storytellers who so chose are listed alphabetically at the end of the book. Some have deliberately made their identity visible in their story.

It has become clear to me that those of us working in this field need to become more acutely aware of the wide range of needs of different religious and ethnic communities and make sure the information we offer is sensitive to that. There is a lot of work still to be done on this. People with learning disabilities have often also been overlooked. The LeDeR programme at Bristol has worked to address some of this. And, until quite recently, the dying and bereaved in the LGBTQIA community were often treated with profound insensitivity.

This is not a book about what happens after we die, although that is sometimes referred to. Rather, it is about how to prepare for and accompany the dying and the bereaved. I do not imagine you will necessarily read all the way through at first. Perhaps you will just read the stories or seek out a particular chapter that seems relevant to you and then return when you need different advice. I hope the book will accompany you through life and enable you to help others too. It may be that your work means you are very familiar with some aspects of the content but not with others. I hope the book will become a trusted friend.

I have chosen to embrace abortions with pre-term deaths because, although I know the journey towards them is very different, I wanted to acknowledge the pain that suffuses all of these losses with the judgements that can be projected or felt. The chapter on animal deaths is important because for many people their primary relationship is with an animal, or becomes so, and the impact of these deaths is constantly underestimated. There is little written currently about dementia and death, so I am delighted to include this. Funeral poverty is rising exponentially and is a national scandal of which we should all be aware. The final chapter is perhaps the point of it all for me, because it speaks to the enormous value of death as a teacher about life. The remaining chapters are, I think, self-explanatory.

The commentaries were contributed by a range of people with special expertise, interest and experience in the particular topic of the chapter. They are intended to provide a wider context for the stories and to offer the reader helpful advice and some resources. The resources can never hope to be comprehensive; they are chosen by the commentators, sometimes with my own additions.

Some of the stories have been cut slightly but the words are as I received them from the contributors; I have not changed the language. This is how the teller chose to express themselves and I have honoured their individual voices.

The images are intended not to illustrate but to thread their own narrative through the book. The invitation is to let them speak to you in their own voice and see what memories and meanings they evoke for you. It may be that simply spending some time looking at one of them brings more insight than any number of words.

Finally, this is not the end of the story. I invite you to contact us and share your stories so this resource of human experience and wisdom, of which this book is only the tip, can continue to grow and offer comfort and inspiration. Your story might make all the difference to someone who comes across it just at the moment when they need it most.

To get in touch and share your stories, visit *www.fullcircleproductions.org.uk*

Liz Rothschild
Westmill Woodland Burial Ground
September, 2020

Outside the Box

1 – Getting ready

Writing a will

A will-writer told me that, when she sits down with most people to start planning their wills, they say 'If I die'. She wants to say 'When, When!' but she doesn't. She picks up her pen and takes notes.

Alone

I have spoken to 'death professionals' and told them I wish to have a quick cremation. No coffin. No ceremony. No celebration. Then I realised it was like I felt I didn't matter. Just body disposal. I believe this is what awaits me. No family. Few friends.

Bad advice

I have been talking to my insurance people about my funeral plan. I have already paid the full amount and I am not dead yet. I said, 'Can I stop paying now?' They said, 'No. If you do, you lose the lot.' That's not right is it? I am going to make an appointment with the Citizen's Advice and see if they can help me. I don't think it's fair, do you? I have been paying too much every month. £30 – it's a lot of money. I was badly advised.

What do you want?

I asked my mother what my grandma wanted for her funeral (my grandma was very unwell at the time and had Parkinson's, so I thought it a pertinent question). My mother got so angry at me. I then asked my sister if she knew. She started crying and said she didn't want to think about it. What surprises me about death is that the people you thought you knew really well react completely differently.

A Korean solution

Recently there has been a sharp rise in depression and suicide among office workers in South Korea. In 2016, the national suicide rate was almost double the global average. The solution? Living funeral courses. Workers get to write their own will and read it out. They dress up in a traditional hemp burial robe and lie in a coffin with the lid nailed down for 10 minutes. I picture rows of them lying there. Imagining not being. Imagining not imagining. Turns out mortality can be quite bracing. They go back to work with a spring in their step.

Call me by my name
A friend, an old lady, always known by her middle name, hated her first name and, at 94 years old, changed it by deed poll so that when she died, or was in hospital, she would be referred to by the name of her choice.

Sticky labels
My 90-year-old stepmother-in-law has put sticky labels on the bottom of all her favourite ornaments and pictures with the names of who she wants to give them to. She's also highlighted in her phone book all the numbers of the people we need to contact to tell about her death and invite to her funeral.

My possessions
I talked to my children about which of my possessions they'd like. My son said 'The hose and the car'. Middle daughter said 'Just the book you used to record the wild flowers you've seen'. Youngest daughter went about the house with a clipboard!

We'll make it up as we go along
Nothing prepares you. I really thought I had got my head round my mortality. It has been my habit to live each day in awareness of my inevitable demise. I have contended with the social taboo around death by talking about it a lot. But, just as there are no rehearsals for being born, no induction, no info pack, no mentoring, there's no knowing what it's going to feel like and how the world is going to look when the doctor with the biopsy results tells you that you have cancer. No white-out shock in my case; more a growing realisation over the succeeding days that my membership of the living had been quietly revoked. The eyes of others gave me to understand that I was different now, no longer one of them but… detaching. On a different trajectory. Dying.

When I was first diagnosed, I saw myself as the central character in the drama of my dying. I soon learned that I'm not; I'm incidental. In the run-up to my death, it's my partner and loved ones whose lives will be disrupted by chores and ordeals. They need to have agency. After I have gone, they're going to have to carry on and reconfigure their lives. So I have learned the vital importance of keeping nothing to myself. I share my feelings, I negotiate plans and I'm prescriptive about nothing. Some people plan their funerals in narcissistic detail. What dreadful manners. My funeral will be about me, yes, but, and here's the point, *for them*. If we talk enough about everything while we can, they'll know what they need to do.

Together we'll make it up as we go along. Because that's how life is. And there'll likely come a time in this protracted, medically induced process when the doctor will say, 'I'm terribly sorry but there's nothing more we can do.' And I suspect that, when she does, it will come as a relief. Lord now lettest thou thy servant depart in peace. Death is a perfectly normal and natural event, after all.

My dad

I am very proud of my dad, James O'Hare. He has always been extremely hard-working and put his family first. He never complains, despite many health problems, and has always picked himself up, dusted himself off and started all over again! He still lives completely independently as a widower.

I wanted to mark him reaching the grand old age of 90 in a unique way. Old age is a time when we reflect on our lives and consider our regrets, achievements and what our life has meant. But this is seldom acknowledged or talked about. I believe it is an important part of preparing for death. I work with the elderly, the bereaved, people who have been preparing for their death, and I help out at a woodland burial ground. It occurred to me that deep emotions were being expressed and wonderful things were being said about people at their funerals. But the person wasn't hearing or experiencing any of this. It felt like something we should be expressing and sharing before the person we love dies. For me this was an opportunity to celebrate my Dad's life while he was still living it so that he could hear, see and be part of a commemoration of who he is and the things he has achieved. I contacted his family and friends for photos and memories and I recorded his occasional reminiscences of his youth. I then produced a book of memories and photos of his 90 years and a short Life Story based on his and others' reminiscences. I also wrote a song, as did a friend of his. These were all shared at his party. He loved every minute of it. Now he has them as a testament to the people who have known and loved him through his life and the people he has influenced and loved.

A celebration of life

When my daughter, Harry, aged 30, was told by the medics that there was no more they could do for her spinal cancer and that she had about a year to live, she decided to have a pre-death get-together of the people who were significant to her, to celebrate her life and mark the approaching end. She invited 24 people to a wheelchair-accessible venue with a large kitchen/dining room and a spacious, comfortable lounge. People came from far and wide, as they do for funerals. Most invitees felt nervous about the event; some felt it was inappropriate. Harry was an actor/musician/artist and had many friends and family with similar skills. Her invitation had requested that, if guests would like to offer a memory, story, poem, song, interpretive dance or suchlike – for the 'after lunch spot' – that would be welcomed. As her mother, I wanted to contribute, but felt that I wouldn't have the emotional strength to stand up and say how much I loved her or tell stories of her childhood. What could I offer? I had given her life and had not been able to prevent her death. With those haunting thoughts, I decided the only thing I could do was dance. A musician friend turned a choral composition of Harry's into a street-dance piece, which included Harry's partner rapping and various young friends singing the three-part melody. Another friend of hers did the choreography for two boys aged eight and 12 (who had been invited to the party) and me. I was 61 years old. We met about five times to rehearse. It was exhausting. I found it hard to remember the moves. But we danced brilliantly and gradually the audience got more and more excited. Harry said afterwards, 'I was in ecstasy watching you – thinking, That's My Mum.'

Finally, she took three photos because there were so many of us. We printed them out and joined them together. The photo is extraordinary because 23 people are looking at Harry, the photographer, with love and attention. They are all seated on sofas and the floor. Like they're on a magic carpet that will go with her wherever she goes. I put this photo into her coffin with her four months later. It was a comforting feeling for me that these people accompanied her into the fire. By holding that pre-death party, her family and friends were able to face the loss of her publicly, in the safety of her live presence, and it was an unmeasurable gift.

Transition and rebirth

I took part in a profound ceremony that involved digging my own grave and then spending the night in it. Once in, it was covered with planks, tarpaulin and then earth. The idea was to meet one's own death and to reflect on life – a transition and rebirth. I spent the night singing! Very moving and profound experience.

Wardrobe coffin

I wanted to tell you about my father's coffin – made by him, to fit, about 10 years ago. A beautiful work of art. It serves now (he's still alive) as his wardrobe. Shelves for folded shirts. Rail to hang clothes. Coats to hang on the side, handles fashioned into hooks, his shoes at the bottom. The beauty of this is how he has made into furniture, made commonplace, what scares the rest of us to death. On the outside front are pictures (framed photographs) of his four wives and four children. The four wives are at his feet!

Visions of the future...

I am quietly preparing myself for the inevitable… the day my husband dies and

I am alone. He is quite a bit older than me, so this seems the likely course of things. I was speaking with a friend who lost her husband six months ago and she said one of the things she misses most is hearing her husband's footsteps on the drive and him putting the key in the lock and coming in to greet her.

Several hours later, I was at home and I heard the latch to our back gate open and my husband walked in the back door and greeted me. My eyes filled with tears and I felt first-hand what my friend was speaking about. Thankfully, my husband and I were able to talk about the feelings and dissipate the fear, knowing it will happen one day.

Understanding death

My son James has a learning disability. He is 43 now, but it took him well into his 30s to understand death. An old drama teacher of his, and a good friend, died suddenly. James was bereft. I tried to normalise it for him. I explained that all people die. 'One day Grandad will die, James.' 'I know,' he replied. 'And Grandma will too.' 'Yes, I know,' he said. 'And me and Dad.' 'Yes, yes, I know,' he said. 'And then, one day, you'll die too.' He was visibly shocked. 'What?' he shouted. This was complete news to him and took him a long time to understand.

Turn away or turn toward

My friend was diagnosed with inoperable pancreatic cancer in January 2013, a few months after she had returned from a three-month retreat in the mountains of northern Spain, where she had received her new Buddhist name, Candrasri, meaning 'She who is the light of the moon'. Candrasri gave a talk to a gathered group of Buddhist friends and some of her family in June of that year, in the auditorium of the beautiful Georgian theatre that is home to the Cambridge Buddhist Centre. During the course of a moving and inspiring evening, Candrasri told us how confidence in her Buddhist practice was helping her to face her death at 68, when she still had so much to live for. She described her shock, sadness and grief when she was given her prognosis. But gradually she found herself becoming more reconciled. She realised, as never before, that she had a choice – to turn away, or to turn towards the situation. With that simple awareness, she reflected, came relief. I still feel the ripples of her words years later. 'The times of most suffering can also provide us with the greatest opportunities,' she said. 'If only we can embrace what might seem to be irreconcilable feelings.'

When I die…

When I die, I would like my ashes to be put into (good quality!) transparent pens with my name and dates of birth and death on the side in beautiful gold letters. These can be given to as many people as want them (and refilled as required if someone bites off the end absent-mindedly!).

In the way

As a farmer's wife, I decided I'd like to be buried right in the centre of our biggest, flattest field, with a fabulous view over several farms. I told my family to bury me (using a fore-end loader to dig the grave) and plant an oak sapling on top, so that every time my son ploughed, drilled, cultivated and harvested this field, he'd have to go around me, so I'd be remembered (and probably cursed!) for my independence and bloody-mindedness.

Practical solution

My mother died in Somerset. We live in York. At the time all our children were in the middle of exams. We decided not to have a funeral in Somerset and instructed the undertaker to cremate her body and send the ashes to us in the post. We later scattered her ashes in a family ceremony in a lovely green lane near York. Her (few) friends in Somerset discovered later and were appalled and held a memorial tea party to remember her. My mother had expressed no wishes. I still wonder what I should have done.

Not for resuscitation

In the day unit of our hospice, it is policy to have a conversation with all new patients about their resuscitation wishes. I was approaching the topic with the usual sensitive explanation when the woman in front of me unbuttoned her blouse and proudly displayed a tattoo emblazoned across her chest. It showed a large red heart and below that the words 'Do not resuscitate'. The easiest and most entertaining DNR conversation I've ever had.

Digital legacy

I was driving to work and just pulling into the car park when my phone rang. It was my father-in-law, sounding very wobbly. I said, 'Is everything OK?' and he said 'No.' Eventually he said that my husband had died. He told me he had hanged himself in a churchyard. My biggest concern was what I was going to tell our daughter. She was our only child and she and Matt were so close. She was only seven at the time. What would she remember? I got loads of information from charities who help with bereavement and suicide about how to help her. They suggested I make her a book with lots of photographs so she could remember all the wonderful things she had done with her dad. To keep the memory alive. And that was when I realised I didn't have many photographs. They were all on his phone, and I did not know any of his passwords. I went to the Apple shop and asked them to unlock his phone. They were very sorry but no, on privacy grounds. I was told the only way you can change this is with an order from the court and that would mean you would have to sue Apple – take them to court. Then, by amazing luck, a friend introduced me to a man who is a reputational lawyer working with a lot of celebrities, and he was intrigued by the case and shocked at what had happened and said he would like to help. When we finally got to court, the judge agreed it was ridiculous and we won. It took us three years to beat Apple but now we have those precious photographs back. We have our past back. I really hope my case will make it easier for others who find themselves in the same position through no fault of their own. We all need to wake up.

Commentaries
Making a death plan – Jane Duncan Rogers

Jane is founder of the social enterprise Before I Go Solutions and author of *Gifted By Grief: a true story of cancer, loss and rebirth* and *Before I Go: the essential guide to creating a good end of life plan.* Jane is also a popular and inspirational coach and motivational speaker. Under the training arm of Before I Go Solutions, she leads the B.I.G. accredited training for those wishing to train in the Before I Go Method® and spread this work to their local communities. Jane's mission is to have end-of-life plans become as commonplace as birth plans.

When people think about getting ready, or planning in advance, they almost always think about the funeral. It is easy to assume that, if you have a funeral plan, you have everything taken care of, but a funeral plan is, in fact, just one small part of a whole end-of-life plan.

However, even when people do know about all the other components required to prepare well for end of life, they still don't really want to do it – or they say they do, but just can't get round to it.

Even with the will, although most know they really ought to have one, still 60% don't. Why is this?

Here are some of the most common reasons given to me:

- What if I change my mind about what I've written down?
- It seems so final.
- My husband won't talk about it.
- I haven't found a solicitor I like for the legal stuff.
- I can't decide what to give to whom.
- It's a minefield and I just don't want to go there.
- I can't decide who could be my executor/guardian of my children.
- I'm worried I will upset family members.
- I think I should distribute it all equally, but I have a much stronger relationship with some family members than others, therefore that's not fair.

- I'd rather focus on life while I can.
- I'll be dead, so why should I care?

Do you recognise any of these?

Statistics show that 100% of us will die. That means you, reading this book. It means your family, your friends, your neighbours. When my husband died, I discovered that the only way to cope with the feelings was to allow them to be there, fully, even though I would rather have locked the door and barred the windows against them. What I learnt was that, if I opened the back door of my house wide too, then the feelings came and went again. It was when I was trying to keep them out that they hung around and caused trouble.

It's the same if you feel scared or some trepidation about contemplating your own or someone else's death. However, it almost always happens that, once faced up to, once the fear is admitted and given a bit of space, it is less emotional than people think. Especially when someone is in the last years of their life, or has a terminal diagnosis.

So, having acknowledged that it might be alarming to think about someone else's death (even if you're okay with your own end of life), let's look at what it really means to 'get ready'.

Getting ready for anything is often made easier with a plan, and it's my aim to have a world where end-of-life plans are as commonplace as birth plans. We all know that a birth plan doesn't necessarily go according to that plan, but it really helps the mother, the father and the professionals to know how everyone wants the birth to go, as an ideal. Because then it can be prepared for.

But traditionally we haven't done this with the end of life. Yes, people know they need to make a will, and they are familiar with funerals and making the choice between being buried or cremated. If you have all this clear in your own mind, you're probably patting yourself on the back. And it *is* good – it's just not quite good enough.

Why? Because these days we are all living longer, but not necessarily in good health. And poor health, or just the effects of ageing, requires us to think about it in advance; otherwise, we minimise our chances of living a vibrant life to the full, right up until we die.

So, part of thinking about ageing and end-of-life matters includes having a plan.

Some of the stories in this chapter illustrate aspects of what is in a good plan, but they also illustrate that people find this subject difficult to talk about. But talking about end-of-life matters is crucial to the planning stage; otherwise, after you've gone, there may be unwelcome surprises for those left behind.

The chapter on funerals expands our thinking about funerals, and the chapter on what dying is like advises on how to prepare for the physical process of dying. I am going to concentrate on the equally important but often overlooked areas of:

- powers of attorney (for healthcare and finance)
- advance decisions or directives ('living wills')
- advance statements and care planning
- your household (finances, secrets, emotional wills and all your stuff!)
- living legacy.

And I will start with the very obvious suggestion: that you create a death folder or workbook where you store the information below, or where it is lodged and can be readily accessed.

Powers of attorney (for healthcare and finance)

A power of attorney (PoA) is when you appoint someone to act on your behalf in respect of your health and finances, should you be unable to act for yourself. There are separate powers for health and finances and they can be held by different people. A PoA is a legal document and needs to be applied for and registered. But setting it up takes time and it's important to note that you can complete the registration in advance. You only activate the PoA when you need to, but if you wait until then before applying, you may be too late, especially if the problem is dementia and loss of decision-making capacity.

If you are not fazed by legal language or the thought of completing a legal document and you are okay with filling out forms online, then you can do it yourself, and it is not that difficult (see Resources). Or you could get together with a group of friends or family to complete the forms. Make it a project; it could even be enjoyable! You will need to pay the fee to have it registered.

If you are someone who can't bear the thought of this, then get a solicitor to help you. The cost will be worth paying if trying to do it yourself is going to distress or worry you. You will pay for the registration (as above) and any legal fees for the solicitor to do it on your behalf.

Shop around, as prices for this can vary enormously.

You can ask anyone to be your PoA. It doesn't need to be a family member; it can be a suitable friend, colleague, your accountant or solicitor. It *is* a big responsibility – but it is also an honour. So, think widely and wisely about who would be suitable, from both the financial and healthcare points of view.

Advance decisions/directives

This used to be called a 'living will' and is the document where you state what kind of medical treatment you *do not wish* to be given in your last days/weeks. In England and Wales, where it is known as an advance decision, it is a legal document. Not everyone (including doctors) knows that this is so, but it is, and it has to be respected (so long as it is valid). In Northern Ireland and Scotland (where it is known as an advance directive), at the time of writing, it is not a legal document, but doctors are required to consider your wishes if you have written them down as such.

In my experience, this is one of the areas that many people find the most challenging. It's no wonder – who wants to think about being incapacitated and unable to make their own decisions about their finances and how they want to be treated if they are dying or very unwell? It is really uncomfortable. But there is a way to do this that makes it much easier. Simply ask yourself: 'If I had become incapacitated yesterday, what would I have wanted?'

The more you do right now, the easier it will be later on, should you find yourself in that situation. Think of it like insurance – you hope you will never need to use it, but it's there just in case. Bear in mind, it needs to be regularly reviewed, because the forms have a limited shelf life, but this is as it should be – our circumstances and perspective change as we grow older. If you make an advance directive with your GP, it will not necessarily be automatically recorded on any hospital system, so someone needs to keep track of this – ideally, the person you have nominated to have PoA for your health and welfare. If you request a Do Not Resuscitate (DNR) form, bear in mind that this is very specific to cardio-pulmonary resuscitation (CPRDNR); it doesn't cover other treatments that could be life-prolonging, such as treatment with antibiotics.

Advance statement and care planning

Your advance statement is where you write down the care you *would like* in your final days – for example, where you would ideally like to die – home, hospital, hospice – what kind of atmosphere you would like, who you would like to visit you and be there at your death (if anyone), as well as the kinds of food and drink you prefer, music and TV preferences and so forth. Research by Compassion In Dying (2015) has found that people who have recorded their wishes in this way are 41% more likely to have 'good death'. Ideally you will also have discussed these preferences with the person who holds the PoA for your health and welfare.

Together, the advance statement, the advance directive or advance decision and your wishes about resuscitation form your advance care plan. In Scotland, there is also a document known as an anticipatory care plan, which more usually applies to people with long-term health conditions and covers what they would like to happen if their condition changes, as well as health improvement issues and staying well, but it is also applicable to palliative care.

Your household

Hardly anyone I have met has thought about this subject in advance, and nor would I, except that I found out the hard way how important it is. My husband had died about three weeks earlier and I was on my own in the house for the first time. I turned on the TV and it didn't show the screen I was used to. I could not for the life of me find my way to where all the programmes were showing. It sounds mad now, but I was grieving and all sorts of odd things happen then. All I could think about was that my husband would have sorted this out if he had been there. It made a horrible situation much worse.

Many of us take on different roles in a shared household, so it is understandable that, when one person dies, another family member has to take up that role. But it is not easy at the best of times, and especially not when you and/or other family members are bereaved. Think about it – who knows how to work the appliances in your house? The washing machine, the boiler, the cooker, the computer technology, the garden machinery? None of this is utterly crucial – but having thought about it beforehand and written down simple instructions, or even where the instructions are, is really helpful. If you live alone, this is incredibly useful information to leave out in an obvious place where others can easily find it – a kind of household manual that describes the running of your house. Whoever comes in to take care of things is likely also to be in the throes of grief, and is quite likely to be someone who doesn't know these things, so anything that can be done to make their lives easier is a very good idea.

Finances also feature highly under this heading. If you had died yesterday, would you be leaving a mess or a muddle for your spouse/partner/children/executor to sort out? Can you put your hand on your heart right now and say that they would know exactly where to find all your bank account details, how many there are, how to get into them if they are online, all your relevant passwords and where to find your credit cards? A simple spreadsheet that you keep up to date will be fine, so long as you make sure the relevant people have easy access to it (and take the necessary security precautions as to passwords, of course). There are companies (see Resources) that will keep your passwords safe and enable you effortlessly to connect to all the websites you regularly use. Simplifying all these can improve your everyday life, never mind your death. The more you do now to ensure this information is up to date, the easier it will be for those you leave behind because, when you are grieving, it is really common to find even day-to-day decisions impossible and for muddled thinking to be the norm. This is a time when people can more easily be taken in by a scam (that happened to me; I lost £400) or discover their ready-meal supper has ended up in the bathroom cabinet.

Another issue that comes under the 'Household' heading is often forgotten about – secrets. If you know somebody is likely to find out something about you or your family by going through your papers after you die, and it may be harmful in some way, then you need to take care of this in plenty of time. A friend of mine with a terminal illness decided she was going to burn all her journals. That was a lot of journals – she'd been writing them for 50 years and she had kept them all. She decided she didn't want her children or grandchildren to read everything she'd written. So she had a big bonfire of her journals and felt amazing doing it. She hadn't expected to feel so released. If you have this kind of information, whether in journals and diaries or on your computer, consider whether you really want what is written there to be read after you have gone. If you want it read, then why not when you are alive? Make a conscious decision about this.

If you are the holder of an actual secret in your family or among your friends, it's important to realise that, if you die without telling it to anyone else, that secret will die with you. That is not necessarily a problem, but in my therapeutic work I have seen how a secret can filter down through the generations with nobody really understanding why the family dynamics are the way they are. It can often feel like there is a missing piece of the puzzle, and when it is found, it explains a lot of family patterns and behaviour. So it is important that you make a conscious decision about this too. Ask yourself:

- Is there something that only I know (even if I don't think of it as a secret) that needs to be told to someone else?
- Is there anyone I need to speak to about anything?
- If this secret dies with me, what effect might that have, if any?
- Who would benefit from being told this?
- Who would it harm?

If you choose to tell your secret, then you don't have to say it before you die. You could write it down and specify that it is only to be read after your death, and by a particular person. You could tell someone else who you trust not to say anything until you authorise it, or until after a particular person has died. It really doesn't matter how you deal with it, so long as you make a conscious decision. Having said that, you may find you achieve greater connection and intimacy if you do decide to risk exposing what has previously been a secret.

You may have heard of the term 'emotional will'. This is a list of items you own that you wouldn't put in an ordinary will because they are not valuable enough, but they are of sentimental or personal value to you and/or your family. Sometimes this is known as a 'letter of wishes' and it can be attached to a will, even though it is not legally binding. Whatever way you do it, a list of items that mean something to you and who you want to have them is incredibly helpful when it comes to tidying up your affairs.

Last but not least under the 'Household' heading, and something that will make writing an emotional will a lot easier, is death cleaning! This is just another name for decluttering towards the end of life. There is no doubt that this makes life a lot easier for those you are leaving behind. Just look around your room or your house right now. How much stuff do you have that someone else will have to sort through after you've gone? Do you care about where it goes? Because if you don't do anything about it, almost definitely it will be packed up by a house clearance company, emptied into a skip and taken to landfill or burned. So get going – or, at the very least, write down in your death folder or workbook that you want it all to be given to a charity or that you don't mind it going to landfill.

Living legacy

A living legacy is something you create right now, while you are still alive. All those old black-and-white photos that the older generation still have, often in albums – those are a form of legacy (assuming someone has recorded names, dates and a bit about the people in the photos). Audio and video recordings of your memories, or even creating a performance piece of your life can be incredibly precious to those coming after you. There are more and more people offering these services nowadays, as we cotton on to the idea of how important it is that our loved ones have something to remember us by. And if you care about how you are remembered, this is an essential part of getting ready for your death. I call it a living legacy because you start creating this while you are alive and continue it until you just can't do it anymore.

People who have 'living funerals' or arrange a 'last party' (see the stories *My Dad* and *A Celebration of Life*) are creating a living legacy – a memorial for themselves right now and their family and friends later that lives on long after they have gone. That is something their loved ones may really treasure and can become a family heirloom and part of your family's social history.

Talking about it all

This is arguably where it all starts. It's practically impossible to have a really good end-of-life plan without having talked about at least some aspects of it with someone who will be affected by your death. However, as we saw in the stories in this chapter, relatively few people actively want to talk about dying, death or grief.

The thing is, death does not have to be distressing. Of course, no one wants to lose a loved one; that's natural. It can be painful and sad. In fact, there is a place for *all* emotions when someone is coming to the end of their life – that is normal. While there may be situations where the deaths themselves are distressing, we ourselves invite the possibility of added distress when we have not prepared for it, have not talked about it, and have not been honest and truthful about the one thing we know for sure will happen to us.

So have the courage to begin a conversation. You are likely to discover that there are many others who secretly want to join you.

Write it down

I also want to make a case for writing down all your thoughts and ideas and thereby creating your plan. It's quite amazing how different people can remember things differently, even about the same event. If you don't write it down, you risk not getting what you wanted (and it can be a huge source of comfort before you die to know that those you trust and love will be carrying out your wishes). Because the act of writing things down (whether typed on a computer, written longhand in a death folder or workbook, or even recorded in your own voice or on video) can really help you clarify in your own mind what you want. Just putting something in writing or hearing yourself in a recording can in itself make you change your mind. And you should review it regularly, to see if you still feel the same.

An enormous amount has to be done to tidy up the remains of someone's life. I discovered this after my parents died in 2018. By this time, I was working in the death field, and they were enormously proud of what I was doing and had completed their end-of-life plans in full. So I and my siblings knew exactly what to do – and we all completely underestimated the solace that it brought. But even with it all organised, it still took six months for probate to be granted. And they did not own a house or have a lot of money in their estate. Just knowing that they had known while they were alive that we were going to carry out their wishes was a soothing balm on the soreness of their deaths.

And last but not least, admitting that you will die one day can be emotionally challenging. Be kind to yourself as you take a peek at the end of your own life – it's okay to feel sad, happy, squirmy, resistant, cross, scared, joyful, at peace, whatever. All emotions are okay, acceptable and welcome. It's only when you think they are *not* okay that they cause trouble. So, do yourself a favour and decide you will invite your feelings along for the ride too.

Advice points

1. Make creating your own end-of-life plan into a project, and break it down into manageable tasks, doing it bit by bit.
2. Dare to start talking about it to someone close to you.
3. Plan in advance for your older age.
4. Write down what you want.
5. If nothing else, make a will!

Reference

Compassion in Dying. (2015). *Plan well, die well: learning from an information service*. Compassion in Dying. https://compassionindying.org.uk/library/plan-well-die-well/

Your digital legacy – James Norris

James is the founder of the Digital Legacy Association and MyWishes. The Digital Legacy Association is a global association dedicated to improving awareness and standards in digital asset planning and digital legacy safeguarding. MyWishes is free end-of-life planning software that enables people to document and share their end-of-life preferences. It was co-designed with hospices, patients and legal and NHS professionals in England and Wales.

In the last 10 years, the internet has changed the ways we communicate with one another. It has changed how we work, how we shop and how we use the media.

With the rise of internet-enabled devices (like mobile phones) and online platforms and services (like Facebook, Amazon, PayPal and others), we are spending more and more of our lives online. Moreover, the assets we own are increasingly becoming digitised. Our photos, home movies, music recordings, videos and so forth all used to be physical assets. Now they are largely produced, purchased, shared and accessed online, through a vast number of online services and password-protected devices. These can all easily be lost if someone dies without leaving instructions as to how to access them.

It is important that we all review the online platforms we use and the information saved on them. Think about how to manage your passwords and enable those you have nominated to access the necessary information. If you have a social media account, you may want to download your photos and videos from the service and pass them on to your next of kin. You may also want to provide administrative access to your social media accounts to someone you trust.

If you have a number of online accounts, you may wish to record them in a social media will (sometimes called a digital will). A social media will is a set of wishes. It is important to be aware that this might not classed as a legally binding document should it be used as evidence in a UK court. Each online platform has its own terms of service. When someone agrees to a company's terms to use their service, this will normally set legal precedence over any conflicting wishes you may have stated in a signed document or the wishes of your surviving friends or family. Knowing of this potential conflict and how complex it can be, I strongly advise people to follow the advice points below.

Advice points

- Think about the online platforms you use, learn about how they work and make plans for your online photos, videos and digital estate in a social media will.

- Set up a secure means to record and manage your passwords.
- Consider how you want your social media legacy to be managed after your death.
- Consider how any online subscriptions or bank accounts can be managed after your death.
- Use an external memory device to store precious photographs or videos and/or share them with a friend or family member.

Resources – making a death plan

Books

Magnusson, M. (2017). *The gentle art of Swedish death cleaning: How to free yourself and your family from a lifetime of clutter.* Canongate.

Films

Dying wish (2008). Karen van Vuuren (Director). Dying Wish Media. www.dyingwishmedia.com (Documentary about Dr Michael Miller, an 80-year-old retired surgeon with end-stage terminal cancer who chose to stop eating and drinking in order not to prolong the dying process)

Extremis (2016). Dan Krauss (Director). f/8 Filmworks. (A short film depicting the challenging emotions that accompany end-of-life decisions, in an American hospital ICU. Featuring Dr Jessica Zitter, author of *Extreme Measures*)

YouTube videos

How to do a good death. Jane Duncan Rogers. (2017). TEDxTalks. www.youtube.com/watch?v=An0k3s8pTXc

Webpages

Advance Decisions Assistance: www.adassistance.org.uk (Supplies suggested and necessary wording for particular situations and adaptable templates)

Age UK: www.ageuk.org.uk

Ageing Well Without Children: www.awwoc.org

Before I Die: www.beforeidieproject.com (A global public art project that invites people to share their hopes and dreams in public spaces)

Before I Go Solutions: www.beforeigosolutions.com (Groups and resources to help you actually get your plan done)

Compassion in Dying: www.compassionindying.org.uk

Conscious Ageing: www.consciousageing.org ('Building community support and sharing information')

The Conversation Project: www.theconversationproject.org (How to help start the conversation about your wishes for your end-of-life care)

Dying Matters: www.dyingmatters.org (A coalition of 30,000 members across England and Wales that aims to help people talk more openly about dying, death and bereavement, and to make plans for the end of life. Nationwide events every May)

Final Fling: www.finalfling.com

Good Life, Good Death, Good Grief: www.goodlifedeathgrief.org.uk ('Working to make Scotland a place where there is more openness about death, dying and bereavement')

Macmillan Cancer Support: www.macmillan.org.uk

Office of the Public Guardian: www.gov.uk/government/organisations/office-of-the-public-guardian (Very helpful staff and a relatively straightforward procedure for registering your power of attorney)

The Probate Department: www.theprobatedepartment.co.uk

Resources – Digital legacy

1Password: www.1password.com (A secure online method to record all your passwords, so you only have to remember one. Other companies offer the same service, such as Dashlane: www.dashlane.com)

Digital Legacy Association: www.digitallegacyassociation.org/for-the-public

My digital legacy. We Need to Talk About Death (Series 2, episode 2). BBC documentary. www.bbc.co.uk/programmes/b09jf1zb

My Wishes: www.mywishes.co.uk (End-of-life planning software)

Outside the Box

2 – The departure lounge

Unreality
A funny story about my Mum. She never really acknowledged (at least to me) that she was dying. She was in her 80s and had lung cancer after a lifetime of smoking. One day, close to her death, she said to me, 'You know, I don't think I'm taking this seriously enough.' I recognised the feeling – that sense of unreality in the face of something you know is happening. I loved her deeply.

How she laughed
My gran was 97 when she died, but the coroner said she couldn't die of old age (it's not allowed in Cornwall!). We fought to stop the post-mortem. Two days before her death, she sat up in bed, eyes shining, and we started to share memories. How she laughed! We talked of being stranded on boats, baking pasties, Papa and singing, and all the family came. She loved having us all together. She talked of forgiveness for her daughter for putting her in a home. When she died, I and my daughter Ellie, aged 19 at the time, bathed and dressed her, and then we all raised a cup of tea to her.

A lovely cup of tea
When my father died recently, I was not there, so I wanted to know everything that had happened just before he died. He was in hospital after a broken hip. I was told he had just thanked his nurse for a lovely cup of tea. I have thought about that many times – just so like him, he was such a gentleman.

The value of silence
I met Peter as a volunteer befriender. We knew each other for six years – meeting in his room at the care home. Limited by his physical disability to the four walls, the television and his tablet, he would be ready for me, with coffee machine warmed up and a dark chocolate KitKat in the fridge. We very rarely talked directly about dying, although we both knew that he was waiting

for it. Not a taboo subject at all, rather one taken for granted between us. No verbal communication about it, rather an awareness in the very occasional silences. Peter's health started to fail and there were two, three, four emergency admissions to hospital. The savour of life drained away for him as he lost the use of his hands and became dependent on others for almost everything. After his last hospital session, back in his room, he decided it was time to die. He never told me, but I knew it when the staff said he was refusing to eat. It took six weeks. On two or three of the last visits we would be together there for an hour in a deep silence. That felt both hard work and rewarding. The hard work of intense concentration, of listening, of affirming him wordlessly and being grateful for all that he had given to me, for his friendship. Nothing to say. Nothing that needed to be said. I am deeply grateful for that final gift.

Reaching out

I worked in a hospice in Cape Town, using a body technique to help patients release pain and fear, working on the spine and the feet. It really seemed to work. I could feel them relax. One day I was asked to go to see a man who was dying. There was his wife next to the bed and the man lying curled up, facing the wall. The room was cramped. I did what I could. I could see his wife was struggling. I suggested we talk in another room. For days he had not spoken or looked at her. She was desperate for a smile or any sign he knew she was there. I could feel this when I was working on him, like hooks reaching out from her. I said, 'Would you try something? Can you feel the love you have for him in your heart?' 'Yes,' she said. 'Can you remember a special time together, at the beach, at home, at a movie perhaps? A time when you were really happy and close.' She nodded. 'I want you to go back in and just sit with that feeling. Let it grow inside you. That's all. Don't try and get a response from him, just feel your love.' She said she would try. The next week I was back in the hospice and the woman came rushing up to me. 'I did what you told me to do and it worked. I just sat there remembering and feeling my love for him and suddenly he turned on his back, stretched out his legs, looked at me and smiled!'

Finding our way

I tended to my beloved auntie as she was dying. She had dementia and had stopped eating. Towards the end she was very weak, and it seemed death was near. One afternoon, as I sat with her, she became very agitated, trying to get out of bed. 'I'll have to stand up and be counted!' I talked about her remarkable life, standing up for the underdog and living with zest. 'When you stand up to be counted, I think it will be a celebration of what a wonderful person you are, what a great blessing.' She was trying to get up and walk round the block. I responded that maybe we could just imagine that together and stay here in the warm. She agreed and calmed down. After a long pause she said, 'I'm in the water already.' She held my hand. After some time, she put my hand aside very definitively, looking at me, and said, 'We have to separate, we have to say goodbye. I have to go to the river alone.' After another long pause she said, 'I'm in the last movement now.' And later, '*Lovely* music' (as if we were listening to it together). For the next few days she was peaceful, dozing quietly, ethereally already somewhere else, until she died, having shared her final gift – that a slow dying of old age and dilapidation, as she called it, can be a journey made with soul, as well as feistiness and humour. I feel sure there is wonderful music wherever she may be.

Best interests

I am a learning disability nurse and worked with a man in his 40s living in his own flat with staff support. He had Down's syndrome and a moderate learning disability. He was diagnosed with oesophageal cancer. He did not have the ability to understand that he was going to die but knew he had a sore throat and that we were trying to help. The thing that he really struggled with was not the cancer but the people that descended on his life. Endless people wanting to visit interrupted his model-making and this really upset him. So the staff (eight of us) agreed that we would trust each other and that one person would visit per week and report their findings to all the others. This really changed things and his level of distress dropped as his normal routine and quietness of his flat could resume. We carers also felt supported as we laid out a clear plan as to who to contact for which issue. Common sense, wouldn't you think? It felt pretty scary, trusting our fellow professionals in this way, but it was in the patient's best interests.

Please tell me the way to Heaven

A young man I was working with, in his 30s, with a moderate learning disability, saw his parents every week. His mum was diagnosed with a terminal cancer. She continued to visit her son but did not feel he should know as he 'wouldn't be able to cope'. In my experience, many people who say this actually mean, 'I wouldn't be able to cope if he knew,' because of painful questions and seeing their loved one's distress. So he wasn't told. Mum got worse and stopped coming so regularly. When she died, the family told the carers that her son couldn't come to the funeral or be told that she had died. This young man was clearly very confused as to why Mum stopped coming, and felt abandoned. The carers didn't agree with the family but didn't feel they could go against them. The family finally told the young man that Mum had 'gone to Heaven'. Now all this man asks is 'How do I get there?' He thinks Heaven is a place like London and wants to know what bus or train he can get. No one has yet told him he will never see his Mum again. Surely this shouldn't happen, but how do we stop it happening?

Acceptance and allowance

When my dad was dying, we couldn't really discuss it because my mum was coping by believing he would get better. I learnt many things about my dad in those two weeks – not material things but more about his core character, including his understanding that he couldn't discuss this and his kindness in allowing it to be so.

In denial

Do not entirely dismiss denial as an unsatisfactory but effective palliative measure. (Patients should not be 'made' to know.) 'Life-shortening illness' may be the most that some patients can take. My wife and I had one good last year in 'denial'.

Tongue-tied

I have lived under a sentence of silence with a friend who was dying. The truth could not be uttered for fear of excommunication from her presence. To name it was to make it happen. I am removing from her thin, frail chest a forgotten piece of equipment left in by the hospital many miles away – afraid of hurting my friend. A slip of a daughter watches me from the doorway. A nurse on the end of the phone is instructing me in what to do. I thought, this is not OK. Being alone here with you and the children and no medical support. Still I dared not speak. So the next day I wrote her a poem.

> *Deathly silence*
> You have stopped up my mouth with your hope.
> How can I swallow your hope?
> And I need to speak.
> I want the word spoken between us.
> It might be mine we are talking about
> but yours looks more likely now.
> I am cold with your fear, I am freezing and I cannot move.
> If that hot word could be spoken,
> if it could sit in this cold place with us,
> I believe there would be thawing,
> meltwater tears and that we would begin
> moving gently together in the flowing current of our lives,
> still cradling the pebble of your hope.

She read the poem while I sat carefully beside her, then she smiled and quietly put the paper down on the covers. We were both naked in that moment. The door I had been leaning on for many months suddenly gave with my weight. I could not quite step over the threshold to meet her. We talked of other things. Next day she did ring the hospice.

Home visit

A palliative care nurse was visiting a family at home for the first time. The door was opened by a grown-up daughter and son. 'Thank you so much for coming. Go on in. Mum is down the hall there on the left. You won't tell her, will you? She doesn't know how sick she is.' Down the hall and into the bedroom. The woman is sitting up in bed. 'Hello, you must be the nurse. Shut the door will you and come over here please. I am so glad to see you. There's something I want to tell you. Don't tell the children I'm dying, will you? There's no need to upset them.'

Life's a lottery

Volunteering at St Wilfrid's, I entered the room of a man who was clearly very unwell and approaching end of life. He asked me to buy him a large number of lottery tickets. I clearly looked surprised. He smiled broadly and said, 'You never know, this could be my lucky day.' You are living until you take your final breath.

We were ready

My Dad was in his mid-60s at home, having outlived his prognosis from his brain tumour by nine months because he wanted to meet the girl my brother would marry. New Year's Eve, he sipped the celebration champagne. Four days later, he changed; Mum and I told him he could let go. He died. That night, Mum slept as always in the bed next to him. The next day, his grandchildren put flowers round his body and played on the floor. The second night, Mum slept there as normal, and on the third day we asked the undertaker to take his body. We were ready.

A little bit excited

Peggy Preece, my mum: 'I'm a little bit excited. I'm going to meet Jesus and be with your Dad again. Try topping that bill!'

I felt her weight

My friend was dying in hospital. I'd been with her for the last few weeks of her life, had travelled for hours in the ambulance with her when her liver had started bleeding out. She had lived with terminal cancer for five years, having been told she had 18 months to live, aged 28. She never wanted to acknowledge that she was 'dying' or talk about it – even in her last weeks in the hospital as she lay, disappearing in front of our eyes. To me, it was so painful to not get the chance to speak of her dying, particularly in those last weeks. To not say to her the things I wanted – what she meant and what she taught me that I still don't really have words for. When the hospital staff upped her pain meds in the last days, it was routine for them, but they never told us what it signified –

that she would no longer be able to communicate back. I still feel angry about that. The sudden shift into a different state she was never to return from. The last conversation I had with her, we were laughing. It is still a shock, the whole experience, and one I cannot get a hold of. I carried her coffin, her body inches away from me. I felt her weight and still my mind cannot grasp that she is dead.

Every detail

My daughter aged 27 was diagnosed with spinal cancer in May 2007. The surgeon treated her on all occasions with respect, reassurance and honesty, which was how she wanted to be treated. She asked what his advice was regarding how to approach her life now. He said, 'No one knows what is going to happen tomorrow, I try to appreciate every detail – the trees, the sky, the detail of each day. There is only the present moment.' When she returned two and a half years later to have a second tumour removed, he gave her some ukulele sheet music (they had discussed both playing the ukulele). A friend wheeled her outside and she played her ukulele and sang the song as the snow gently fell.

You are dying

I was caring for a patient who was very close to the end of life. He was in and out of consciousness, not eating, barely drinking, and had been refusing his nursing visits. But he allowed me to come. It was the first time I had met him. I had given him a hand massage and he asked if we could hold hands for a bit because my skin was soft. Then he looked at me and asked if I would answer a question honestly. I said yes. He asked, 'Am I dying?' With a lump in my throat, I said, 'Yes, you are dying.' We sat together, holding hands, with quiet tears running down our cheeks.

What are you afraid of?

Patients often tell me that they are 'afraid of dying' and I always feel it is important to ask them what aspect of dying they fear. Sometimes it is the thought of leaving loved ones and how they will manage without them; sometimes it is the thought of what happens after death, but most frequently their concerns are about what dying is like. As an oncology nurse, I have been present at the death of a number of patients, but many of the patients I see have never experienced any aspect of death or dying. Explaining how we plan to manage end-of-life care can be a comfort for patients. I tell them about how we control pain, about the process of dying and that we aim to keep our patients calm and as free of distress as possible. Occasionally death isn't so neat. It is possible that a patient may have, for example, a catastrophic bleed because of the position of the tumour. We would discuss this with the patient and explain how we would manage this rare situation. A patient said recently, 'You have made dying less scary.' That felt like a good day at work.

Uncarers

We sat with our 94-year-old father while he died all day of pneumonia – at about 8pm we thought maybe our presence wasn't quite enough and called the district nurses, in the hope that they would somehow help him, make him more comfortable, do things for him we hadn't. They came – two of them – and were grumpy and brusque. They uncovered him completely to wash him with wet wipes and, even in that last hour of life and having had morphine by mouth, he tried to cover his willy up. An awful invasion on the calm, warm, chatty atmosphere, and they offered nothing. We knew what was right for him ourselves.

Long goodbye

My mum had a stroke soon after my dad died. She could not eat. The doctors spoke to us carefully and tactfully – we had to let her go. Mum was moved to a stroke ward in a cottage hospital. What a remarkable ward. We were very lucky. We visited constantly, we stayed nights, sleeping on chairs or even in empty beds. From the end of November, my mum lay there, breathing on and on. No food and no water! She breathed on. We played CDs, we sang hymns. We read poems. We played them again, we sang them again, we read them again. You know a baby will, eventually, come. We knew that Mum was going to die. I cannot express how much all of us appreciated the time we had to just sit with Mum. She died on December 23rd.

Give me the night

My mum was given three weeks to live with bowel cancer. She lived well for 16 months, then she took a sudden downturn. I asked the GP, 'How long?' Like asking, how long is a piece of string? 'Will she survive the night?' When the GP and nurses left at midnight, I sat with my mum and asked her to give me the night as my younger brother had just gone to Weymouth and would have had a drink. I promised her I would call him at daybreak and, once he arrived, she could go. He walked in at 8.50am and I said, 'You can go now, Mum.' She left us at 9.20am.

Far and near

I remember rushing to see my uncle before he died. From Bristol to London. I took the bus, all the while on the phone to my brother, who I asked to hold the phone to my uncle's ear as he was about to go. I just had to tell him I loved him and I thought he was totally hard core for being one of the most soft, gentle beings I've ever known and so quiet about his struggles with diabetes that had ended up with him having both his legs amputated and leaving us so (apparently) suddenly. I felt him listening. I was in floods of tears, surrounded by people on the bus on the motorway. And when I arrived to his dead body, I felt his soul still very present. It was all perfect.

Volvo for sale

When my Nan was on her deathbed she was asked about her obituary. She said: 'I want… Margret Hampson / Died peacefully / Volvo for sale / £500 or nearest offer.'

Commentaries
Preparing for death – Bob Whorton

Bob is a Methodist minister, pastoral supervisor and trainer. The first part of his working life was spent in traditional ministry settings and the second part in chaplaincies. He worked as a chaplain in Broadmoor and Rampton high security psychiatric hospitals and for 12 years at the Sir Michael Sobell House Hospice in Oxford. He now lives in France, running a small reflection and hospitality centre with his wife, Sue (*www.lesjardinsdesarts.com*).

I write out of the time when I was a hospice chaplain, and a word of explanation about this role may be helpful. Chaplains accompany and listen to anyone who wants us to be there. Usually coming from a religious background, we are all things to all people, including those without any religious beliefs. Some want to share their spiritual or religious exploration, or tell the story of their life, and others do not. We are simply *there alongside,* if and when patients, relatives and staff want us.

Some people die at the end of a long life, with a sense of fulfilment, passing on the baton gladly to the next generation. Helen Kewell writes below about how older people face their dying. My starting point is with those who find themselves in the departure lounge long before they are ready. Most of us have a certain idea of how life is going to pan out, and this idea does not usually include an early death. We know in theory we could die at any time, but we are designed for survival, and our natural impulse is to push thoughts of our own death away. When life lurches towards dying, a revision of every assumption about our life is necessary. We cannot overestimate how difficult this can be.

There will often be a sense of rage, fear, deep distress and a feeling of being cheated out of life. This is not how the story should go. Other people are healthy and happy, so why is this happening to me?

In the middle of our 'normal' lives, we inhabit roles that we usually do not reflect upon – such as healthy person, worker, partner, parent, member of an interest group or friend. Within these roles, we do certain things like driving a car, walking, getting on a bus and meeting colleagues at work. When we are dying, the roles we used to have change or disappear. For example, colleagues may find it hard to visit, not sure what to say or how to be, underlining the fact that the worker role has now gone for ever. There is a particular suffering experienced by a parent who is dying and knows that they will never see their children grow up and travel through the different milestones of life. The role of a parent is to love, care and protect. It is very hard to live with the knowledge that others will now take over those responsibilities. For a couple, the intimacy and sex they took for granted changes also. Bodily changes, lack of privacy and the knowledge that death is near can inhibit the natural expression of an intimate relationship. Bridget Taylor (2014) has done some helpful research on this.

Human beings are, of course, incredibly flexible. What was unthinkable a few weeks ago becomes the norm today. What helps in making these adjustments and living as well as one can in the last months and weeks of life?

Practical help can be very welcome – for example, rearranging furniture to accommodate a hospital bed in the living room, baking a pie or looking after the children for a while. At the same time, it is helpful for the person who is dying to do as much for themselves as possible. Friends and family can be too helpful and can unwittingly take away the last means of staying in control.

Good professional support perhaps goes without saying; the control of symptoms and help with personal care enables a person to keep feeling human. Those who care professionally for the dying need both excellent boundaries and the ability to create human connections. Without good boundaries, the professional's inner being and needs become entwined with the distress of the person they are there to serve, and ultimately they become exhausted and useless to themselves and those around them. But without human connection, a professional is simply a robot performing certain tasks. The story *Uncarers* shows vividly and painfully the distress and disconnection that result from thoughtless care that does nothing to preserve human dignity. A dying person needs professionals who will reach out to them with kindness (an under-rated quality), and who will offer the particular skill relevant to their role. *Every Detail* illustrates the reverse – the care of the expert health professional for the person, not just their illness.

Someone who is in the last months or weeks of life does not need to be treated as if they are from a different planet. They are still the same person they have always been. A friend who can come to the house or hospital and talk about vintage cars, Brexit, artichoke sticks, miniature railways, the startling news that Janet is having a baby, golf, *Love Island*... is likely to be a welcome friend. This friend needs to remember that energy is limited, so short visits are preferable to long ones. And humour is allowed (if the person is open to it). Death is a weighty business, but laughter at this time can bring release and comfort.

Is talking about death and dying going to be helpful or unhelpful? I was struck, when reading the stories here, about how different strategies worked for different people. For some, naming death was important, and in other situations denial meant getting on with the life still to be lived. It will be easier for certain people to talk to a healthcare assistant who is giving them a welcome, relaxing bath than to a loved one.

Dying can be a lonely business and to share concerns and fears can be incredibly helpful. Sometimes the same ground needs to be covered over and over again, and in this way an abnormal situation is 'normalised'. Most health professionals who care for those who are dying believe that truth-telling is healthy. The story *What Are You Afraid Of?* shows how helpful and reassuring the giving of clear information about the dying process can be. People can then make realistic plans, talk about the future, get married, look at finances and discuss the care of children. It also means there is an opportunity for people to say those important words 'Thank you' and 'Sorry', and 'Do you remember when…?' and 'We didn't do so badly, did we?' These can be precious moments of connection and intimacy that help everyone in uncertain days.

> Intimacy is based on clear and honest communication (by word, behaviour and touch) as well as attentive listening. In this way, safety, trust and inclusion are established… The other person is wholly appreciated for who that person is. (Kuhl, 2002, p.172)

In the story *Reaching Out*, we hear of a very natural reaction in 'turning to the wall'. Death is too much. There is too much uncertainty, too much anger, too much pain, too much… And so there is a closing down and a turning from life. But in turning away, a dying man cuts his wife out of his life. She is encouraged to sit with him without resentment, lovingly and with good, positive memories. He turns to her and they can again share life, and the process of dying, together.

There is a difference between giving information clearly about death and dying and assuming that everyone will want to talk about their feelings. Healthcare professionals can make the assumption that all people are like them and need to talk about how it feels to be dying. As a chaplain, it took me a long time a to realise that not everyone needs to do this. And people often live with two attitudes to death in balance: one of acceptance and one of denial.

In the story *I Felt Her Weight*, we read: 'She never wanted to acknowledge that she was "dying" or talk about it – even in her last weeks in the hospital as she lay, disappearing in front of our eyes…' There will be different reasons why talking about dying is hard. It may seem like defeat or failure and giving in to something that should not be given in to. Or it may be that there is a belief that, by not talking about death, it will not happen. Or it could be the fear that, through talking about dying, everyone will be plunged into the abyss, not just the person who is dying.

When life is coming to an end and such a lot has to be surrendered, spiritual beliefs or a particular way of seeing the world can be helpful for many. Some have a spirituality or faith that helps enormously, and this may be easily articulated, or is so personal that it is hard to put into words. In a time of great uncertainty, the reading of sacred words that are deeply familiar or the sharing in a religious ritual with family and friends can be very helpful. Beliefs that have been laid aside may be picked up again. Occasionally, somebody who has lived a very devout life will 'lose' their faith completely at the end of life. It may be that faith has been a way of keeping in control of life, and now nothing is within their control. The end of life can be a time of intense questioning, and the existential questions have to be worked through or simply lived. Equally, some people do not have a need to explore the spiritual dimension to life. Some are practical and have an ability to live deeply in the moment with great love and attentiveness, without the need to reflect spiritually; some approach death with their minds and a rich conceptual world satisfies them.

It needs to be noted that a faith or belief can sometimes be positively unhelpful to a particular person. They may feel they have to be 'strong' as a witness to others and will find it hard to admit to members of their faith community that they are fearful or depressed. Keeping up this façade can be a tremendous burden.

Whatever a person believes or does not believe, as we come to the end of life, we are all in a liminal, literally 'threshold' place. This is like a sandy winter beach between the solid land behind and the moving sea in front. As I read the stories, I am aware of our need for images and symbols to describe death. Approaching a river and crossing it, the birth of a baby, a door and a departure lounge in an airport are some of the images used. It is hard to be comfortable in liminal space, because it is a place where we are not in control. We do not know whether the river will flow or freeze; we are not sure what the onward journey will be like. And we human beings like a degree of certainty and order in our living. But, as time goes on, the liminal space may reveal its gift. It can be a time of beautiful connection, when a love is experienced that goes deeper and wider than we had believed possible.

I remember a man who was dying in the hospice and was quite isolated and full of complaint and misery. The staff and volunteers treated him with kindness and hospitality, as they would treat anyone. After a time he said to me, 'I have such love for every person who comes into this room.' That is a little miracle of liminal space. If people are given the opportunity, there can be a blooming of creativity in this time. It can be a time when words are written, songs are sung and pictures that are full of depth and meaning take form on a piece of paper. I have a picture on my study wall that was painted by a young man who died more than 30 years ago. It shows beautiful trees and bushes around a lake, with snowy mountain peaks in the distance. The water is completely still. What an image for a young man to paint at such a time! The act of painting enabled him to express very clearly his inner experience as he approached his death.

Liminal space is full of mystery. Doubtless there can be 'explanations' for what happens as people approach death, but I am not sure I want an explanation. The ordinary and the extraordinary do a dance with each other in this time, zigzagging in and out of each other.

Of course we must not idealise this time. Fear, anxiety or panic are natural responses to being in the departure lounge. It can sometimes take a while to get physical symptoms under control, and I suspect it is hard to have interesting thoughts about liminal space if you are feeling nauseous all the time. And it may simply be boring after a while, when someone does not die when they are supposed to and the waiting drags on and on for everyone. This, as much as crisis-laden times, can be a test of love. But life continues as death approaches. And sometimes, without willing it, there may be a sense of otherness, of the world opening out, or roots going deep. A moment in time is filled with love and there is shared music.

Advice points

1. As someone adjusts to dying, accept rage and distress as normal.
2. Acknowledge the changing roles.
3. Professionals who care for the dying need to be kind as well as boundaried.
4. Treat someone who is dying in the same way you have always treated them.
5. Be open to someone's spiritual and religious beliefs (if they have them), whatever your own beliefs are, and be open to mystery.

References

Kuhl, D. (2002). *What dying people want: Practical wisdom for the end of life.* PublicAffairs.

Taylor, B. (2014). Experiences of sexuality and intimacy in terminal illness: a phenomenological study. *Palliative Medicine, 28*(5), 438–447.

Counselling at death's door – Helen Kewell

Helen qualified as a humanistic counsellor in 2015, having spent most of her career as a management consultant. During her training, Helen became profoundly influenced by existential and experiential approaches to therapy and, almost inadvertently, became fascinated and inspired by working with older adults. She considers this area of psychotherapeutic work to be under-represented in literature and under-resourced, and hopes to continue to promote a wider dialogue on it and prompt others to do the same. She runs her own private counselling practice in Sussex and previously volunteered as a counsellor and supervisor for Cruse Bereavement Care. *www.helenkewell.co.uk*

When someone we love is dying, even at the end of a long and full life, speaking the difficult truth together can be difficult. To say it out loud can invite untold grief into our hearts. For those who are dying, when others refuse to talk about our lived experience of it and our fears, it can make the process much harder. In the story *Home Visit*, we see, almost with comic timing, the way denial can be silently held between loved ones. We protect the ones we love; we tell gentle untruths if we must. During my counselling training, I was taught that one part of our role is to 'tell people the things they don't want to hear in a way they can hear them', and this orientation means that we bravely step into conversations that are difficult. When someone who is profoundly old and nearing the end of their life wants to fantasise about how they will die or wants to ask questions about what will happen afterwards, it can be comforting for others when we go there with them, even if it is painful for us. In *What Are You Afraid Of?* we see a lovely example of how an oncology nurse discusses the process of dying with patients, giving them reassurance and restoring their sense of control.

It also works in the reverse: when someone is dying but feels they can't acknowledge it, it can be hard and we can feel held at a distance. In *Hope Amid Silence,* we see a friend writing a poem to say what seems difficult to voice out loud: 'If that hot word could be spoken / if it could sit in this cold place with us / I believe there would be a thawing.' Those of us in the helping professions and those caring for others at the end of life can help ease families into these realities. We can sit gently with them all in the departure lounge, as it were, and help bridge those conversations.

However, this is not about pushing conversations into difficult places when people are not ready. One of the best rules of courageously engaging in difficult conversations is to follow the flow of narrative alongside the other person and not minimise or redirect the conversation somewhere brighter. Humans are social and kind by nature. Most of the time our objective is to make things better for others, especially when we care about them, so it becomes a socially conditioned response to move people onto cheery topics or distract them from their fears. It feels counterintuitive for most of us to simply sit with someone and feel the weight of their experience and pain and validate it. Using phrases like, 'That sounds painful for you to say' or, 'When you say that, I can feel the sadness you might feel,' or asking 'What is it like to say that out loud?' allows you both to stay inside the painful conversations without pushing them into places the dying person isn't ready for. Moving people on to talk about the weather or cheery subjects is inauthentic and overrides the lived experience of the person we are with. We see a beautiful example of this in the account *You are Dying*, where the simple confirmation out loud of the fact that he is dying, along with the sharing of tears and touch, appeared to be a very releasing and therapeutic experience for the patient.

As we all know, less than 10% of communication is through spoken words (Mehrabian, 1971). The rest is communicated by tone of voice, body language, eye contact and the energy of our presence. If someone is at the end of their natural life, cognition and short-term memory, as well as one's grasp on immediate reality, can begin to fade. Mental stamina for long conversations also wanes. Those who are experiencing dementia often inhabit other spaces while we are with them – places from their past or from their imaginings. Their 'reality' may feel very different to ours, which makes communicating purely through normative narrative confusing for them at best and terrifying at worst.

Likewise, inevitable physical decline can make ordinary, turn-taking verbal communication difficult: hearing may be compromised, eyesight may be weakened and conditions like osteoporosis can mean a hunching of the upper spine, meaning eye contact is difficult to maintain. Our inability to communicate with people experiencing some or all of these frailties is entirely our failing, not theirs, so we must get creative with the way we communicate. Like the commentator in *Finding Our Way*, we must find a way to listen at a deeper level.

This is a wonderful way to engage with people from within their reality rather than trying to anchor them in ours. Who is to say which is real and true anyway? One of my counselling clients was 95 and had dementia. He spoke every week about escaping the home he was in, to go away and die quietly alone. Each week we would arrange our chairs near to the open door in his room, as one of his greatest fears was that the bus to Southsea would arrive and he would miss it. This simple gesture calmed him and allowed us to reach a deeper way of relating. By living inside their reality, we can reach for meaning and understanding far more easily than by trying to force upon them what seems real to us.

Senses are also a wonderful way of engaging with people when they are older and dying. What follows are some other ways we can communicate with others who may be very late in life or nearing death without specific conversation having to happen. In Chapter 6, 'Dementia', Hazel May explores this in more detail.

Reflection and validation
Talk quietly and gently about what can be seen around you both. Notice and state how the light is, the smells that you can sense, the background sounds that can be heard. Reflect what you see them doing or how they are moving, such as 'I can see your breathing is quiet today, but your hands are tightly in fists.' Affirming someone's physical presence and immediate environment can be validating and comforting, without you or them having to do anything about it. Don't expect that they will respond directly; to sit alongside them and affirm what is happening may be enough. Although, by drawing their attention to their body, you may open a channel for communicating about other things. If someone is in pain or their body is failing them, the sensations and limitations within their body can dominate their awareness. If we meet them within their felt sense of the world and how their body is, we have more chance of forming a meaningful and deep way of relating to them.

When we come into the world, we rely on the presence of others to reflect back that we are a whole human being (remember the surprise you see in an infant when they grab hold of their foot for the first time and suddenly realise it belongs to them?). In the same way, at end of life, we can experience ourselves as fragmented, like a newborn does. Dementing or not, people often find themselves not recognising or acknowledging parts of their bodies as their own. Or we can reject the part that is no longer working or is in pain – an arm rendered numb and lifeless by a stroke or legs no longer able to hold our body weight. By mirroring the wholeness of a person, reflecting their gestures and words back to them, we can help them experience safety within themselves. Those who are profoundly old or at the end of their natural lives often cry out for and return to thinking about their mother or father, believing they can see or hear them. This is part of the same process. So, as a caregiver or family member, we can help create a self of whole self and safety by our presence and by connecting them and us to their bodies. Sometimes even touch and movement alone can do this.

Engage with your body rather than words
Try something, if you will. Sit somewhere where there are other people and close your eyes. Bring stillness to your body and try slowing your thoughts. Tune in, instead, to your proprioception first – your sense of where you are. Then see what else you can sense behind your closed eyes. Are those around you noticing you or do they seem indifferent? Are they near or far? Are they relaxed or angry? Sad or happy? Hopefully you sense something. But how do

you know this? The purpose of this exercise is to understand first-hand how vulnerability can also make us highly attuned to the presence of others, even if they are not talking.

The story *Reaching Out* reveals this so powerfully. When someone seems to be sleeping or in and out of verbal contact with us, our thoughts can drift or, worse, we begin to speak over them or about them to others, as if they are not there. This can be frightening and isolating. A very simple thing to do is look them in the eye, even if no talking is happening. Sometimes this might mean you have to sit on the floor or move position. Or you could hold their hand or arm for gentle reassurance or, as in the story, simply sit alongside them holding kindness, love or warmth in your heart, not needing to talk.

Engage all the senses, be creative

All communication is about sharing space and experiences with another person. If we can't share words, we can share many other things. Looking at photographs, either in albums or on walls, can help you climb into someone's memories and feelings with them. Familiar objects, food that is enjoyed and scented candles can also be experienced together, held and tasted or smelled and then explored. Music is incredibly evocative. If you know what music or artist someone loves, then listening to this with them and noticing how they respond can be helpful. 'When this music plays, I can see that you frown. Does it remind you of something?' Naomi Feil, creator of Validation Therapy (Feil, 2015), writes and talks beautifully about how to enter the world of older people who are withdrawn. In one, now famous example, she sings a gospel song to an 87-year-old lady, Gladys, who was so withdrawn from the world and from others that she could not even maintain eye contact or speak. Within a few short minutes, Naomi is singing and Gladys is smiling, grasping her arm and beating time. It is one of the most moving examples I have seen of communicating deeply with the elderly through music and movement (Priddy, 2018).

Finding meaning and purpose

Sometimes there is a misconception that the last few years, months and days of life are about finding a place of quiet contentment from which we can slip away. While this may be true for some, it couldn't be further from the truth for others. As Dylan Thomas (2003) urges us: 'Do not go gentle into that good night, / Old age should burn and rave at close of day; / Rage, rage against the dying of the light.' What I think he meant, and development psychology would agree with him, is that, as we approach the later stages of our lives, we naturally reflect on and often seek to resolve past conflicts, find acceptance for things that we might be less proud of (Erikson & Erikson, 1998), process the many losses that have stacked up across the years and establish a meaning and purpose for our existence. We may also start to question the meaning of life itself and the nature of death. These are times when our bodies may have become less vibrant, but our psyche may have a lot of things to process and, hence, a lot of work to do.

Existential philosophers believe that an inescapable part of being human, and of simply *being,* is that we are acutely aware from a very early age that our life has both limits (our death) and infinite possibility (we are free to choose). This philosophy considers the many expressions of emotional distress we see, such as anxiety or obsessive behaviours, as an expression of this ultimate knowledge and fear of dying. It also encourages us, in the face of this, to anchor our self in the meaning and purpose of our life and to take full responsibility for how we live it. It is invigorating and incredibly freeing to live this way. When someone is at the end of life, naturally the idea of death is in much sharper focus, but we can also give more attention to the meaning and purpose of our lives and the choices we still have. An example of this, when supporting people at the end of life, is simply to encourage them to think about what their life has meant to them, what they feel their legacy is, and to express choice within the limits of their parameters. For example, where would they like their bed to be placed, is the music loud enough, what are their wishes about their final moments?

When we become dependent on others due to ill health or old age, we can feel we have no choices left. Learned helplessness and/or resentment can set in. We can help liberate those we are caring for by promoting and finding spaces and opportunity for them to have agency, even in the smallest ways. One person I worked with lived in a nursing home and felt totally helpless in every aspect of his life. Asking him each week which chair he'd like me to sit in gave him autonomy in a space where his choices were few, and it seemed to calm him. I also asked each week if he would like me to come back and asked each time we began our sessions if it was OK for me to be there with him that day. My hope is that these small moments created a feeling of freedom, within the limits he found himself in.

It can be very powerful, too, to be the gatekeeper for someone towards the very end so that they decide who gets to visit them. Sometimes there is no choice – for example, if someone needs constant care and can no longer live alone – but we can explore these choices and live in them together in our imagination. What would it be like for them to be living in that house? How would they feel? Simply exploring freedom and choice can also be powerful, even if we feel powerless to give people access to any of what they are expressing.

Storying our lives

Psychologically speaking, as the end of our life becomes closer and more of our life lies behind us, inevitably we naturally begin to be more reflective. Telling stories of our past is a logical way of processing that, particularly for a generation who (when this book was published) grew up during the hardships of the Second World War, when people learned to soldier on and not make a fuss. If emotional language is hard, simple storytelling helps us process our feelings out loud in an acceptable way. I loved reading *How She Laughed*, where the narrator's 97-year-old gran suddenly sat up in bed and shared (maybe even 'shed') her memories and in doing so was able to find forgiveness for her daughter before she died.

Storytelling is more than telling stories. At a time when we might not have so much autonomy left, it gives us control over the narrative of our lives. It allows us to author who we are and what has happened to us. It can pass family lore through generations and it helps to connect people to their past. It is no coincidence that, before babies can speak, we read stories to them; it helps them learn how to sequence and how to engage with others. Stories communicate meaning, teach lessons, communicate feelings and give the gift of imagination. In the absence of knowing what to say or how to comfort someone who is older and dying, encourage them to tell the stories of their lives. In the telling and the retelling, many tiny things are happening. We, as travellers in these stories, can gently ask questions and help clarify and weave meaning through them in our responses.

People often comment to me that my work must be hard, and I feel genuine disbelief. Working with people who are at the very end of their natural lives is a privilege. I am invited into the internal world of someone facing the greatest challenge of life, to walk with them, witnessing the richness of the lives they have lived and helping them release themselves from, or at least acknowledge, past regrets. I get to sit in deep silence and feel into their darkest and also most tender spaces. I am able to do this without also grieving and feeling my own deep pain if it is in a professional capacity, treading that careful path between boundaries and connections that Bob describes above. I have also been there with family members of my own and borrowed from my experiences with clients, and still I have found the experience formative and life affirming.

Advice points

1. Don't ignore the person who is dying. Even if they seem asleep, try not to talk as if they have already gone.
2. Seek to communicate in whatever way you can, even when words are difficult, or simply allow the silence and use your presence to create safety and reassurance.
3. If someone wants to talk about dying, engage with the conversation bravely.
4. Gently invite reflection and the telling of life stories. It can be comforting and powerful.
5. Encourage and help people find agency, however small and limited their choices may seem.

References

Erikson, E.H. & Erikson, J.M. (1998). *The life cycle completed.* W.W. Norton & Co.

Feil, N. (2015). *Validation, communication through empathy.* [Video].TEDxAmsterdam Women. www.youtube.com/watch?v=ESqfW_kyZq8&feature=youtu.be

Mehrabian, A. (1971). *Silent messages.* Wadsworth.

Priddy, J. (2018, January 11). *Gladys Wilson and Naomi Feil.* [Video]. www.youtube.com/watch?v=zm0gyUOBYlg

Thomas, D. (2003). 'Do not go gentle into that good night.' In: *The Poems of Dylan Thomas* (D. Jones, Ed.). New Directions Publishing. [Original work published 1952].

Resources

Books

Carstensen, L. (2011). *A long bright future.* Public Affairs.

Carstensen, L. (2011). *Older people are happier.* [Video]. www.ted.com/talks/laura_carstensen_older_people_are_happier

Cavendish, C. (2019). *Extra time: 10 lessons for living longer better.* Harper Collins Publishers.

Dowling Singh, K. (1998). *The grace in dying: How we are transformed spiritually as we die.* Harper One.

Dunmore, H. (2017). *Inside the wave.* Bloodaxe Books.

Feil, N. (2012). *The validation breakthrough: Simple techniques for communicating with people with Alzheimer's and other dementias.* Health Professions Press.

Gawande, A. (2015). *Being mortal: Illness, medicine and what matters in the end.* Profile Books.

Kalanithi, P. (2016). *When breath becomes air.* Random House.

Kearney, M. (1996). *Mortally wounded: Stories of soul pain, death and healing.* Scribner.

Kewell, H. (2019). *Living well and dying well: Tales of counselling older people.* PCCS Books.

Murphy, K. & Whorton, B. (2017). *Chaplaincy in hospice and palliative care.* Jessica Kingsley Publishers.

Prouty, G.F., Portner, M. & Van Werde, D. (2002). *Pre-therapy: Reaching contact-impaired clients.* PCCS Books.

Slater, R. (1995). *The psychology of growing old: Looking forward.* Open University Press.

Viney, L. (1993). *Life stories: Personal construct therapy with the elderly.* Wiley-Blackwell Publishing.

Whorton, B. (2015). *Voices from the hospice: Staying with life through suffering and waiting.* SCM Press.

Yalom, I.D. (2008). *Staring at the sun: Overcoming the terror of death.* Jossey-Bass.

Radio programmes/Podcasts

Facing death creatively. (2019). Four Thought. R.M. Sanchez Camus (Presenter). BBC Radio 4; 20 July.

The future of medicine. (2014). Reith lectures series. Dr Atul Gawande (Presenter). BBC Radio 4; 20 December. www.bbc.co.uk/podcasts/series/reith (Dr Gawande examines the nature of progress and failure in medicine)

Films

When I die: Lessons from the death zone. (2013). Adrian Steirn (Dir.). https://youtu.be/S2eUw0CUuMc (Philip Gould shares his thoughts and insights as he confronts his impending death from oesophageal cancer)

Outside the Box

3 – Far too soon

Letter to my first child

I vividly remember the feeling of shock when they told me. It had only been three weeks since I'd been at the hospital and seen a heartbeat on a monitor. The woman operating it had said there was a 99% chance our baby would be OK. I relaxed. So now, even though I was bleeding a little, to hear the heartbeat had gone was a real shock. I remember the walk to the canteen, carrying their brochures, to think about 'what to do'. I couldn't fathom it or believe it. Because to me you lived a life here, though only inside of me. To me, you're my first child and the first one I lost. I said I'd wait, take the weekend to review their leaflets. My instinct to let your life end naturally. Theirs to caution that 'You might not want to do that since it might take a long time'. A funny thing to worry about when you're losing someone who's lived inside of you. But you didn't take your time in the end. Me knowing was, I think, the catalyst to letting go of you. Within an hour we were home on the sofa when the labour pains began. I'd had no preparation for you to leave me so abruptly, for contractions, for a mini-labour as I let you go. They said nothing at the hospital of how important I would later find it to bury you in my mother's garden. I weep now to think that in general we mark miscarriage in no way at all. You made me committed to be a voice that was willing to speak of baby loss. I have felt compelled not to hide you, nor the other four children whom I have subsequently lost and who are at rest and remembered with you under the same Dorset apple tree.

The box

I was five months pregnant. Up on the bed ready for the midwife with her listening device. 'I'm afraid I can't seem to find a heartbeat.' Health centre to cottage hospital. Cottage hospital to the maternity unit. 'I'm so sorry.' Chemically induced labour. The unit was very good. They gave us time. They gave her to us to hold. There was a book to write her name in. Then we hit a problem. We had brought a basket and a little white sheet to wrap her in, a soft blanket to go over her and a bunch of tiny forget-me-nots from our garden. There was consternation and a stout, ordinary box. 'You cannot take her home like that.' 'Why not?' 'What if there is an accident? I mean how would you explain it? A dead baby in your car?' She was not a parcel. We did not want to post her anywhere. We simply wanted to wrap her tenderly and place her in a familiar, woven basket and take her home. And we did. Because there are in fact no Health and Safety regulations pertaining to the transport of a body of any size, except that it should not be in public view.

Choice

We brought our little dead baby home. Cara. We asked our two children if they wanted to see her. One did. One didn't. Their choices were not what I would have predicted.

Swept along

Christopher was born dead. He would be 13 now. I was 25 at the time and lots of decisions were expected of me very quickly, some of them in labour. I was young, heartbroken and scared. If I could go back, I would have made different decisions, in fact I would have actually made decisions. I think I just got swept along. I will remember this when caring for other parents in my practice.

Regret

In 1973 our baby boy was born with serious health problems. The doctors took over to some extent and decided he would die quite soon. From then on, he was treated with care by nurses, but we were made rather distant from the process. When he died, the funeral directors took over and, again, decisions were made for us. I can still remember the funeral, which was rather distant and seemed to have little relevance. The sadness was ours, but little else. It would have felt so much kinder to this little soul to have prepared him, carried him and buried him without any interference. One never forgets but remembrance is tinged with regret.

I am a different person now

After nine months of trying for a baby, my wife Mary fell pregnant with our second child. We told family and friends pretty much as soon as we knew, about six weeks. I also told customers on my weekly veg market stall that Mary was pregnant, to general congratulations and excitement. We had had a conversation and agreed that, if the worst were to happen and we lost the baby, that we would want everyone to know, and that it would be harder to tell them we'd had a miscarriage if they didn't know she was pregnant. Then, after a totally uneventful pregnancy, Mary had a late miscarriage at 16 weeks. She lost two and a half litres of blood, was on the verge of needing a blood transfusion and had to have emergency surgery. All through the ambulance trip and around the hospital, I carried our dead son wrapped up in one of my favourite T-shirts and a towel. The paramedic Clive had offered to take him, but he was happy for me to keep hold of him, and in the hospital they inspected him but then returned him in a basket. This simple kindness of treating us as bereaved parents and looking after him really helped and is bringing me close to tears even now. What was also striking was how many people – nurses, drivers, doctors – who we met had also lost babies. This was continued into the next weeks and months as we had to tell all those who knew we were expecting what had happened. At this point, I felt that telling people early had been the right decision because of the sense of community and support that helped us to get through the next days and weeks, although it was hard facing anyone for the first time and having that difficult conversation again. Losing our baby, who we named Rowan, was one of the worst experiences of my life, but somehow it made my relationships stronger; it gave an edge of reality to conversations with strangers and friends alike. I am a different person now; I have lost a baby, I have dug a grave and laid him in it, I have shared grief with my wife and family. As I write this, Mary is pregnant again, we are now at 13 weeks, and yes, we told people as soon as we found out. This wasn't hard to do, because we know that, if we suffer another miscarriage, we will need our support network again, and we are not ashamed to use it.

Precious

I have been involved in the funeral profession for 20 years, still learning. Eighteen years ago, a client requested that her little baby (who was born early and lived for one day) came home with her for the weekend. I made sure all legal requirements were met, just in case (there were none). She spent quality time alone, in her own home, with her precious baby. It was very special for a person who did not have the usual celebrations associated with a birth.

Talk to the baby

I was a midwife. When washing and dressing a baby who had died, I always asked the parents if it was okay to talk to the baby as I found it hard not to. They were always comforted by this.

Collusion

My brother died at one week old; I was almost three. It was never spoken about; his name never uttered again. This denial of grief imploded my family at the core; we sucked it up and never recovered. I lost my parents that day. They went to the hospital and never really came back. I took it upon myself to protect them from feeling any emotion, mirroring what they were showing me. I thought it would destroy them to feel something and I wanted to protect them. It was quite a task. Being the gatekeeper of emotion, endlessly on guard. We all colluded. It took me another 32 years to finally crack.

Connection

I am 20 and I have been surprised with two pregnancies and have gone through the process of having an abortion/saying goodbye to my child twice. I have a bit of the blood I bled into a tissue in a pretty bag by my bedside, which sounds creepy but I am just not ready to part with the physical connection.

Liberty

I spent 44 years accusing myself of murdering my child. The date of the abortion was 6th November 1973. I sat in the four-bedded ward ALONE! with fireworks going off. It was the night before. There was a large window on my right. The first year I had nightmares every night, mostly about drowning. I went on a retreat in November last year and received such healing. Part of which was to again see the fireworks through a large window near my bed and once more on my right. In the current run up to Bonfire night, seeing the fireworks for sale and hearing some go off, I feel none of the anxiety I felt for the previous 44 years. I have now named my baby Liberty because I am now free.

Taboos

I met an old lady who told me that when she was a little girl her mother handed her the wrapped body of a newborn, her sibling who was stillborn or quickly died, and told her to take the body to the undertaker to be top or tailed – tucked into a coffin with a stranger's body. She did this. What is remarkable is that, although it was thought appropriate for her to run this errand, she had not been told her mother was pregnant. That, apparently, was the more taboo subject.

My daughter Charlotte

My story is about my daughter Charlotte. When I was 20 weeks pregnant, we found out she had Patau's syndrome. After much turmoil, we decided to have a medical termination. The medics made the appointment for the following week and I duly went in, took the tablets and gave birth to my very poorly baby girl – stillborn, of course. What I later found out was that I could have waited. I could have carried her for longer, getting over the 24-week mark, which would have given her a birth and death certificate. Very sad not to have had this option – or known this option was available.

Conflict of interests

My 22-month-old son died in hospital. It was evening. I knew I wanted either to spend the night with him next to me in bed on the ward or to take him home with us that evening and put him in the cold spare room at home. Medics were horrified at each, pointing out (perhaps correctly) that others on the ward would be horrified/that my husband/parents/four-year-old son would be horrified. One cannot be totally selfish in the presence of death.

Commentary

The death of a child: stillbirth, neonatal and postnatal deaths – Jen Coates, Sands, and Helen Pepler, midwife

Jen is Director of Bereavement Support and Volunteering at Sands, the Stillbirth and Neonatal Death Charity. Jen has 25 years' experience in loss and bereavement, having worked with children and families with eye cancer early in her career and since in medical charities, the children's hospice movement, cancer support and counselling. Her passion and commitment is to give people choices in situations where it feels there is little choice, to empower them to make decisions, grow around their grief and find a new, healthy normal. She has a particular interest in the impact of bereavement on children and how to support them effectively through this, as well as ensuring that Sands' support and prevention work reaches diverse communities at higher risk of stillbirth and neonatal death.

Helen's career spans more than 40 years within the NHS, first as a registered nurse at St Bartholomew's Hospital, London, then as a midwife in Swindon. Her passion and special interest always lay with supporting families suffering bereavement through pregnancy loss and child death, and the staff caring for these families. Helen undertook a bereavement counselling diploma and set up a maternity and paediatric support service in the hospital. The team now also provides a unique 'Birth Matters' service. Helen is a founding trustee of the bereavement charity Wiltshire Treehouse (*www.wiltshiretreehouse.org.uk*), working with Child Bereavement UK, offering support to bereaved families and providing training for the education and healthcare sectors.

Bereavement through the death of a child is surely one of the most challenging forms of grief. Grief when the child dies before, during or shortly after birth, when relatively few family members and potentially even fewer friends have met them, can be even more challenging and isolating and yet this remains one of the last taboos. Some 75% of all child deaths from 24 weeks of pregnancy to 15 years are through stillbirth or neo-natal death (Campbell, 2019), and yet, because society finds it hard to acknowledge this type of loss, parents can find it hard to talk about their babies and to grieve in a way that is helpful for them.

If 14 toddlers were dying every day, which is the equivalent to this national statistic, there would be an outcry and wider recognition, making a parent's bereavement journey that much less isolating. Past medical care of stillborn babies and those who died shortly after birth has also left a legacy of long-ago bereaved parents who were never allowed to meet their baby, to know where they were buried or to feel it was permitted to grieve for them.

Parents who elect to conclude a pregnancy early due to social or physical concerns can feel a conflict of emotions and reactions, especially guilt, judgement and responses to the perceived denial of the right or permission to grieve. They may feel isolated from grief support groups and forums when they perceive that other families had no choice and they can feel that somehow their own grief is not real, valid or genuine.

Thankfully, healthcare practice has evolved with the advent of specialist bereavement support midwives and non-clinical, designated bereavement suites or rooms, empowering healthcare professionals to hold a space for parents to start developing enduring bonds with their baby. In a situation over which parents and families have no control, to give them information and choice can be healing and empowering. Time spent with the baby who has died, creating memories and allowing friends and family to meet the baby if they so wish, can set the tone for a healthy, if challenging, grief process and bereavement journey.

Phases and tasks of grief

The foundational building blocks of early human experience serve to influence how we face bereavement and grief in our lives, both as children and as adults. They also serve to help equip us with the ability to secure continuing bonds with those to whom we have an emotional attachment and who then die (Renck Jalongo, 2008).

Bonds with our adult family members, ties with siblings, interaction with peer groups and connections outside the family with caregivers, teachers, administrators and service providers have a profound effect on who we become and how we respond to life events such as bereavement. One important distinction to make between grief and bereavement is that bereavement is a permanent state of being, whereas grief is a journey with a beginning and an end. Both can be extremely lonely places and almost impossible to navigate alone.

Baby death affects parents but also often young siblings, children born after a baby has died and, increasingly, step-siblings, who may be older teens. The process of grief may follow a similar pattern for adults and children alike, but patterns of behaviour will depend on the stage of emotional development of the child, which will be discussed later in this commentary.

Adult grief can follow phases and tasks of mourning that may well overlap or reappear over time during the journey (Parkes, 1996; Worden, 2008).

An initial numbness, sense of shock, and denial with a sense of unreality may occur, and in the context of the death of an unborn baby or young child, this can feel acute. During this phase, the first 'task' is to accept the reality of a loss. Going through the rituals of a funeral or memorial and beginning to speak and think about the baby in the past tense are made much harder by the sudden juxtaposition of anticipated new life with unexpected death.

> ... now, even though I was bleeding a little, to hear the heartbeat had gone was a real shock. I remember the walk to the canteen with their brochures to think about 'what to do'. I couldn't fathom it or believe it. (*Letter to my First Child*)

Acceptance is always a challenge and moving in and out of this state when bereaved by stillbirth can be particularly difficult. Parents will not have actually 'met' their baby alive before they have to start accepting that he or she has died. After receiving the devastating news that a baby has died, the mother may still feel 'movements' in her womb – when standing up, for example – as the baby's body moves, and this can be extremely distressing.

For parents of babies who die in the days or weeks following birth, the start of their baby's life may well not have been as they expected during pregnancy, and they will already be adjusting to this different reality before having to adjust to their baby's death.

Another common struggle with this task and the process of grieving is around acceptance of the circumstances of the death. If a baby dies due to unanticipated complications or mistakes in care, this can add significantly to difficulties around grief and acceptance. The ability of family or friends to acknowledge or accept the reality of the baby's death is incredibly important to parents and made harder by the fact that many will not have met the baby. It takes confidence and communication on both sides for friends and family to come and meet a baby who has been stillborn or died soon after birth, but the benefits are immeasurable for the family. There may be practical challenges to meeting a baby who is seriously ill in a neonatal or special care baby unit but, if the parents wish it, again the support from having friends and family who are able to share memories can be great.

The first aspects of this unique grieving journey are swiftly followed by the formidable second task: that of working through the pain of grief. Sadness, fear, isolation, despair, yearning, hopelessness, anger, guilt, blame, shame, relief... there are many emotions to process. Waves of grief, irritability, loss of appetite, anxiety, tension and an inability to concentrate are all normal responses to the feelings bereaved parents may experience. Not only are there massive hormonal shifts and natural mood swings/bodily changes that accompany childbirth for women; the first weeks and months following pregnancy or baby loss can also be lonely and overwhelming. Birth mothers will still produce milk, and this is acutely painful both physically and psychologically. Isolation can be one of the most challenging aspects for bereaved parents to deal with. This, coupled with widespread ignorance about stillbirth and discomfort with the emotions around baby death, can lead to further isolation at an incredibly challenging time.

Once the family returns home after the baby's birth, unrealised plans and dreams for life with a new baby accentuate the void, and the third task, of adjusting to the environment in which the deceased is missing, can feel impossible to achieve.

This is complicated in stillbirth and neo-natal death by the fact that the baby may not have come home. Parents must face an empty nursery, unused baby equipment and bereaved siblings who were excited about meeting a new brother or sister. It may take a significant period and specialist support for any siblings to adjust to their new role as bereaved. It is vitally important that the parents and any siblings can clear nursery and babycare equipment in their own time – it should not be undertaken by well-meaning friends or relatives. Coming home to an environment stripped of any 'painful reminders' further reduces the world in which the baby existed and denies acknowledgement of their brief life.

The potential for the onset of postnatal depression is very real. Grief and postnatal depression can share similar symptoms, so it is important for grieving families to receive the support of family and community healthcare teams, perhaps along with community support agencies, especially in the short and medium term. 'Grief triggers', such as real or imagined physical pain, sights, smells or noises, can immediately and unexpectedly reignite the intense feelings and emotions experienced at the very beginning of the journey, compounding the grief burden even more.

> Telling people early [about the pregnancy] had been the right decision because of the sense of community and support that helped us to get through the next days and weeks, although it was hard facing anyone for the first time and having that difficult conversation again. (*I Am a Different Person Now*)

Peer support from other parents who have lived a similar experience can be extremely beneficial in reducing isolation and helping couples to navigate their different grief journeys.

> Losing… Rowan was one of the worst experiences of my life but somehow it made my relationships stronger… I have shared grief with my wife and family. (*I Am a Different Person Now*)

The potential for conflict and communication barriers between spouses may build if one partner feels a physical emptiness and unfulfilled need to nurture and the other struggles with oft-times unexpressed feelings of helplessness, protectiveness and sadness.

Physical or emotional abuse within families can become a reality or worsen, especially where blame, guilt, anger, hurt, frustration and other very real and damaging feelings are constant and unrelenting.

It is not unusual, or indeed abnormal, for feelings of failure, guilt, remorse, regret and blame of self or others to accompany the loss of any pregnancy. In situations where a pregnancy has been marred by complications, or perhaps was unexpected or unwanted, responses and emotional reactions to the baby's death or an untimely end of a pregnancy can sometimes be accentuated. Feelings of this nature can be extremely profound and far-reaching, especially if they are not acknowledged or disclosed. Where a pregnancy is disguised or grief denied, these feelings may be suffered silently for a lifetime, and many longer-ago bereaved parents only find the opportunity to be released from their pain as they walk alongside another newly bereaved friend or family relation.

Making the decision to end a pregnancy due to life circumstances, complications or the health of baby or mother raises complex challenges. Choosing to end a pregnancy, whatever the reason, may also leave long-lasting guilt and pain. It can feel as if the bereavement is somehow less valid in comparison with others' loss, and there may be fear of stigmatisation and perception of judgement, especially from others whose pregnancy ending was not chosen. This can make it impossible to seek sympathy or to forge common bonds with support groups and forums. Details of the pregnancy ending may be deliberately glossed over or hidden from others, and the ongoing weight of hidden truth and resulting guilt, self-judgement and punishment can cause chronic emotional pain and distress if not shared. The lack of confidence or opportunity to seek appropriate support may further cement emotional isolation, leading to chronic and unresolved grief. Crucially, validation of the pregnancy and giving an identity to the baby who is the subject of the grief can be liberating and therefore a conduit for emotional healing.

> I spent 44 years accusing myself of murdering my child… I went on a retreat in November last year and received such healing… I have named my baby Liberty because I am now free. (*Liberty*)

Some bereaved families may find it almost impossible to think of embarking on another pregnancy; others, albeit with trepidation, move into a new pregnancy with single-minded drive, renewed hope and anticipation. Some find they are unable to have further pregnancies, and this is an additional grief to come to terms with on top of the loss of a baby.

> As I write this Mary is pregnant again, we are now at 13 weeks, and yes we told people as soon as we found out. We know that if we suffer another miscarriage, we will need our support network again, and are not ashamed to use it. (*I Am a Different Person Now*)

The extremes of emotions felt during this time can cause periods of acute anxiety, which require sensitive and empathetic support from family, friends, caregivers and healthcare teams. The transition and often vacillation between the desire to move forwards and the fear of doing so can cause acute physical and emotional unrest (Stroebe & Schut, 1999). It is very normal that a new pregnancy will be filled from beginning to end with these opposing emotional forces, which can be extremely unsettling, but this is not always appreciated by those alongside. Emotional support is crucial where these feelings are present during pregnancy, and the practical reassurance gained from midwives, other professionals and support services involved is invaluable.

The phase of emotional investment in the future (and perhaps a new pregnancy) can help to provide the context for Worden's fourth task of mourning: to find an enduring connection with the baby who has died, while embarking on a new life. This is perhaps the most challenging phase of all. Placing the identity of the baby who has died within the framework of the family and giving them significance are vital for future conversations. The baby can then be freely acknowledged, mentioned and referred to by name, seen in photographs and talked about and lovingly remembered.

Personal, tangible reminders such as hospital name bands, photos and hand and footprints and casts take on incredible significance. Re-visiting these important reminders of a baby through the subsequent years of bereavement is an important part of healing and discovering a 'new normal' life without the baby.

Creating new memories or reminders, such as buying named decorations, including a soft toy in family photos as an acknowledgement throughout the growth of the family that the baby remains an important part of it, and dedicating trees as new life are all ways of developing enduring bonds and allowing the grief to sit more easily within continued life.

> I have a bit of the blood I bled into a tissue in a pretty bag by my bedside… I am just not ready to part with the physical connection. (*Connection*)

Control, choices and memory-making

The choices made initially are of vital importance for the future. Having said that, many people, in the spotlight of new grief, are unable to recognise what is actually happening – unaware of the choices they may have, or even how to make them.

> I was young, heartbroken and scared. If I could go back, I would have made different decisions. In fact I would actually have made decisions. I think I just got swept along. (*Swept Along*)

Control has been snatched away; the task of making decisions and choices can often be too much to bear.

> I said I'd wait, take the weekend to review the leaflets. My instinct to let your life end naturally. Theirs that 'it might take a long time'. But you didn't take your time in the end. (*Letter to My First Child*)

Knowing what needs to be known is hard both for parents and for the professionals supporting them. Information about choices must be conveyed in a timely, empathetic and professional way, in order for both to explore the transition between not-knowing, knowing and acting on that knowledge for the best possible long-term outcome. Frequent checking of each other's understanding about what has happened is crucial to providing the appropriate level of support and care and empowerment in a disempowering situation.

Bereaved parents have to create memories almost retrospectively; experiences surrounding the birth and the memories made of the baby are what new parents will take home as they leave the cocoon and security of the hospital environment. The onus therefore is on staff and caregivers to support families with these while the opportunities arise.

The burden of responsibility of choices should not rest with the family alone; shared decision-making, based on enlightening conversations encompassing practicalities, legalities and family culture and preferences, are vital to give control back to the family.

> All through the ambulance trip and around the hospital I carried our dead son wrapped up in one of my favourite T-shirts and a towel… In the hospital they inspected him but then returned him in a basket. This simple kindness of treating us as bereaved parents… really helped and is bringing me close to tears even now. (*I Am a Different Person Now*)

No matter at what stage of pregnancy or how the new life ended, naming the baby is an important step. Some families wish to keep a name originally chosen for their baby; others will prefer to give this little one a different name of significance that will endure, so forming the beginnings of an enduring bond. In circumstances where the pregnancy has been ended by choice, giving identity to the baby may be difficult due to the conflict of choice versus the experience of acute grief. The naming of the baby need not be hurried; for some, recovering some clarity of thought before decisions are made feels important.

Maternity staff can make a real difference to families if they refer to the baby by name and write the name on cot cards, name bracelets and certificates.

> I was a midwife. When washing and dressing a baby who had died, I always asked the parents if it was okay to talk to the baby as I found it hard not to. They were always comforted by this.
> (*Talk to the Baby*)

The importance of having the opportunity to spend as much time as possible with the baby following birth, if the family wishes, cannot be underestimated. Creation of a safe, emotional space in which this can occur is crucially important.

Bathing, dressing, cuddling and getting to know the baby can be extremely helpful. Finding familial features, such as 'toes just like yours', or 'long fingers like mine' can cement enduring bonds with the baby in the here and now and provide lasting proof of the reality, especially if these images are captured through photographs. A teddy or similar soft toy placed with the baby can become of great significance and bring much comfort to families. These can either be taken home or remain with the baby once the time comes to say goodbye. Many hospitals keep a book of remembrance where the name and date of birth of the baby is entered as a permanent reminder of a brief and real life lived.

The final parting of parent from child is of immense significance. The opportunity to spend time lying close beside one's baby for as long as needed can be one of the most important moments for facilitation of a healthy grief journey.

For many, photographs are important, whether taken by an expert who can spend time and make suggestions for family members to be involved, or by the parents with support and suggestions. Inclusion of siblings, parents, grandparents or friends may at first seem an alien concept. However, for many the long-term benefits of capturing these precious moments on camera will be appreciated further on the journey, as time passes.

Good quality hand and footprints can be made for the tiniest of babies using inkless wipes and special card. These may be copied and even replicated into pieces of jewellery at a later date, as can locks of hair. When offering such services, staff should always be aware that this will not be felt appropriate to some communities, so this needs to be done with that awareness. There are many ways to treasure these tangible pieces. Likewise, plaster casts of tiny hands and feet can later be made into highly tactile bronzed pieces that last a lifetime.

Toys, blankets, hats, clothes and name bracelets that the baby has worn following birth can all be brought together and placed in a memory box, provided either by the hospital or baby-loss charity, or perhaps sourced and even decorated by the family or siblings of the baby.

> We had brought a basket and a little white sheet to wrap her in, a soft blanket to go over her and a bunch of tiny forget-me-nots from our garden. There was consternation… (*The Box*)

Some are fearful of the thought of taking their baby home, or do not wish to do so. For others, it provides a much-sought-after connection with the baby and an opportunity to make new memories with siblings and family. Many hospitals have arrangements in place to facilitate this; likewise, many funeral directors can help.

> Eighteen years ago, a client requested that her little baby came home with her for the weekend… It was very special for a person who did not have the usual celebrations associated with a birth. (*Precious*)

There are, in fact, no legal requirements or prohibitions. However, on a practical note, if the family plans to take the baby home in this context, the local police service should know in advance of the journey. The registration number of the vehicle and place and time of departure and destination should be provided, so that, if the vehicle were to be involved in a collision on the journey, any attending emergency services would be aware of the status of the little passenger.

Funerals for babies should now be provided at no cost to families. Many funeral directors are a source of inspiration and support for families in creating a unique rite of passage that can be shared with family and friends.

> It would have felt so much kinder to this little soul to have prepared him, carried him and buried him without any interference. One never forgets but remembrance is tinged with regret. (*Regret*)

Again, it is important to take time to make decisions that are right, maybe with advice and support from a funeral director, faith leader, burial celebrant or crematoria staff.

Sibling/other children support
This subject is dealt with in more detail in the next chapter, but there are specific issues that may be helpful to consider around stillbirth and neo-natal death.

Children sometimes have mixed feelings when a new brother or sister is expected. A child who felt jealous during the pregnancy might feel guilty after the death of their sibling. It can be helpful to try to reassure a child that the death was nobody's fault and that nothing they did or thought made the baby die. This can be especially important to address when older, possibly step-children are involved. Within a blended family, a new baby can cause a wide range of emotions and responses within an environment where stable communication is not always easy, and alliances and support are possibly just beginning to evolve.

Some children may feel angry towards the baby who died or towards their parents. Children may also fear that they or others close to them may die as well. They may be more upset than usual at being separated from their parents, especially if their mother is critically ill or must stay in hospital. As with adults, children – especially younger children – may find it difficult to express their feelings. Look for changes in behaviour, especially regression to younger behaviours.

Even very young children can sense when something is wrong. If they are not told what is happening, they may be frightened and imagine they are at fault for making parents feel sad.

> My brother died at one week old, I was almost three… I lost my parents that day. They went to the hospital and never really came back. I thought it would destroy them to feel something and I wanted to protect them.
> (*Collusion*)

Consider what external support you and your child(ren) might need, either from relatives or friends or through play therapy. Professionals, such as the health visitor, teachers and childminders, should be informed so that they can support your child accordingly.

Children may also make the baby an imaginary friend. You/your child's nursery may find this unsettling, even though it is a common way for children to cope with loss. Children will often play funerals with toys or friends, and this too is a normal way of making sense of what has happened.

Subsequent pregnancies and pregnancies within the wider family circle may be confusing for children and they may ask when/whether that baby is going to die too. This can add to the anxiety of a parent already concerned about a pregnancy.

There are many ways to involve younger children and help them feel part of what is happening around them. They may include, in the short term:

- going to the hospital to see the baby to say goodbye
- bringing baby home to say goodbye as a family
- helping to plan and participating in the funeral
- adding something like a drawing or letter to a memory box or the baby's coffin
- helping to paint the coffin
- having a photo of or with the baby
- visiting the baby's grave or choosing/visiting a special place where the baby's ashes are scattered.

In the longer term, important dates, such as the anniversary of the date when the baby was born, died or was due to be born can be especially sad for parents. It can be helpful to talk to children in advance about any dates that might be more difficult than others, so that they are aware that their parents may be sad again for a while. Important dates and the lead up to them may trigger feelings of grief for children too. Holidays and other times when families gather together can be a time when the baby is especially missed. Family birthdays, and especially those of a surviving twin or multiple birth, can also be bittersweet. Some families do something special to remember their baby on these occasions, such as:

- lighting a candle for the baby or choosing a special decoration together
- having a family day out
- baking a cake for the baby or visiting a special place
- hanging a stocking for the baby or putting ornaments on a Christmas tree or lights at Diwali in their memory
- creating traditions and involving family and friends.

> I have felt compelled not to hide you, nor the other four children whom I have subsequently lost and who are at rest and remembered with you under the same Dorset apple tree. (*Letter to My First Child*)

Advice points

For parents

1. Grief is a journey and may feel lonely but does not have to be walked alone. Meeting others who have experienced a similar loss can be very beneficial.
2. It is very normal, if challenging, for partners to grieve very differently

For those supporting the family

3. Talk about the baby who has died and mention them by name. Remembering special dates and anniversaries will feel very comforting to bereaved parents.
4. Give time and be ready to listen, hear and empathise; everyone is different and will make different choices.
5. Help parents to take time to acknowledge their loss and make memories so they can travel their grief journey feeling supported and acknowledged.

References

Campbell, A. (2019). *Vital statistics in the UK: Population and health reference tables – 2019 update.* Office for National Statistics. www.ons.gov.uk/releases/vitalstatisticspopulationandhealthreferencetables2019update

Renck Jalongo, M. (Ed.). (2008). *Enduring bonds: The significance of interpersonal relationships in young children's lives.* Springer.

Parkes, C.M. (1996). *Bereavement: Studies of grief in adult life.* Tavistock Pubications.

Stroebe, M., Schut, H. (1999). The dual process model of coping with bereavement: Rationale and description. *Death Studies, 3*(23), 197–224.

Worden, J.W. (2008). *Grief counselling and grief therapy.* Routledge.

Resources

Books

For adults and professionals

Heineman, E. (2014). *Ghostbelly.* Feminist Press. (A personal account of a stillbirth, and the harrowing process of grief and questioning that follows)

Schott, J., Henley, A. & Kohner, N. (2016). *Pregnancy loss and the death of a baby – Guidelines for professionals* (4th Ed.). Sands UK/Bosun Publications.

Wright, E. (2018). *Ask me his name: Learning to live and laugh again after the loss of my baby.* Blink Publishing.

For siblings

Crossley, D. (2001). *Muddles, puddles and sunshine: Your activity book to help when someone has died.* Hawthorne Press.

Durant, A. & Gliori, D. (2013). *Always and forever.* Random House Children's Publishers.

Faithfull, K. & Kitson, S. (2018). *In the stars.* Sam Kitson Publishing.

Gliori, D. (2003) *No matter what.* Bloomsbury

Heegard, M. (1988). *When someone very special dies: Children can learn to cope with grief* (Drawing Out Feelings). Woodland Press.

Heegard, M. (1991). *When something terrible happens: Children can learn to cope with grief* (Drawing Out Feelings). Woodland Press.

Poore, E. (2019). *Where are you Lydie?* Emma Poore Publishing.

Stickney, D. (1997). *Waterbugs and dragonflies: Explaining death to young children.* The Pilgrim Press.

Films

Up. (2009). Doctor, P. & Peterson, B. (Dirs.). Pixar Animation.

Return to Zero. (2014). Hanish, S. (Dir.). Canonball Productions.

Journal articles

Butlin, H. (2020). A box full of memories. *British Journal of Midwifery, 28*(2), 767–77.

Blogs

Figlioni, K. (2019). *When it comes to talking to children about death, it's better to be honest.* Marie Curie Talkabout; October 24. www.mariecurie.org.uk/blog/when-it-comes-to-talking-to-children-about-death-its-better-to-be-honest/259629

Websites

Child Bereavement UK: www.childbereavementuk.org

Dopeblackdads.com (Website 'to heal, inspire, educate and celebrate black dads')

Dopeblackmums.co.uk ('Digital safe space for black women to navigate motherhood together')

Kidspot.com: www.kidspot.com.au/baby/real-life/reader-stories/even-though-our-babies-have-died-the-bond-with-them-continues/news-story/99ecd628c75a5c3024daddec72b40b28

Lullaby Trust: www.lullabytrust.org.uk

Miscarriage Association: www.miscarriageassociation.org.uk

Reflect: https://reflectyork.co.uk/what-we-do/support-advice-and-counselling/unintended-pregnancy

Stillbirth and Neonatal Death Society: www.sands.org.uk

Outside the Box

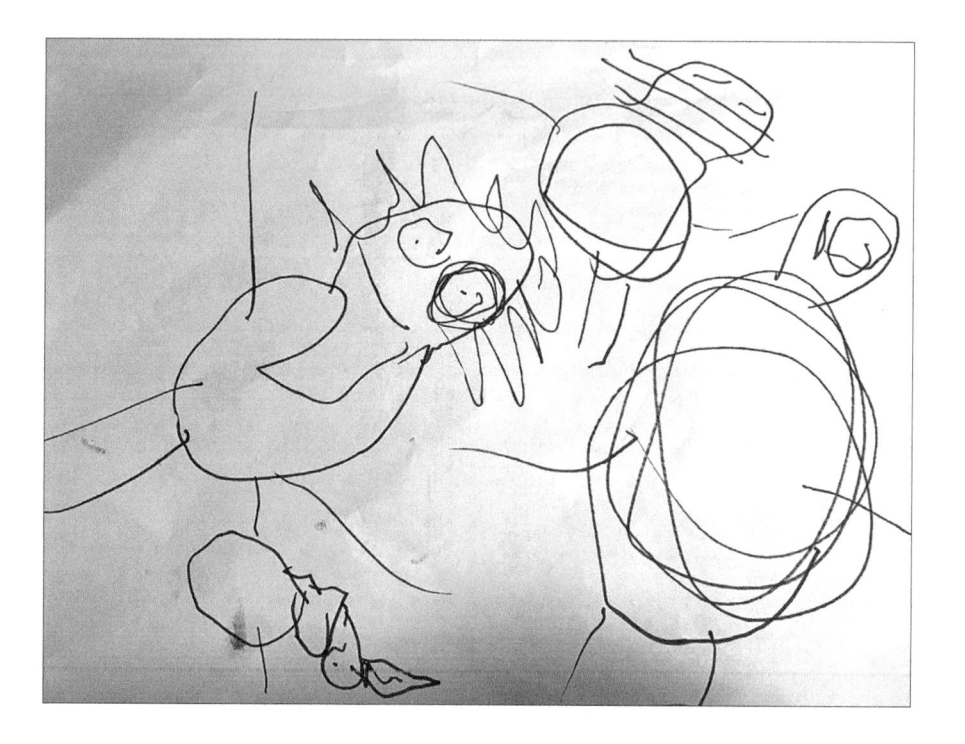

4 – The wisdom of children

Why will he die?
I have a six-year-old son, and my own father is 93. We've obviously been aware for a long time that Alfie's Grandpa isn't going to be around forever. Over the last two years, we've talked totally openly about this with Alfie. 'But why will he die?' 'I don't want to die.' 'I don't want you to die.' We haven't shied away from anything. I've talked with him about how we can die when our bodies have had enough. When he says he wants to live forever, I exclaim 'Oh, I don't!' We have discussed what a relief it must be, when the body has had enough, to let go. Naturally, he's also talked about what happens after. I don't know and he knows I don't know. We've talked about different beliefs. About a year ago he decided it would be okay for us to die, because we would be reborn and I would be his mum all over again (in the same house… and his toys would all still be here). I don't belittle his beliefs; I merely add them to the list of beliefs I've heard of.

Strong together
I was very young when Mum was first ill. I never felt like I didn't know what was happening. I knew she was sick. It didn't matter if it was cancer or any other sickness; that isn't important when you're nine. Of course I was upset and scared and sad, but I knew my mother; I knew her right to the core; she was strong and true and courageous. I never felt as though she hid the truth from me. I saw the injections she had to give herself, the colostomy bag, the cupboards full of medicine, the morphine-induced fits, and it didn't scare me. In fact, I often think I may have seen more than anyone else did. I did ask her once, 'Please promise me you won't die,' and she said, 'I can't promise that,' and then we talked about it. I felt strong when we were together.

Can I come with you?
My husband died when my daughter was three, but he told her all about what was happening. He showed her four cards in different colours – black for sin,

white for purity, red for Jesus's blood and gold for the crown of gold. And she said to him, 'Are you going to be with Baby Jesus?' 'Yes, I am.' 'Then can I come with you?' 'No, you can't. It's not your time. But one day you will, and we will be together again.' And she remembers that, and it helped her.

Taking teddy

A young child was dying in a hospice. The parents had been there for hours and found the waiting unbearable. They went away to have a short break and a cup of tea. One of their other children stayed behind with her sister, quietly holding her hand. The little girl died and, before she went to get her parents, the older girl reached over and tucked a teddy bear into her sister's arms.

Another daddy

Sitting on a bench on the top of a hill, after shouting 'Hello' into the world, my three-year-old niece asked my sister-in-law, 'Mummy, can you grow another Daddy in your tummy?' That's a year ago, almost. Honesty has been hard but good.

Milestone

My mother took her own life when I was seven years old. The real irony of this is that her mother died two months before and she couldn't go on, so left her own daughter behind. I have often avoided telling people as I feel bad that it makes them feel awkward. I didn't go to the funeral and it was never ever talked about after. I was brought up by my father, who had his own emotions to deal with, in an era where everything tricky was swept under the carpet. However, last year was a milestone. I feel allowed to reflect and celebrate. My son reached 7½ years. I've been able to provide him with a mother for longer than I had one for! Milestones such as my graduation, wedding day or even the day I had lived longer than her seem to be more about me, but this one feels more worthy of note.

Under the blanket

Me and my brother often got off the school bus at my gran's farmhouse to chat with Gran and Grandad about our day and have a drink. That day (we were about nine or 10 years old), we noticed a blanket over the chair by the aga. Gran explained that Victor, the elderly farm worker (who lived in a hut on the farm by choice since the war), had just died. He'd come into the kitchen to rest as he felt unwell and had died peacefully. Gran made this normal. She said we could fold down the blanket and say goodbye. I remember thanking him for making us laugh so often and for helping so well on the farm, giving him a kiss and then heading home. Maybe this introduction to death, as relaxed as introducing us to new life in the family, played a part in my choice of career as a nurse in palliative care.

Oma Wacka's stick

When Oma Wacka died, I was probably 12. She had always been somewhere around, in the garden or the house, chasing us children with her walking stick. I don't know why she loved doing that – maybe because she liked the idea of being a bit of an old witch. We sometimes were a bit afraid of her, but not really. Then she stopped walking and we had to feed her (I usually did that – I somehow preferred to help her than the little children). Then she got sick and we (the children in the house) somehow felt the need to go into her room with our recorders and music and start playing and singing. Max even told a story. Oma Wacka was there, her eyes even open (sometimes). I'm sure it didn't sound very good but we had the feeling we had to do it not because someone pressurised us but because it felt good. After we finished our concert, we said goodnight and went to bed. I can't remember any adults being around. The next morning we went down to look after her. When we saw her dead there was no surprise. Max again (he was the oldest at 14) had the idea to search for all the candles we could find. So in the end the small room was filled with candles, with Oma Wacka in the middle! I remember it as one of our adventures in childhood, not spooky, not weird and no one was crying (usually there was someone crying when we had our adventures). I only cried when we were at the funeral run by the adults. My best friend and I still love to share stories connected with Oma Wacka, who loved us children so much that she had to chase us with her old-people stick. Long after she died, we still played with her sticks.

Peaceful departure

1963 or 1964, summer. A hot, still afternoon in my great grandparents' house. Great Grandma was in the garden. Great Grandad came in from his walk 'uptown'. Light summer suit, tie, straw hat. He sat in his usual chair by the window next to the table. I was about five years old. He asked me 'Would you get me a glass of Lucozade?' I, pleased to be asked and trusted, gladly went and unscrewed the orange bottle and poured the golden liquid. Using both hands, took it through to Great Grandad, who had fallen asleep. Glass on the table, I sat at his feet and waited. He often fell asleep. I waited and waited a bit more. It was all very peaceful. I thought it odd he wouldn't wake up, so I went and found Great Grandma. She realised what had happened, shepherded me across the lane to Grandma's and then much incomprehensible adult chaos let loose… I wasn't allowed to go the funeral, but it was a lovely introduction to death.

Bye-bye body

I took my four-year-old grandson to see his grandfather at the undertakers. As we left, he said, 'Bye-bye, body.'

Cheerios

I helped to organise the funeral for a 14-year-old boy who died of an accidental drug overdose. His favourite food was Cheerios cereal. We had big bowls of Cheerios at his graveside and all the guests sprinkled them over his coffin, along with or instead of earth. Then we let off huge fireworks. Before that, we arranged for his body to be brought home and he lay tucked up in his bed for a couple of days. His mother said it helped her so much to have time to say goodbye – his death had been so sudden.

Hairy moment

My three- and five-year-old boys were involved in their Nanny's death from the moment that she knew she had a few months left. She had a cardboard coffin at home and they helped decorate it and she told them she was going to be buried in it. My son placed the pictures and letters they had drawn into her coffin so she would have something to read. At her funeral, the children played at her graveside with their toy cars and at one point someone had to stop one of the kids falling into the grave. It was a hairy moment, but we did giggle loads after.

Let the children decide

There were four children in the shared house where our friend Xen lived. Their adults were undecided whether the children should go to the funeral. We visited the household and read Britta Teckentrup's *The Memory Tree* to the children and some of their adults. After this, the children decided they would like to visit the cemetery before the funeral and see where Xen would be buried. We were shown around by the wonderful cemetery manager on a sunny Sunday afternoon. We saw the chapel where we would congregate before the burial to talk about Xen, and then walked up to the lovely natural burial ground where she would be buried. Three of the four children came to the funeral.

Can I ask you a question?

Our grandson came with us to his auntie's funeral. He said, 'Nana, can I ask you a question? Has she got any clothes on in there?'

No ice cream

When I was eight years old, my brother died. I begged my parents to let me go to the funeral. They let me attend, but they didn't let me watch the coffin be lowered into the ground. Instead, my uncle took me for an ice cream. I didn't want ice cream, I wanted to be able to comfortably grieve for my brother in my own way. Ice cream didn't help me do that. Children are resilient, but they don't always need ice cream.

Choosing the coffin

A young mum had cancer. She was dying. She had a son aged seven. She decided she was going to share each step of the journey with him, answer any questions he had. Together they created a memory box; she wrote cards for the birthdays she wouldn't see and a letter for him to open when he was 21. They both took great comfort and pride in these shared and private preparations. And she asked him if, when the time came, he would like to choose her coffin. This he did, with great pride, selecting one with floating candles on the side because she always liked to have them in her bath. A few weeks after the funeral, he came back to visit the funeral director and found her with an elderly widower, quite unable to make the same choice for his wife. Sam asked if he could go in and see him. The man agreed. Sam went in and told him all about his mum, the funeral and the coffin. Then together, old boy and young man, they made the choice.

Being strong

I was with my mother when she died at home of cancer. My aunt and I were supporting my father. The most difficult time was afterwards when my aunt told me not to cry in front of my dad as I had to be strong for him.

Don't upset the bairns

My grandfather died at home when I was three. He knew he was dying and had given my parents explicit instructions about what to do, including, 'Don't upset the bairns, I don't want them at the funeral.' So he was taken away by the funeral director and I never saw him again or had the chance to say goodbye. All the grown-ups thought they were doing the right thing, but it couldn't have been more wrong. I hope things are more progressive these days.

Don't ignore the children

My dad put me to bed (as usual) and as usual in the morning I heard him come up the stairs to check if I was awake the next day – but it wasn't him. He had died in the night. I was 10. I was not allowed to see him, not allowed to go to the funeral. 15 years later, I still used to search the hospital record system to check he wasn't hiding. Even though I knew he wasn't really. Don't ignore the children.

Grief and grievance

When I was 13, my mother died of cancer. She had been dying for nine months but nobody told me. I came back from a holiday with friends and called 'Hello' into our house. My mother apparently responded 'Hello' upstairs and then promptly died. So I never got to say goodbye to her, and two weeks later I was sent off to boarding school, where it was hard to grieve. I became resentful of my father for not telling me and stayed angry with him for 17 years. At the end of this time, a therapist suggested that I might write my father a letter, expressing my anger towards him and giving him my reasons. When I did this, he wrote back: 'I wanted to tell you – but your mother would not let me – she could not bear to see your pain.' He also apologised for sending me to boarding school, and acknowledged: 'This was a mistake.' Hearing this, I realised that I had mistakenly born a grudge towards my father for 17 years and relations between us immediately improved.

Hello Grandpa!

My father died in 2008 and was buried in early October. On Christmas Day, the family gathered again and went to the village church. My six-year-old nephew skipped along the path, turned right and waved at the grave, 'Hello Grandpa!!' Then he waved up at the sky and waved again, 'Hello Grandpa!'

Not just yet

When my four-year-old niece asked my mum if she was going to die, my mum said, 'Of course not.' I jumped in and said, 'Yes darling, everyone dies, but hopefully not for a long time.'

Ssssh!

When my children, five and six years, said to each other, 'Be quiet, Dad's coming,' I asked why. They said I got too upset when Mum was mentioned. So a lot was never expressed amongst us due to fear of emotional upset. I somehow knew this wasn't OK but didn't know what to do. I saw a programme about [the children's charity] 'Winston's Wish'. We managed to get a weekend with them. The freedom we got at that weekend of being able to encourage openness with death and grief has led us to becoming a more intimate and loving, happy family. I wish we had more knowledge of death.

Friends and family

When I was a child, a girl from our primary school died at the age of seven. The parents and the teachers in school talked very openly about it with us and explained it to us, although we were quite young, which really helped us to understand why she had died. Before her funeral, all her friends and children from school who felt connected with her drew on her coffin so that it was full of beautiful colours. It looked very nice and made it really personal. It seemed to help the parents to see that they were supported by so many people and that all her friends took part in her funeral by painting on the coffin.

Done the course

A five-year-old in my class died. She had been ill for several years. Her death happened over half-term. On the day we returned, my head teacher came to say that a woman had turned up to counsel us because she had 'done the course'. I said that I would be leading the session as my class and I had actually known the little girl. We sat in a circle and shared our memories of our friend and classmate. We laughed together. We cried together. None of us had 'done the course'.

Not in front of the children

As a teacher, I was reading *Charlotte's Web* and I got upset as it reminded me of my son who died as a baby. I felt the need to explain why I was upset in a very brief manner. I later found out a parent had complained about me mentioning it.

We didn't know how

My dad died of cancer just before I was 17. I was an only child and very close to my dad. My mum was devastated but I couldn't connect or communicate with her. I just shut off my emotions and disconnected from the situation. Mum desperately wanted and needed that emotional closeness and to talk about my Dad; she just didn't really have anyone else to share her feelings with and friends stayed away. But I just didn't know how or want to connect with her. I had a lovely boyfriend who is now my dear husband, and I shared my grief with him. My mum died four years ago and I was never able to connect with her emotionally and talk about 'Daddy'. I wish I had been able to. I wish we had had access to support to help both of us, but we were just left on our own and we didn't know what to do. I hope things will be better for our children and I hope that my mum knew in her heart that I cared.

Green highlights

My friend passed away suddenly in October 2016. She and I used to have competitions at church of which hair colour would shock the old ladies the most. I was winning with green highlights, then she dyed her hair a bright aqua colour, which took the winning spot.

A week before she died, she'd had to dye her hair a bog-standard brown to be a bridesmaid at a wedding. All I could think of during her funeral, and still to this day, is that she died with a hair colour that didn't match her personality, and it didn't seem like she would be dead, because she needed to re-dye her hair like she'd planned and shock the ladies one more time.

It's okay to get personal

Kirsten is my mum's best friend. About a year ago, her dad died. On the day of the wake, we all gathered together in a room and it was quiet. I felt quite uncomfortable. Then, Kristen went to her dad's casket and began to sing. At the end of the song she cried out, 'I LOVE YOU DAD.' In between the sobs and the screams, I felt peaceful and safe, because I realised getting personal around death is allowed.

Such a bitch

One of my friends had terminal ovarian cancer. About a week before she died, I went to visit her and got into bed beside her – she was at home. I turned to her and said: 'When you die, can I have all your jewellery?' She replied, 'You are such a bitch. If I had the strength to kick you out of this bed, I would.' We laughed until we cried, and I held her and told her how much I loved her. It was a wonderful moment.

Commentaries

Helping children and young people through bereavement – Sarah Harris, Director of Bereavement Support & Education at Child Bereavement UK

Sarah is a qualified registered child and family social worker with more than 20 years' post-qualification experience working with children, young people and their families. Before becoming a qualified social worker, Sarah worked in social care and the voluntary sector, in adult mental health and disability. Before joining Child Bereavement UK, Sarah was a principal child and family social worker, developing and leading nine centres of excellence. She is an experienced training facilitator and has designed and delivered training to statutory agencies, including schools and NHS trusts, as well as to third sector and voluntary organisations.

The overriding themes that have come out of these childhood, children's and young people's stories are those of curiosity, honesty, memories and, of course, loss. Much of what follows is taken from guidance freely available on the Child Bereavement UK website and our information and guidance sheets, short films, case studies and associated literature, which is based on what families have told us is helpful to them, and evidence and research.

We often forget how many children at any time will be experiencing or anticipating a bereavement. National figures suggest that the equivalent of one child in every class group of 30 will be affected by the death and dying of a carer, sibling, grandparent, classmate, teacher or other important figure in their lives. As responsible adults in their lives or professionals working with them, we need to be ready to offer appropriate support.

It is important to remember that every child is unique and will cope with the death of someone important in their own way. There is no magic formula, but things that help include:

- clear, honest and age-appropriate information
- reassurance that they are not to blame and that different feelings are okay
- normal routines and a clear demonstration that important adults are there for them
- time to talk about what has happened, ask questions and build memories
- being listened to and given time to grieve in their own way.

Younger children – curiosity

When a parent, main carer, sibling or other important person is not expected to live, the prospect of communicating this to a child can be very daunting, especially when you are yourself upset or in shock. For a parent who is seriously ill, the thought that their children will grow up without them may be devastating. Not knowing what course the illness will take or how the child's life will be affected makes it harder to know what to say. To protect children, and themselves, parents or carers may want to avoid the subject for as long as possible. Stories like *Strong Together* and *Can I Come With You?* demonstrate how helpful it can be to overcome this natural reticence, while *Grief and Grievance* illustrates the lasting damage that failing to do this can cause.

Even very young children tend to pick up when something is wrong, although they may not fully understand what is happening. They will feel more secure if they are kept informed in a way they can understand, as avoiding the subject may leave them afraid that they have done something wrong or too worried to ask questions.

For young children, it is helpful to explain the illness or situation in basic terms – for example: 'Daddy's illness is called cancer. Because of it, his body can't work very well. You haven't done anything to make this happen, and you can't catch cancer, like some other illnesses.' This direct reassurance is very important for children to hear. Or, 'Eddie was driving his car and it crashed. He was badly hurt and is in hospital, but he is so hurt that the doctors can't make him better.'

What you tell children will depend on their age and understanding and how much they already know. It is best to start giving them information early on, in bite-size chunks, allowing them time in between to process what they've been told and ask you any questions. Only give them the information they need at the time; you can add more later.

Children may ask repeatedly, 'When's Nanny coming back?' or, 'Where has she gone?', even though they've been told clearly what has happened. They may hunt everywhere for a 'lost' person, and so a clear explanation of what 'died' means may help. Children may play games where the person dies or is still alive. They may seem fascinated with death, play-act about death or ask repeatedly about it. All of these are ways that children show that they are processing their understanding of what has happened.

If the child knows something already, acknowledge this: 'You know that Joe has been ill for a long time, and the doctors have been trying to make him better.' Their response may help you to understand how much they already know. You can ask what they've noticed about Joe recently. They might say something like, 'He's too tired to play with me.' They might go on to say more about what they think is happening or you can ask what their understanding is of the situation. The answers you get to these enquiries will guide how the conversation continues.

Young children (under six years) are unlikely to understand fully what death means. They can switch quickly in and out of feelings, as they are not able to stay with very difficult feelings for long. However, they are still very much affected and still need support.

However, even very young children are interested in the idea of death in birds and animals. They can begin to use the word 'dead' and develop an awareness that this is different to being alive. Children of this age do not understand abstract concepts like 'forever' and cannot grasp that death is permanent, and their limited understanding may lead to an apparent lack of reaction when told about a death. They may ask many questions about where the person who has died is and when that person will come back. Children at this age expect the person to return.

Children of all ages watch adults closely and overhear adult conversations. They are usually aware that there is something seriously wrong, even when adults think they have successfully hidden the signs. Children who are seriously ill often know more than their adults realise. It is important to note that, just as adults seek to protect children, so children may try to protect the adults around them by not showing their feelings. We see this in the story *Openness*, where the children try to avoid upsetting their father by not talking about their mother in his hearing.

Honesty

Young children also tend to interpret what they are told in a very literal and concrete way. It is important to avoid offering explanations of death such as 'lost', 'gone away' or 'gone to sleep', as they may cause misunderstandings and confusion.

There is often uncertainty about when someone will die. Some people die much sooner than expected; others live longer than anyone thought they would, surviving treatment after treatment. Young children often only understand things in very concrete terms and it is hard if you can't provide them with a definite answer. The family may have had to live with uncertainty for many months or years and may have prepared for the worst several times. In such circumstances, it can be hard to believe that the person is going to die, and so children may not be willing to accept what is now being said to them.

As adults, we might fear the questions children may ask. They may be the very questions we dread or can't bear to think about, but it is vital to try to respond to children at the right time for them and not to put them off, as opportunities to support them may then be lost. Answer any questions honestly and simply, and check that they have understood what you have said. If you don't know the answer, it is okay to say, 'I don't know, but if I find out, I'll tell you.'

When a child asks, 'What happens when people die?', a simple answer that can be understood by most children is: 'When someone dies, their heart and breathing stops, and their body doesn't work anymore.' You can also acknowledge that this is a good question that can be hard to answer and ask the child what they think. This can help you to find out the child's level of understanding and correct any misconceptions they may have. It can also be a chance to share thoughts according to family culture and beliefs.

Memories and remembering

Remembering is helpful. Feelings may be too raw initially, but looking through photographs, recalling experiences or visiting places where you remember being with the person who died can help children connect with their grief. It can also be helpful to explain that tears are there for a reason. They indicate that the person crying needs support and, on the physiological level, they enable the body to release chemicals that make us feel calmer. In time, you may want to do something in memory of the person who has died.

Thinking about the person and what is right for them will guide your choice about what to do in their memory. Here are some ways that people have found helpful:

- plant something – a tree, bush or spring bulb display
- create a memory box in which to keep photographs, cards, toys and small items. If for a parent, it might include a scent bottle, a piece of jewellery or a small item of clothing connected with the person
- make a memory jar, using coloured sands to represent different memories
- create a place in the house with a photograph, perhaps a candle and some flowers and some snuggly cushions where people can go and relax and remember the person who has died
- wear something with the person's picture on it or a small badge or piece of jewellery
- erect a bench in a special place you associate with the person
- create a book of memories, inviting everyone who knew them to contribute pictures or stories, or do an online version
- keep a journal or write poetry or a song about the person

- do something specific to that person and what they liked to do. For example, paint a mural on the wall of a music venue a young person went to regularly. One group of friends created an online football team in memory of their friend, who loved gaming.

There is no right way or wrong way of remembering. Each child or young person or adult is unique and that is how you will want to remember them. Whatever you choose, do not put pressure on yourself to make a perfect item or memory activity. The process of creating these things is as important as the result, because it is an enduring connection between you and the person and enables you to spend time thinking and talking about them with others and makes you feel closer to them.

Funerals

People often ask if children should be present at a funeral, and the answer is that the best person to answer that question is the child themselves, as demonstrated in *Let the Children Decide*. Clear and age appropriate explanations about how the funeral will work and a visit beforehand to the venue can all help normalise the experience. If the child chooses not to come, it can be very helpful to take a few pictures or film it, so that, if they have any questions or are curious at a later date, you have something to show them. Visiting the grave site or another place of remembrance can also be very helpful when the child or young person wants to remember a key anniversary or just feel closer to the person who died.

Bringing flowers or gifts or sharing a key piece of news is an important part of mourning. Some adults keep children away from the funeral for fear of breaking down in front of them but, in fact, this honest expression of feeling does not usually create a problem for the child. Being excluded and not knowing how the story ended can bring a lifetime of unhappiness, as *No Ice Cream* exemplifies. Older children often gain a lot from contributing in some way – reading out a letter or poem, putting a drawing in or on the coffin, or simply lighting a candle or placing some flowers on the grave or other remembrance site. There are so many ways children and young people can be invited to get involved, and they will have their ideas too, if given space to contribute.

Loss and grief

It is very important to explain to children that they will experience a wide range of emotions and that all of that is normal and okay. They may feel sad, or angry towards the person who died for leaving them, or numbness, or fear about the future, or regret that they did not do or say something to the person before they died. They may feel guilty when they have had a good day and for a few hours forgotten about the person. They (and their adults) need to know all and any of this is to be expected. There is no set order for children and adults to 'move through' grief; most people move back and forth between these feelings. At times it may feel very difficult for the adults to hold their grief as well as that of their children, especially if their children's grief is manifesting in behaviours that are hard to understand. This is when the support of a child and family bereavement service can be invaluable.

It is also crucial to inform other adults working with your children about what is happening or has happened and to tell them when a key anniversary is approaching, such as a birthday or deathday, so they can be prepared for any changes in your child's behaviour and respond in a creative and supportive way.

Young people

Teenagers face different challenges in facing death and bereavement. They are already coping with all the impact of hormonal changes on their life, making them subject to mood swings and vulnerable to pressure to fit in with their cohort. They may find it hard to talk to the adults in their lives, but equally not find support for their experience from their peers. They often turn to online information and social media to find answers to what they are dealing with. Youth workers, teachers, religious leaders and other key non-family adults can sometimes play a crucial role. Offering young people opportunities to open up is very important and they benefit enormously from having contact with other young people who are also coping with bereavement, as it reduces the sense of isolation. There are now a wide range of county-based charities that offer this kind of service and also the national children's bereavement charities, Child Bereavement UK and Winston's Wish (see Resources for details).

Some teenagers may be the primary carer for the person who is dying and they will have very particular practical and emotional needs. They often do not realise there is support for them and keep the situation secret for fear that social services may step in and remove them into care. Advice is available on the NHS website for young carers and there are specialist organisations, like the Carers Trust and Action for Children, who work specifically with young carers.

Young people may also be particularly vulnerable when they become the confidante of a closely affected adult. If the adult is without appropriate support, the young person can be placed in an emotional caring role that prevents them from expressing their own needs.

These stories about the wisdom of children and young people are both powerful and informative and point towards their strength and resilience and the importance of honesty and enabling the grieving process to unfold naturally.

With the right support, children, young people and their families can rebuild their lives and find a new sense of normal after the death of the important person in their lives. There is more detailed discussion of the grieving process and models for understanding it in the commentary to Chapter 11, 'Grieving and Remembering', by Dr Marilyn Relf.

Advice points

- Every child is unique and will cope with the death of someone important in their own way.
- The best person to decide if a child should attend the funeral is the child him or herself; being excluded can bring a lifetime of unhappiness.
- Memorialising at the funeral and after is an important part of grieving. Children should be invited to memorialise in their own ways.
- Tell other adults working with the child about what is happening or has happened, and when a key anniversary is approaching, so they are prepared and can be supportive.
- Young people may find it hard to talk, so offering opportunities for them to do so and to meet with other bereaved young people is very important.
- Children and young people who are carers may need particular support through bereavement.

Deaths in military families – Helen Fisher, Family Bereavement Support Practitioner, Winston's Wish

Helen is a counsellor and play therapist who has supported bereaved children and their families since 2007. She joined Winston's Wish in 2013, from a local children's bereavement charity, and extended her work to support families nationally where the death was as a result of or connected with military service or homicide.

First, an important note: some families whose loved one was serving in the armed forces when they died may not have a positive experience of the military, and wouldn't necessarily consider themselves a bereaved military family.

All families are unique and have numerous challenges that life throws at them. Life as a military family is no exception and has a number of differences that may feel like challenges or advantages when compared with a non-military family. When a death has occurred in a family that has a connection to the armed services, there will be aspects of military life that contribute to how individuals and the family grieve and how the family manages their combined grief as a unit as they find their new normal and their path into their future.

One of the key determinants of grieving is the relationship with the deceased person prior to their death. When a loved one is often away on service for long periods of time, the routine of family life can follow the patterns of their tours of duty, with the family functioning as a lone parent unit for many months at a time, then adapting to the return of their loved one. This can bring major shifts to the family dynamic. The returning parent may make up for lost time and be hugely fun and less strict with routine or boundaries. They may continue to delegate to their spouse, or the family may have to manage the emotional fall-out of their loved one's experience on active service and how they are coping with this.

The child's experience of a parent being away from the family home for long periods of time and not having the felt sense of their presence with them, despite the wonders of video calls, can make it hard for them to comprehend the finality of death. They may rationalise that their absent parent is just away on service, maybe on a 'secret mission', and they will be back when they can. Such magical thinking can hinder a child's acceptance of the reality of their parent's death and thereby postpone or delay their grief, which will impact on how the family as a whole grieves.

Often, while service personnel are away, their families are held by the military through its established structure and within a rich community of other military families. We hear of strong and close friendships, which are enriched further when families live on military bases, both at home and abroad, that form significant support networks. However, following a death, some families report that they have felt isolated from the community, as their friends struggle to find the words or distance themselves as they wrestle with their own fears about the possibility and reality of what could happen to their own loved one.

Moreover, while it may be some weeks or months down the line, families who have lived on a military base will ultimately have to move following the death. The children will have to leave their schools and friends and the surviving parent their job, if they have one, as they will have to relocate, sometimes from another country back to the UK and civilian life. These secondary losses and the fragmentation of what was their supportive network, impact further on the children's experience of bereavement.

Among the families I have supported following the death of their loved one, whether killed in action overseas or where the death occurred while they were on active service, I have heard polar extremes of families' reactions to how the military establishment responds following the death. Some families have embraced and been relieved by the military arranging and planning the funeral, with due ceremonial rituals and honour; others have felt that their goodbyes have been taken out of their hands by the image the military seeks to portray, and they then have to manage those regrets too as they continue to process their grief.

The nature of the death and the circumstances around it may also hold significance to the bereaved family and to the support networks around them. A person who was killed in action is commonly put on a pedestal, their life honoured, as they have paid the ultimate sacrifice. They are seen only as a hero. Sometimes the family can feel under pressure to maintain this public front. Yet the reality of their parent may be completely at odds with their portrayal by the military or the media, which may be an incongruence that is hard to manage. For other families, their loved one may have experienced a life-altering injury or a mental health condition such as PTSD that contributed to them ending their own life. The family may hold a level of shame and remorse that their loved one's accomplishments, contributions and life have not been celebrated and they have not been held in such high regard as a hero. (For further information about PTSD symptoms and treatment, see Chapter 5, 'Out of the Blue', and the commentary by Dr Pat Johnson.) It is important that children should be allowed to remember their parent as a complete human being, as they were, with their gifts and skills, and not as they are defined by the nature of their death or the image the military wants to portray.

A number of families I have supported have blamed the military for the death of their loved one, for a variety of reasons. They may believe or have been led to understand that the equipment used wasn't adequate or checked, that too much was expected of their loved one, or that they were not sufficiently supported through their mental ill health. In circumstances like these, families can divert their distress into seeking justice and ensuring policies and procedures are amended, or into a memorial to support others in the name of their loved one. Challenges can occur within the family when this is driven by a parent as a way for them to process their grief and is not necessarily echoed by the child(ren), who may feel they are unable to grieve authentically or that their voice is unheard.

Finally, a challenge that a number of military family members experience following the death of a parent on service is the ethos of many serving personnel – that they should be stoic, strong and just get on with life. When a child has experienced their parent or caregiver in this way and has learned it is brave to not cry, to 'man up' and that the only acceptable emotion to demonstrate is anger, it removes permission from the child to grieve authentically and limits the possibility of grieving healthily. It is important that children are encouraged to grieve openly and cry when they are upset, laugh until their sides ache, and remember that, whatever they are feeling, it is okay. For that is the true gift of love.

Advice points

- Do not make assumptions about how a bereaved family will experience the military; not all families want to continue to wear that badge after a bereavement.
- The cycle of tours and experience of their parent working away from the family for periods of time can hinder a child's acceptance of the finality of death.

- Enable and encourage families to remember their loved one as a real and whole person, as they knew them, not only as a hero on a pedestal.
- The death of a serving parent may lead to the multiple secondary losses of home, friends, school and community and may break up the supportive networks previously available to the family.
- Encourage the children to express emotions, memories and worries authentically and not to take on messages about stoicism.

Resources

Books for children and young people

Cain, B. (2001). *Double-dip feelings: Stories to help children understand emotions.* Magination Press.

Davies, N. & Fisher, C. (2017). *The Pond.* Graffeg.

Dowling, S., Blackman, N. & Hollins, S. (2003). *When somebody died.* Books Beyond Words.

Duffy, C.A. & Ryan, R. (2010). *The Gift.* Barefoot Books.

Halliday, N. (2006). *The lonely tree.* Halliday Books.

Hollins, S. & Sireling, L (2004). *When Mum died.* Books Beyond Words.

Huebner, D. & Matthews, B. (2008). *What to do when you dread your bed: A kid's guide to overcoming problems with sleep.* Magination Press.

Ironside, V. & Rodgers, F. (2004). *The huge bag of worries.* Hodder Children's Books.

Mellonie, B. & Ingpen, R. (1983). *Lifetimes – The beautiful ways to explain death to children.* Bantam.

Ness, P. (2011). *A monster calls.* Walker Books. (For teenagers,)

Pudney, W. & Whitehouse, E. (1998). *A volcano in my tummy: Helping children to handle anger.* New Society Publishers.

Rosen, M. (2004). *Sad book* (illustrated by Quentin Blake). Walker Books.

Teckentrup, B. (2014). *The memory tree.* Orchard Books.

Verley, S. (2013). *Badger's parting gifts.* Anderson Press.

White, E.B. (1952). *Charlotte's web.* Harper & Brothers.

Books for adults and professionals

Bowlby, J. (1981). *Attachment and loss, vol 3.* Basic Books

Gardener, K., Nugus, D. & Stubbs, D. (2008). *Hope beyond the headlines: Supporting a child bereaved through murder or manslaughter.* Winston's Wish.

Klass, D., Nickman, S.L. & Silverman, P.R. (1996). *Continuing bonds: New understandings of grief.* Taylor & Francis.

Stokes, J. & Stubbs, D. (2008). *Beyond the rough rock: Supporting a child who has been bereaved through suicide*. Winston's Wish.

Journal/Online articles

Levenson, J. (2017). Trauma-informed social work practice. *Social Work, 62*(2), 105–113.

Macmillan & Winston's Wish (2015). *Preparing a child for loss*. www.winstonswish.org/wp-content/uploads/2018/01/MAC15372childforloss Ellowrespdf20151223.pdf

Websites

Action for Children: www.actionforchildren.org.uk

Carers Trust: https://carers.org

Child Bereavement Network: www.childhoodbereavementnetwork.org.uk

Child Bereavement UK: www.childbereavementuk.org

Together for Short Lives: www.togetherforshortlives.org.uk

Winston's Wish: www.winstonswish.org

Resources for military families

There are few specialised resources specifically for military families. Those in the general list for this chapter will often be applicable and some from Chapter 3. One resource specific to military bereavement is:

Winston's Wish. (2020). *The family has been informed: Supporting grieving children and young people from military families* (2nd ed.). Winston's Wish.

Outside the Box

5 – Out of the blue

The Japanese windphone
In the coastal town of Ōtsuchi in the Iwate Prefecture in north-east Japan, looking out over the Pacific Ocean, stands a white telephone booth with an old black rotary telephone in it. The telephone is not connected. It is for calling the dead. Itaru Sasaki created the *Kaze no Denwa* (literally, phone of the wind) for his own personal use to mourn the death of his cousin. Then, a year later, in 2011, the tsunami struck. Some 2,000 people died in Ōtsuchi, and up to 20,000 in the whole affected area. More than 2,000 remain unaccounted for. Unimaginable degrees of loss. Sasaki decided to allow others to come and make use of his windphone. He said, 'I want people to resume their lives as soon as possible by expressing their feelings.' Word spread and now it has become a place of pilgrimage, attracting more than 10,000 people in the first three years. People come, some from quite far away, every year to mark a significant anniversary or when they feel the need. They dial the number of the person who died. They share their news, cry, tell people how much they love them. The wind carries their message out over the waves.

The Southall train crash
It was 19th September 1997. I was 23 years old and in my second proper teaching job. I was at work during the afternoon at the college where my father was the principal. His secretary came to find me in the staff room to tell me that there had been a train crash just outside London and that they thought he might have been on the train. There followed an agonising seven hours. At home with my mum and siblings, we tried in vain to get any information from the helpline that had been set up for relatives to locate their loved ones. Phone calls to the hospitals also drew a blank. As the hours went by and we did not hear from him, there was a dreadful dawning realisation that it could only mean one thing. Towards midnight, I knew what had happened for sure, although the rest of the family and my dad's devoted colleagues who had stayed with us were still holding out hope. I

felt alone with something then. At midnight, a police car crawled up the drive and I watched my family's hope turn cold. Inside I felt several things rising – grief and shock, alongside a feeling that I had to be strong to deal with what was to come.

I remember that the community police were young and inexperienced. They came bearing tragic news but didn't know how to help us and didn't stay long. We were alone and it was the middle of the night. My mum said we should sleep, and I had to come into her bed because I was trembling. I felt desperate to do anything I could to have relief from the grip of grief. I felt white and cold and empty and unsettled to the core. For weeks afterwards, we had cousins and dear family friends come to stay, which was a comfort and a welcome distraction. My father's death was reported in the national news, so long-lost friends came unexpectedly out of the woodwork. His funeral was huge, with people standing outside the church. I sang, but could hardly keep my voice together. All too soon came the end of compassionate leave and time to go back to teaching. Being in his workplace meant another wave of grieving with his colleagues. My father was exceptionally convivial and on friendly terms with everyone, right through to the cleaning staff. Everyone had something to say and one staff member had received a message from him in a dream. I stumbled through. A few weeks after he died, I found out that I had been pregnant at the time of his death. Not having known, I had been having a large nightcap of whisky every night to try to get to sleep, and unsurprisingly I miscarried four weeks after his death. This double grief was in some way a blessing. For a time, instead of 'staying strong', I just howled like a baby.

For such a long time when I saw a car like his, I thought it was him, and I had fantasies that somehow he was still alive. At the time, when we had been asked to identify his body, a police officer advised us not to, suggesting that it would be better to remember him as he was. We took that advice… although I'm sure for all of us it set our imaginations on fire and that was the stuff of nightmares.

For the months that followed, part of my role in the family was to liaise with the BBC, who were making a film about the train crash and some of the more political issues around it. The railways had been privatised and one of the cost-saving exercises had been to dispense with having a second driver in the cab. My dad's train had crashed because the one and only driver had turned around to pack his bag and missed a signal. Seven people died on that train and dozens were injured. The crash was a political hot potato we were caught up with. Unpicking the events leading up to the crash was an important and valuable way through the grieving process, and the BBC was very supportive. Realising that the driver too would be in shock and grief grew my awareness to a less personal dimension. I remember the first time I got back on a train. The train company gave me an assistant, who travelled with me to support me. I remember my tai chi teacher who worked with me to contain my energy and settle my nervous system. I remember so many flowers. Flowers on the doorstep every day. I remember my brother-in law, who did all our shopping for us because we were too scared to leave the house and each other. Our lives changed forever and we all gravitated into closer proximity to each other, living close to each other thereafter.

Six months after my father's death, I was pregnant again, with my daughter Freya, who is now 21. She and her brother have always surprised me with how keen they are to hear stories about their Grandad Clive, who they never knew but who would have been so incredibly proud of them.

Lady Diana

I am not a Royalist, but I can remember exactly where I was when I heard that Lady Di had died. I was in a park buying a cup of tea at a kiosk. The woman serving me asked if I had heard the news. It took a while to sink in. What followed was an extraordinary national outpouring of grief, which I felt somewhat alienated from. For me, she was a young woman who had died tragically young and who had done some noteworthy things, especially around AIDS patients. A terrible loss to her young family but not a personal loss to me. I watched the news broadcasts of people coming and laying wreaths, weeping together and supporting each other, lighting candles and reading the messages. I was surprised when some of my friends, who I knew had never followed her in the media or been interested in the royal family, decided to go down and join the crowds outside Kensington Palace. It almost seemed like a badge of citizenship. What I began to realise was that, along with the genuine adoration she had inspired in so many people, it was also the first legitimate opportunity in years for British people to feel able to come together en masse to grieve. I had been taken by my parents to Churchill's lying in state – a much more formal and controlled affair. Soldiers standing to attention at each corner of his catafalque. Crowds quietly queuing for hours and then silently filing past, occasionally dabbing at their eyes with a modest handkerchief. This new expressiveness felt refreshingly un-English, a reflection perhaps of the informality Diana had brought to The Firm. The upper lip trembled and the nation forgot about keeping up appearances. It *was* about her and I believe it was also about more than one loss. It was an upwelling of many small personal, unattended sorrows and losses. These little streams finally found their way to the surface and formed a great, rolling, uninhibited torrent. I felt glad about that, but a bit uncomfortable with the general expectation at the time that I should express huge personal sadness about her death. I kept rather quiet.

Killed for being a Goth

In August 2007 my daughter Sophie and her partner were 20 minutes away from home and decided to walk because it was a beautiful summer evening. They stopped at a local garage to get some cigarettes and met a young man, who invited them to a local park. They had been in the park two minutes when five young boys arrived. They attacked Sophie's partner first, Sophie went to his aid and was then attacked. This attack was motivated by their appearance. Sophie was brutally kicked and stamped on and died 13 days later.

I very quickly knew what I had to do to help myself to try and come to terms with her death and to prevent other people having to go through the same trauma. I perhaps need to explain a little about my background prior to the attack, because I believe it helped inform me about the way in which I had to move forward. I have been a youth worker for 30 years and that entails a lot of training in equality and diversity. I also had a sociology degree, so I saw a way to use my background training and education in a positive way and deflect the feelings of injustice and devastation. I fully believe that a person cannot live with the feelings of despair and red hot anger that surface after such an event.

At the time I worked for a government agency called Connexions, working with young people. The Hate Crime legislation had just been brought into being and the centre I worked in was a reporting centre. Prior to Sophie's death, I had recognised that alternative subcultures should be included. I then decided that I would work towards getting Sophie's case recognised as a Hate Crime and I fully believe that my focus on this and setting up a charity (*www.sophielancasterfoundation.com*) helped me to deflect and focus on something positive rather than dwell on the negative.

Healing, empowerment and resilience

The first loss we experienced was a shooting. He was 15. I was 13. In my community, you don't talk about death and grieving. It was weird; we all were struggling with all these contradictory feelings – grief at someone my age having died like that, someone who got on the same bus as us. My mum was confused when I told her about it because she wanted to know why I was mixing with a bad crowd. There was no support at school. So we all carried on, got used to it, became desensitised. The message was the Black community is violent, which was not the case. No one talked about supporting us, so we did it ourselves. I moved out aged 16 and my new home became a place of sanctuary for my peers, recreating the youth club we did not have. Everyone could talk to me, but I had no one to talk to, but I still kept a brave face.

I realised that I would have to drop the heavy bricks that were weighing me down. I got back in touch with my family and I decided to re-access the education system that had misunderstood me for so long. I got a scholarship to study criminology and youth studies. I had to fight to make my voice heard. I learnt to be eloquent while still standing up for the people that my course clearly had no idea about.

In my second year my closest-ever male friend was killed. Those bricks came piling back on. I broke. Manic depression. I come from a place where you have to do things on your own. I realised this time I needed help. The bounceback. Through working on myself, allowing others in and working as a youth worker, the journey started. However, the feeling of experiencing death professionally was different. Emotionally. But it made me view violence holistically. I realised that we view this kind of violence as affecting Black men and boys, but Black women and girls are always there – trying to keep them safe. Black women and girls are told to be strong for everyone else but not for ourselves. My personal and professional journey allowed me to understand that we can put our armour down and be who we want to be. Black girls deserve it. So, I created it, and that place is Milk and Honey Bees (*https://milkhoneybees.co.uk*). We focus on H.E.R. – Healing, Empowerment and Resilience.

The Manchester Arena

My son, Martyn Hett, was one of 22 young people killed by an Islamist suicide bomber at the Ariana Grande concert on 22 May 2017. The day he died, my job as a counsellor died with him. It feels like I have gone through a sliding door; I can still see my old life very clearly but I can't reach it or engage in it any more.

When Darren Osborne drove his van into worshippers at Finsbury Park mosque, the Imam and four others formed a human chain around him to protect him from the lynch mob. The photo of this inspired me to forgive the bomber publicly on the BBC.

My work now has one simple aim: to stop one single person from doing what this man did in Manchester. So I talk to school children about radicalisation and the dangers online. I talk about Martyn and show slides of his life. I tell them about the methods terrorists use to get to them and how quickly people can become radicalised in their own bedroom.

I also tell them about being kind. I tell them I do one kind act a day, something I have always done, even before it all happened. I tell them about tolerance and that there is only one human race they need to worry about and that is humankind. And if you turn that word back to front, it is 'kind human'.

I want to just catch that one child who is on the cusp of being radicalised and who changes their intention as a result of the talk. Then I will know something good has come out of it all. I ask, 'What is there that you can do to include people who are on the outside of the school community? How can you contribute positively to your community?' I think the answer to a culture of hate has to be more of us subscribing to a kinder way of being. I also ask young people to become more questioning about what they see, hear and read online and in the media.

I want the government to introduce Martyn's Law, which would require every big venue to have a terrorism action plan in place, and I am also doing a Master's degree in counter-terrorism.

There is no doubt that my personal therapy has helped me to function. Last year, I had six sessions of eye movement desensitisation reprogramming (EMDR) to help me get over the visit to the morgue to say goodbye to my dead child, which no mother should have to go through, and to the Arena, to the exact spot where Martyn died. Now I feel the time has come to have bereavement therapy to address the feelings of loss. There is a picture of Martyn on a windowsill in the lounge that I still can't look at. I don't want to move it, but I can't look at it or even open or close the curtains around it.

While on the surface I am resilient and strong and very outspoken, inwardly I often just want to go and crouch down in a dark corner and weep. But that is not going to happen as I am now more Martyn's mum than I have ever been.

Good for the heart

Although it's in my job title, the term 'restorative justice' seems cruelly inappropriate when someone has died as a result of a crime. Things simply can't be restored to how they were. When I first introduced myself to the family of a man who'd been killed, they told me that I wouldn't be able to cope with their anguish, expecting me to leave. The father said; 'If I ever see him, I'll throttle him', horrifying himself with the intensity of his rage. I didn't mention restorative justice or suggest communication with the person responsible (despite knowing that he was deeply remorseful). I simply sat with the family, met them regularly and listened.

After many months, the father suddenly said, 'He doesn't have any idea what he has done to our family.' I concurred and we came up with a plan for me to meet the man and read to him the family's victim personal statement that had been taken by the police. I would then report back to the family on his reaction. I visited the man in prison to ask if he'd be open to hearing the statement, and he said he would (in fact, he was willing to do anything to help). On hearing this, the father decided that it wasn't powerful enough – he would have to tell him face to face.

Through all the preparations, I didn't let on that the person responsible for this tragedy was sorry (I'm a criminal justice professional – why would I be believed?) and the father entered the prison still holding the image of the man 'smirking' in court, and the knowledge that he'd run from the scene of the crime, leaving his son to die. We took plastic cups of water to drink, as the father didn't trust himself not to hurl a cup of hot tea across the room at the man.

Almost as soon as we'd all sat down, the father asked for a break and ushered me out into the corridor. He needed to check what his eyes were seeing, and said, 'He's really struggling, isn't he?' Back in the meeting, the father didn't hold back on describing the impact of his son's death. He asked his burning questions and learnt that the man had run because he'd panicked and was a 'coward', and that he had been petrified and ashamed on seeing in court the family of the man he'd killed. As he recounted his story of the tragic events, he and the father leaned in close and were almost whispering, oblivious to the others in the room and at one point grasping one another's hands. As he was leaving at the end of the meeting, the father asked whether they were allowed to hug. Technically the answer was 'no', but the kindly prison warden didn't stop them.

Restorative justice is not possible or appropriate in every situation and certainly is not for everyone, but it can be transformative for those who do take part (including the facilitator). Studies have found that restorative justice can reduce symptoms of post-traumatic stress,[1] which can be associated with higher risks of coronary disease.[2] I like to think that research is starting to show that restorative justice is good for the heart.

The realms beyond

A very dear brother-friend-of-my-heart was assassinated. I received the news at home. I was more than a thousand miles away and unable to go to the place where he had died. Devastated, never thinking this dear man would be killed (although others had been before him), I wandered round my house, sobbing in shock. All the while I was thinking, 'I must go and pray, I must go and pray.' Still, it took me a quarter of an hour or more to be able to sit cross-legged in my familiar place and be with him.

After the loss of some previous friends to assassinations, I had heard that, when someone dies in a sudden, violent way, the soul can be terribly disoriented and lost in turmoil, not understanding what has happened. I sat with my dear friend and spoke to him through my shock and distraught tears, saying 'It's alright now, Ilko, it's alright. Don't be afraid, don't be afraid. All the other comrades are here, waiting to greet you. They are reaching out their hands to you. See, here are Adam and the others, to show you the way. Don't be afraid. You are loved, you are loved.' As I spoke to him, I felt the turbulence of fear and disorientation calming. I experienced him finding his way towards the hands reaching out to him in love. I became aware of peace and I sat in the company of these beloved brave souls.

This was one of many extraordinary gifts from this dear and courageous friend, a peace warrior in life and in death and the joy in my heart. Through my deep love and respect for him, I was able to experience directly some of the ways in which we can connect to the realms beyond those we understand in our current Western culture. In my experience this also holds true for those in an induced coma who can attune to our conscious love and guidance beyond the limits of time and space.

Inna Lillahi wa inna ilayhi raji'un.
We are of Allah and to Allah we are returning

Walking with the dead

The Hebrew word for funeral is *levaya*, which means 'accompanying' – accompanying the dead to their last resting place, which is a *mitzvah* – a

---

1. https://restorativejustice.org.uk/sites/default/files/resources/files/Restorative%20Conferencing%20Reduces%20Post-Traumatic%20Stress%20Symptoms.pdf
2. www.ncbi.nlm.nih.gov/pubmed/21792377

commandment, a good deed, an act of compassion. A year ago, a very unusual *levaya* took place. A small pile of ashes from Auschwitz containing the partial remains of six Jews, one of them a child, was given a burial in Bushey cemetery. This little heap had lain in the Imperial War Museum for 20 years.

When I heard about this, I was moved to tears. My grandparents died in Auschwitz and, as they had no grave, I had put their names on my mother's gravestone. Although I had visited their hometown, the site of their house and the railway station from which they were deported, I had never been able to visit a grave. It was only the thought of a burial that softened my heart into weeping. I was able to see the *levaya* on screen. There were crowds of people there, many of them, in all likelihood, descendants like me. Walking with the little white coffin, almost leaning on it for support, were elderly Holocaust survivors. There is something so powerful about this simple act of walking with the body.

The Chief Rabbi in his speech suddenly turned to the coffin and talked to the child, imagining how his or her life should have been: a child's world of play and discovery, the life he or she deserved to have. At a friend's funeral in Jerusalem, I was amazed and touched to hear, at the end of the ceremony, the bearded orthodox men who looked after the ritual and the cemetery speak to the dead person with intimacy and humility, expressing hope that everything they had done was as he would have wished it and apologising if they had offended him in any way.

Honour in a foreign field

Everyone in my family was involved with the Second World War in some way, unless we were too young. Three of my brothers fought in the army. One of them, George, was a dispatch rider for the King's Royal Rifle Corps. He was in occupied France in 1940 and then went back for D-Day in 1944. They were doing a reconnaissance before going in to liberate a small town called Airaines, in the Somme district. He was driving in front and behind him came four other vehicles. I found all this out by contacting the War Office. I manage to piece together the story. On the outskirts of the village was a German ambush and he was blown up and all the men in the tank behind him were badly injured or killed. The other vehicles beat a retreat. This was all any of us knew for years. Seven men died. That was war. So many families suffered similar losses. Eventually the town was liberated and the war was won. We did not know what happened to the bodies. I had visited the place a few times but it is a small place and no one spoke much English and I can't speak any French, so I never found out much. It meant something to be where he had been, but that was it.

Then I got a phone call out of the blue. Some local French historians from the village had contacted our local Faringdon website and asked if there were any living relatives of George Dowell. Turned out they were celebrating 75 years since their liberation by the British and wanted to give thanks and honour those who died to achieve it. That is when I found out what happened after they died. People from the village came straight out to help. Under the eyes of the German soldiers, they took away the dead and dying and tried to save them, but there was no hospital and they all died. The people of the town worked overnight to build wooden coffins for all of them. They already had Union flags hidden away, awaiting the liberation, and these were draped over the coffins, which were taken and buried alongside the boundary of the churchyard wall, since they did not know the religious beliefs of the victims. The whole town turned out and wooden crosses were made for each grave, and later replaced by the standard war gravestones. My brother and his colleagues had decent funerals and their graves were covered in flowers by the villagers. Every household had contributed to the flowers. I cannot say what comfort this brings after all these years. Sadly, we are the only British family they managed to trace. We went over and they put us up locally and had made an exhibition about it all. I took over my own display about my family's part in the war, with photographs and documents, medals and so on. The band played God Save the Queen and there were speeches and we placed a wreath on the grave. It was wonderful.

Two Valium

The day after my dad died by suicide my doctor gave me two Valium and that was it. No other support was offered – I was 14 years old.

The phone call

My younger sister took her life in 1999, when she was 33 years old. She hanged herself with her dressing gown cord in a small psychiatric hospital in Wiltshire. I was her older sister by two years. I will never forget the phone call from my mother. It was a workday. We were in the process of relocating offices, everything was being dismantled. All the office furniture gone except the main office telephone, still connected, positioned in the middle of the room on the floor. It rang loud, someone picked up the receiver and said, 'It's for you, it's your mother.' Someone else said, 'Your mother never rings you at work…' Because the phone was on the floor, I crouched down on my knees to take it. My mother just shouted the words 'She's hung herself… she's dead.' There was more that followed but I fell further towards the floor and just let out some kind of strange guttural sound.

It's hard to relay the sensations, the feelings that followed. I could feel the weight of the shock shattering my body as I prepared to travel to my mother's house, knowing I was utterly changed in that moment and so was my family, my life.

Her body. I remember the open wound on her forehead from when she had been cut down – her head hit a table. I felt so sad that now this wound would never heal. I moved slowly and felt her death fill me. I asked the nurse if I could take a small cutting of her hair from the back of her head. This is still plaited in the back of an old school photo of her, me and my other sister, when young girls. I kissed her hands, each eye and her lips before leaving her.

I could not hold her bittersweet dreams or rub up against the desolation of her living tundra.

I've never been comfortable with the phrase 'commit suicide'. It somehow feels weighted with judgement, condemnation. Suicide is no longer a crime. I prefer to say, 'take one's own life' or, 'choose to die by suicide'. It is an act of great violence yet stems from great vulnerability. I have traversed so much grief and have found different ways to remember, to heal, to mark anniversaries, to share, even to try to forget (although that is not really possible). It feels like a thread to weave into and through my entire life, until that itself ends.

I could never imagine that I and my family would be entering similar territory 17 years later when my twin sister's son took his life by hanging at the age of 18. There is a different devastation here, and three years on I am still wading through the anguish of it.

Second chance

My friend died by suicide. Laid down in the woods and took an overdose. Her funeral was strange; it didn't feel enough, and it didn't feel tangible. How could it ever be? So I travelled to the place where she died. Crawled into the undergrowth where she had lain. Into the dirt, to be with her. I needed to feel it, I wanted to be close to it. Her death place. In amongst the minutia of leaves and animals and earth. How I wanted to look up at the trees and sky like she did and let it all go, slip away. Yet after a while I sensed I was done. A force had taken hold and a voice spoke to me. I crawled out the other side of the undergrowth. There was only one way in and one way out. Heaved my body up from the space where she never did emerge. I got a second chance, she didn't.

It could have been any of us

I met Rob and Sal 10 years ago and have watched them revolve around homeless services ever since. Sadly, they struggled, and the world of addiction took a massive hold on them. Their relationship was loving but alcohol became heroin, heroin became crack and heroin, which then became spice. They lived on the streets, adjusting to the lifestyle too well.

In May 2019, they were in their sleeping bags on the streets. Rob said he didn't feel well, Sal called 999 but he was dead on arrival at hospital. He was 32. I thought of him as one of the stronger ones, but the lifestyle had taken its toll.

It was Dying Awareness Week and the next day at the homeless day centre we were holding an event to promote thinking about dying, talking about it, preparing. The elephant was in the room; there was music, barbecue and decorating skulls.

Sal arrived, as I knew she would. I held her while she told me what happened. I then told her what the day was about, how hard it would be, but could we make the day about Rob – celebrate his life. No one expected him to be dead today; we needed to think about how it could be anyone. Sal was amazing. The day was about Rob – everyone talking about him and how it could be them. The timing of the day was meant to be and many learnt from the experience and how we don't know when it's our time.

A lost generation

In 1985 I found myself in the eye of a storm. As a social worker with less than four years' post-qualifying experience, I became the UK's first person employed to work exclusively with people with HIV and AIDS.

In the tabloid press, hysteria raged. The prejudice was transparent: gay men and drug users had brought the disease upon themselves and deserved condemnation, while haemophiliacs were the 'innocent' victims and deserved all the sympathy and compensation. The headlines were despicable: Terror of the plague; Britain threatened by gay plague; AIDS is the wrath of God – these are just a few of the many tag lines reporting on the virus. As a lesbian, I did not at the time personally know many gay men but felt so angry at the way my community was being vilified. The job consisted of doing whatever was needed, from public speaking to training our wonderful bunch of volunteers. It was some time before I realised that many volunteers were also diagnosed with HIV or AIDS.

Once opportunist infections appeared, we all knew that the writing was on the wall and death was usually inevitable, probably soon. It was like living with a time bomb. Patients were ostracised in various ways. Barry, dying in hospital, was put into a side room and barrier-nursed, a common (though unnecessary) practice. The orderly delivering meals would not enter the room, and would leave his food outside the door, although Barry was too sick to get to the other side of the room. Initially, hospices would not consider taking patients with AIDS, insisting they only took cancer patients, even when I pointed out Kaposi's sarcoma was cancer.

One morning, I bumped into Alex in the lift of our building. Alex was a young GP whose surgery was in the East End of London. He told me that he had just been diagnosed with AIDS, and we hugged until we reached the third floor. Then we hugged some more, trying to make the hurt go away. He planned his own funeral and chose 'We Shall Overcome' as the music to be played.

It felt like a battle at times; we lost a generation of young men. They were brothers, lovers, sons and fathers. They had become infected before we knew how to prevent transmission through safer sex. They did not deserve the vitriol, fear and hatred doled out to them. They had only done what millions of other young men did: make love. Thankfully, the diagnosis of AIDS no longer equals death. But the pain of those losses never entirely leaves me.

Two hours

Two friends lost their child a few years ago. They were visiting my friend's mother with their two-year-old son. They left him for Grandma to watch while they went to dinner and he wandered out the back door while she was asleep on the couch. They found him two hours later in a neighbour's pool. I came to help search, along with many people in the community. When they found him, the police tried to take him away immediately to the coroner's. Because I know decomposition happens rapidly with water deaths, I advocated for my friends to spend a few last hours with him while he still looked like himself. We took him to a local funeral home, and my friends cuddled their son for two hours as members of the community, family, friends, police officers and firemen shuffled by to share their condolences. When they finished, I took him personally to the coroner's, 20 minutes away from the funeral home. By the time I got there, he was almost unrecognisable.

In memoriam

A woman was involved in a protracted battle with her local town council about maintaining a shrine beside the road where her son had died. They were concerned that it was becoming a hazard in itself. She felt it was the only place she wanted to leave her flowers and messages and that it was important to other members of the family and his friends. More and more people feel a strong connection to the place of death, particularly when it has been a sudden one. Religious sites hold no comfort for them; nor does talk of an afterlife. The place the body or ashes go to has a secondary significance, but what draws the bereaved back time after time is the sense of being close to that person's living presence before their life was snatched from them. To stand where they were when they took their last breath. This, along with the sense of support and community, is also what draws people to volunteer at a hospice. They maintain a connection with the place where those precious last days were spent together.

A disappearance

When I was in my mid-20s, my best friend disappeared. Two mutual friends had arrived at the little house where she was living in the Himalayas to find a letter addressed to me on the table. They wrote to tell me, enclosing the letter (these were the old days, before mobile phones and the internet). My first response was to laugh it off: they've misunderstood, she's gone walkabout. But, as the days passed, this terrible new reality gradually sank in. When I broke the news to our circle of friends, they reacted as I had initially: 'Not a problem, she's just out and about.' Her parents said the same when I phoned to tell them. I had no one with whom to share my dread. A friend who knew India well went out to see what she could discover and, on her return, the circle of friends gathered to see what she had learned, which was nothing.

We were young and completely unable to support one another in our confusion of feelings, lacking both the emotional resources and the wisdom that comes with experience. We had no elders. We had no structure to hold the unknown. We didn't cry. My circle of friends broke apart, unable to bear the weight of grief – or at least the circle was unavailable to me. One friend had the grace and honesty to say that he could no longer bear to see me because I reminded him of our friend.

After some months, I visited her parents to ask if we could hold a gathering of all the people who knew her. Her parents said it was too soon. A year later I asked them again – they said it was too late. Alone, I held a sacred ceremony for my friend at a Neolithic site we used to love. It was incredibly powerful but resolved nothing. I planted a rose for her on the Western Isle we used to visit every autumn. Nevertheless, I was still waiting for her to return. Seven years after her disappearance, I arranged a ceremony on consecrated ground with the support of a very kind vicar and his bishop and accompanied by two friends from my 'new' life. The occasion was heartfelt and touching. Yet I was still waiting for my friend.

There is a particular agony to losing someone who disappears. No body. No time and place to grieve. She was an empty space walking beside me through life.

In retrospect I think that what would have helped was to bring together all of those who knew her to wish her well on the journey, whatever it might be. For a disappearance as much as for a death, I believe gathering to share a space together in love has a power beyond words - in the absence of anything else, to create a place for grief and praise.[3]

Commentaries

Sudden death and disappearance – Debbie Collins, psychotherapist and acupuncturist

In 1985, as I was completing my acupuncture training (following treatment for depression after the sudden death of two friends in 1970 and 1975), my brother was killed in a car accident. Five years later, I chose to train as a counsellor, probably as a direct result of my desire to provide what had not been there for

---

3. Prechtel, M. (2015). *The smell of rain on dust: Grief and praise*. North Atlantic Books.

me, as well as weaving meaning from pain. Since then I have engaged in many different forms of therapy, talking and somatic, in order to work through the losses, which has considerably deepened my therapy work over these many years. It is an ongoing process. Weaving meaning from pain is still central to the healing process I am privileged to witness and accompany. *www.debbiecollins.co.uk*

On hearing of a sudden death, loss or disappearance, possibly the most important need is to face, and be held in, our feelings, including disorientation. To travel this landscape well, we need connection to experienced others – people who have walked this road before, know how to hold, meet and orient us, not try to make it better or, worse, anaesthetise us. This is our pain to feel.

The importance of this need for connection in loss is to know we are not alone, even years later. The death of a public figure like Princess Diana gives many a legitimate, public focus to express their 'unattended sorrows' (Levine, 2005). For some, and especially in these post-Oprah years, it opens up a new way of grieving, enabling us to express more of our pain with others and bond in our shared experiences.

When we feel alone in our loss, perhaps even abandoned by the dead, we may also feel alone in our intuitive sensing about the death, most especially when those around us are not yet ready to acknowledge the reality. Even when others are with us, we may feel alone together, and still as abandoned by, and disconnected from, a seemingly uncaring world that carries on as normal.

To meet the need to feel the feelings, we also need to ensure that life and time stop to honour the loss. It's not business as usual. We need time and space to feel the feelings. Living in an age that no longer signals bereavement by wearing black, an armband or triangle on the collar means many are walking around in unrecognised disorientation and bereavement, and the need to make time to mark and honour the loss is even more vital.

When the death is sudden, it may be particularly important to go to the actual place of death as a way to feel close to the deceased in their final hours, as well as orient and comfort ourselves, even years later. This can be more of an issue with accidental death, murder or suicide, because the death itself often hasn't been contained – it hasn't taken place within a building, like a house, hospital or care home. The lack of containment can leave us feeling as if the death is flapping in the wind, though some will feel closer to the deceased outside, among nature. If we don't know the exact place, we can make one that has meaning for us.

If we cannot go to the place of death, we can find that sensing the lost person's soul as disoriented and in need of guidance can, paradoxically, give an orientation in the loss – a direction and a sense of purpose. Not everyone believes in the soul, of course – the important point is to be able to orient ourselves, to fulfil the need for connection and ongoing relationship with the deceased, and do something meaningful in the meaninglessness of the loss.

For some, sudden loss results in complete isolation: if we experience intimacy as causing pain, we may choose to stay alone. The pain of being separate is preferable to the pain of loss. We might isolate by berating ourselves for not having done more to prevent the death, or hold ourselves responsible by seeing our love as toxic – and even more so when the person has taken their own life. This will affect all our relationships and infect intimacy, as we avoid others' eyes as reflections of our own. If a family dynamic is based in this belief, it can be blown further apart by the devastating loss of one of its members. For some, it can go the other way and draw family members closer together, perhaps fearful of letting one another out of their sight.

What can accompany and emphasise isolation is a felt need to be strong for others in the midst of the shock. We may believe we are the ones whose role it is to hold it together so that others can fall apart. This again will be influenced by early patterning, potentially family position (older siblings sensing a need to be strong for younger ones, and even for parents). This can be an immense act of love for those left behind, and it can be a distraction from grieving – compassion for others colliding with our human desire to avoid pain. It can postpone our own need to grieve as it vies with the need to behave in a way that brings love, causing intense internal conflict.

Facing loss through accident, disappearance or even murder is one thing; it is another when the deceased chose to take their own life. Most people I have known who took this path sincerely believed the world would be a better place without them, and/or felt they could no longer carry their overwhelming burden of pain. Without exception, they were wrong about the world being better without them, and the pain of their loss ripples out beyond their wildest imaginings. So, what support is needed for those lost in this place? Connection and holding on are key. It is not easy to support another who is feeling such disconnection and disorientation to continue living with their pain. Indeed, it is not always possible, and we have to live with the consequences of the loss – to 'simply hold out and see it through' (Bonhoeffer, 1959).

In *The Japanese Windphone*, the booth is open to countless others facing sudden loss, enabling them to continue the relationship with the dead beyond the grave. As well as meeting the need for continuing relationship, the telephone booth provides a place to mourn, vital for some to anchor their grief, especially if there is no body and so no conscious burial. This is poignantly echoed in many of the stories – no funeral and no place to mourn, or if the funeral is not enough. It is immensely powerful, even years later, to lay our dead to rest somewhere, within and without, and vital to healthy ongoing relations with everyone.

Keleman (1974) introduced the concept of 'bodying' the deceased, remembering in our bodies how it felt to hold and touch the person, even years later. Given that freezing is common with shock, this provides a potent path to connecting to the emotions associated with the loss, to healing, and to providing a continuing relationship.

This continuing relationship can take many forms, sometimes to a new direction in life: how can we keep going in the same direction when everything has changed so suddenly and brutally? To stay conscious and aware is key, knowing this is part of the weave of bereavement and that we cannot avoid the pain. Indeed, we have a choice to soften the heart and feel the pain or stiffen into 'being strong', and many move between the two.

With sudden death, whether or not to view and touch the body of our dead is an intensely personal decision. These issues are explored here in *The Southall Train Crash* and in *The Phone Call*. Those inexperienced in loss may believe that, by trying to prevent us, they are saving us the pain of seeing the lifeless form. But for some, difficult and painful as it is, it's an essential part of making the death real. There is no denying a dead body – it cannot have life breathed back into it, no matter how much we love. It takes enormous courage and can make us physically sick to see the wounds that will never heal. Others prefer to remember the person how they last saw them, though for some this may cause worse fantasies about how the body actually looked and may engender magical thinking.

Magical thinking (Didion, 2005) is particularly common when the loss is sudden. Imagining it was all a dream, we may follow a stranger for miles, 'knowing' they are our lost one. They may visit us in dreams and we wake believing they are still here, warm and breathing, until dawn breaks and we have to re-face the reality of their loss. We may do deals with God or another authority figure, believe that, if we're really good, act as if everything's alright, release them to their next life and conduct countless other self-deceptions, they'll return. This often occurs when people have been raised with a punitive deity – the loss feels like punishment and so we think, with enough 'good' behaviour, we can 'win' them back.

With sudden loss, we miss out on conscious awareness of last times: the last time we saw them, hugged, kissed, made love, fought. With suicide, particularly, we can berate ourselves with 'if only I'd said or done…'. The lack of completion leaves loose ends waving and can mean we become obsessed with completing – needing to tidy the house before leaving for work, striving to ensure we leave every person we love in a good way, because who knows if we will see them again? This can result in anxiety and exhaustion, as we struggle to complete in a world full of loose ends.

In the face of sudden death, the need to make meaning is more apparent. It may come immediately or years later. We can become passionate about being beacons of love in the world, rooting out hatred wherever we find it: 'This can't all be for nothing.' Both *The Manchester Arena* and *Killed for Being a Goth* are stories written with this insight. It can be a way of working through the loss –

mourning through making meaning, creation from destruction. There's an edge here about using it as a distraction from the unbearable feelings of loss (as with being strong for others), and it isn't possible for everyone. It is crucial that we take good care of ourselves in our pain.

Creating meaningful rituals, particularly after suicide, can enable some completion and go a long way to releasing ourselves and our dead from completion anxiety (Collins, 2019). And it can re-enact when relationships of any kind end without warning. Coming to terms with loose ends loosens our grip on the need for absolute completion, which, as far as we know, only comes with our own death.

To end then, a few words about forgiveness in sudden loss. Forgiveness is a process, not an event. Some speak as if it's simply a decision we make – a choice. It's likely we will be unable to forgive if we do not allow ourselves to go through all the feelings of which forgiveness is one part. Being able to hold and share memories, laugh and cry, rage at the injustice of the loss, express our fears about going forward and feel our shame loosens the fibres of the loss and enables us to move more freely with the necessary mourning. And eventually, over time, we may be able to forgive. Not forget, forgive.

Advice points

1. Seek out ways to connect and be met in your feelings in safe, supported environments.
2. Notice the choice to isolate, to close your heart to the pain and carry on alone. Know there is a consequence to that choice.
3. Be aware of the use of distraction from your painful feelings; notice the difference between the need for respite from the pain and distraction from it.
4. Make meaning for yourself, whatever that looks, feels or sounds like, no matter how different it is to others' meanings.
5. Create ways to continue your relationship with the deceased.

References

Bonhoeffer, D. (1959). *Prisoner for God: Letters and papers from prison* (p91) (E. Bethge, Ed., R.H Fuller, Trans.). Macmillan.

Collins, D. (2019). Creating meaningful endings. *Therapy Today, 30*(6), 36–38.

Didion, J. (2005). *My year of magical thinking*. Harper Perennial.

Keleman, S. (1974). *Living your dying*. Random House.

Levine, S. (2005). *Unattended sorrow*. Rodale.

The shock of death – Dr Pat Johnson, PhD

Some years after a dear friend disappeared, I trained as a psychotherapist, in order to accompany others in their suffering. After 10 years' practice, I arranged a one-year sabbatical, prompted by a profound solo pilgrimage to South Africa (my birthplace) after liberation in 1994. While I was staying with my cousin-sister in Kenya, my PhD on conflict resolution led indirectly to meeting some remarkable Somalis engaged in participatory action research for peacebuilding. Ultimately, I worked in this Somali-led team, living in the Horn of Africa for 12 years. During this time, all but two of our inner circle died in sudden, shocking ways, as did huge numbers of other Somali civilians. After returning to the UK, I volunteered several times with a US war veterans' healing programme, also benefiting immensely myself, and trained as a Shadow Work group facilitator and coach. *http://shadowwork.eu/index.php/meet-us/shadow-work-coaches/158-pat-johnson*

In parts of southern Africa, news of a death is prefaced by saying 'Prepare to string your beads,' lest the precious beads of memories of your loved one be scattered amidst the shock and turmoil of grief. It seems to me that this phrase is as gentle a way as any to alert someone to a sudden loss.

The gut response to a devastating sudden loss can be understood as a threat to one's very survival – 'No!', 'This isn't possible', 'How can I survive this?' One's ability to process what follows may be aggravated by shock in one's family, social circle and wider community and their ability to support the bereaved. The challenges may be exacerbated by the disappearance of many of the grief rituals from Western culture.

Shock – learning from wild animals

Our nervous system responds to a perceived survival threat with an instantaneous 'fight or flight' or 'freeze' response. In its natural surroundings, an animal that cannot fight or flee may freeze as a survival response, shutting down to expend as little energy as possible. Crucially, if it survives, afterwards it will discharge the tremendous rush of survival energy by shaking and sighing, before resuming its activity without obvious harmful effects; its 'threat alarm' has turned off and it moves on. Wild animals do not generally appear to be traumatised by routine threats to their lives. When we humans are faced with something that appears to threaten our survival, it may not be possible to fight or flee, and instead we are likely to freeze, which is often experienced as numbing, feeling spaced out and dissociation (Frederick & Levine, 1997; Jensen, 2020; van der Kolk, 2014).

Sometimes the impact of sudden, devastating news bursts out spontaneously, but for many people the release of the surge of survival energy through shaking, crying and shouting may be uncomfortable or socially unacceptable. In some cultures, this kind of emotional expression is seen as shameful. In Western culture, boys and men in particular have been conditioned not to express their feelings, and there are situations in which it may be unsafe to express ourselves in these ways, such as in an emergency, where the first priority is physical safety.

Being with close loved ones, sharing the experience of shock and being able to express it (for example, through close physical contact) may be helpful for some. For others, being alone in a safe place when the terrible news is received may be a blessing in enabling some immediate release of emotion.

Physical sensations may include feeling 'white and cold and empty and unsettled to the core', as in the story *The Southall Train Crash*; trembling, wobbly legs; foggy mind and an inability to think straight, and feeling 'all over the place' or 'not in one's body'.

There are simple techniques that may help with shock. If you feel shaky and it is safe to do so:

- feel your feet on the ground and let the shaking through
- let the body shake
- focus on the out breath
- bring the attention back to 'here and now'
- stay warm
- take Rescue Remedy (a Bach flower remedy)
- reach out to a trusted person who can listen and keep you company – it helps to be alongside another nervous system.

A useful emergency technique for shock is to breathe out with a 'vooo' sound, breathe in again, and breathe out again with another 'vooo'. The vibration of this sound down into the belly helps to relax the vagus nerve, the second largest nerve in the body, which runs from the guts to the brain (Frederick & Levine, 1997; van der Kolk, 2014).

Post-traumatic stress

When we are confronted with sudden shocking loss and are unable, for whatever reasons, to release safely the surge of survival energy, it stays in our system. We stay stuck in emergency mode, even though the crisis has passed. Our nervous system hasn't discharged the survival energy and received the signals that it is safe to 'stand down'. But, because this part of our brain and nervous system is managing the most essential level of survival, it cannot be talked into 'standing down'. The survival response is beyond our thinking mind (Frederick & Levine, 1997; Jensen, 2020; van der Kolk, 2014).

In order to cope with sensory overload or try to 'switch off', people may isolate themselves or 'self-medicate', whether with alcohol or drugs or bingeing on box-set DVDs. *The Manchester Arena* is a vivid illustration of the impact of post-traumatic stress. The writer says, 'It feels like I have gone through a sliding door: I can still see my old life very clearly but I can't reach it or engage in it anymore'... 'on the surface I am resilient and strong and very outspoken; inwardly I often just want to go and crouch down in a dark corner and weep.' She describes finding eye movement desensitisation reprogramming (EMDR) useful – a technique that uses bilateral stimulation to enable the brain to process the memory of event, so it can be safely stored in the long-term memory as something now past and not an ever-present threat.

Physical symptoms of post-traumatic stress may include digestive problems or chronic pain with no obvious diagnosis, and there may be cognitive difficulties, such as memory loss and inability to think clearly. The emotional impact of stuck survival energy may show up as anxiety, panic attacks, being constantly on alert, outbursts of rage, feeling overwhelmed and helpless, social alienation, flashbacks, and so on. As *Good for the Heart,* the restorative justice story, illustrates, the bereaved person may be alarmed by the intensity of their reactions. Alternatively, the coping strategy may be desensitisation, as described in *Healing, Empowerment and Resilience.*

The emotional, physical and cognitive reactions reflect challenges in the nervous system – not the mind. While talking therapies help with aspects of bereavement, 'stuck' survival energy appears to respond better to a level of attention that enables the body to release the stuck energy and reorganise the nervous system.

In *Second Chance*, the author describes a powerful instinctive engagement of the body when she 'crawled into the undergrowth' where her friend had lain to take her life, until 'I sensed I was done… [and] crawled out the other side of the undergrowth. There was only one way in and one way out'. In *The Southall Train Crash*, part of the writer's recovery included getting on a train with a support person, and working with her tai chi teacher 'to contain my energy and settle my nervous system'.

We are more vulnerable to post-traumatic stress when there is a succession of sudden shocking losses, when there is 'survivor's guilt', or in circumstances where we are forced to wait in dread for devastating news, and the nervous system does not have a chance to recalibrate and remains stuck on full alert (van der Kolk, 2014). As *A Disappearance* describes, when someone disappears, the dread that something is terribly wrong is prolonged indefinitely by never knowing what happened. A sudden loss may also resonate with trauma relating to earlier unresolved losses (as reflected in *Healing, Empowerment and Resilience*).

The intensity of post-traumatic stress can be heightened by the reactions of those around us, who may also be experiencing shock. The reverberations may be shattering. 'My circle of friends broke apart, unable to bear the weight...' (*A Disappearance*). 'In my community you don't talk about death and grieving' (*Healing, Empowerment and Resilience*). Sometimes the losses play into a challenging wider social narrative of fear, hatred or 'blaming the victim' and support comes from those in shared circumstances (*A Lost Generation, It Could Have Been Any of Us, Healing, Empowerment and Resilience*). In devastating situations, we are fortunate if there are those around us with the personal resources and experience to hold the space – to be elders (of whatever age).

If you suffer from post-traumatic stress, it can be useful to make a list of shock symptoms and what works for you in managing them, and keep it handy. It sounds basic but it is hard to think or remember what helps when one goes into a shock state.

If someone goes into a panic attack or flashback, ask permission before touching them; encourage them to look at their hands and suggest they focus on the out breath and, if possible, use the 'vooo' sound. It may help to acknowledge their feelings by repeating, 'And it's not happening now, you're safe now.'

Professional help for post-traumatic stress includes EMDR, somatic experiencing, neuro-feedback and tapping (acupressure), cranial osteopathy, acupuncture, yoga, mindfulness practice, meditation, collective dance and grief ritual workshops. If none of this is possible, Peter Levine's videos may be helpful (see Resources below). Be aware of ways you may try to avoid reaching out for help: for example, through self-medicating, isolating from social contact for prolonged periods, or somatising (getting physically ill instead).

Reclaiming ritual

Given that engaging with the body and breath provide ways to reorganise the nervous system and 'stand down' from emergency mode and bring us back to the present, it is not surprising that body and breath are intrinsic to myriad traditions that involve communal rhythmic movements. They include the prayer rituals performed five times daily by Muslims, Native American stomp dancing, Maasai rhythmic throat singing, dance, yoga, tai chi, deep belly vibrating humming by Tibetan Buddhists, and so on. In the same way, many grief and healing rituals are rooted in communal movement and chanting, engaging the body and breathing in pulsing rhythm with others. These practices can be found all around the world, from the people of the Kalahari desert to Central American Indian tribes and beyond (Prechtel, 2015). They are used as ways of healing individuals, the community and the land, of releasing shock and enabling grief to flow and of unleashing the river of tears to bring the deceased home. Communal ritual provides both containment and release (Weller, 2015, p.73), enabling our nervous systems to disengage the 'alarm' response and feel present again in the here and now.

In South Africa in 1996, the public hearings of the Truth and Reconciliation Commission opened and closed with collective singing and swaying dance. When witnesses recounting terrible atrocities became overwhelmed, Archbishop Tutu paused their testimony to lead the audience in prayer, singing and rhythmic dance until they could contain their physical collapse and grief, enabling them to move in and out of reliving the horrors (van der Kolk, 2014, p.333). Similarly, in Rwanda, village meetings of perpetrators and survivors of the 1994 genocide conclude with gentle swaying communal dance and song.

In British culture, many of the old ways that engaged our bodies in grieving have been lost, such as the filing past the coffin to pay our respects at the wake, as in *Two Hours*, and walking the body to its resting place, as in *Walking with the Dead*. We too might benefit from physical engagement through collective movement, dance or singing or participating in the ancient grief rituals now being brought to the UK from West Africa and elsewhere.

Anniversaries (deathdays, birthdays or other occasions with special resonance) can feel overwhelming after a sudden loss, triggering the initial shock. It helps to hold this awareness and plan in advance for extra support for what may seem impossible to bear.

In some traditions, the first anniversary of the person's death is marked by gathering ceremonially to share food and celebrate their life – in Lakota tradition, this is seen as a way to support the bereaved collectively to 'wipe the tears'. For some people, there is value in reclaiming past rituals, such as Samhain (Hallowe'en), creating an altar for the dead with flowers, candles, pictures or symbolic representations (as in the Mexican Dia de Muertos, see Chapter 11). This brings us back to *The Japanese Windphone* – a communal means to express grief and praise and cherish the beads of memories.

Advice points

1. Recognise signs of shock and what to do.
2. Use 'vooo' out-breath practice to relax the nervous system.
3. Write a list of your shock symptoms and what helps you manage post-traumatic stress.
4. Seek help for post-traumatic stress and be aware of signs that you are avoiding getting help.
5. Take note of significant anniversaries and be aware that extra support may be needed.

References

Frederick, A. & Levine, P. (1997). *Waking the tiger: Healing trauma*. North Atlantic Books.

Jensen, C. (2020). *The 'freeze response' when trauma energy is trapped: Symptoms of post-traumatic stress and how somatic experiencing works*. www.christine-jensen.co.uk/somaticexperiencing.php

Prechtel, M. (2015). *The smell of rain on dust: Grief and praise*. North Atlantic Books.

Van der Kolk, B. (2014). *The body keeps the score: Mind, brain and body in the transformation of trauma*. Penguin Books.

Weller, F. (2015). *The wild edge of sorrow*. North Atlantic Books.

Resources – Sudden death and disappearance

Books

B'Hahn, C. (2002). *Mourning has broken*. Crucible Publishers.

Didion, J. (2005). *My year of magical thinking*. Harper Perennial.

Levine, S. (1987). *Healing into life and death*. Doubleday.

Weller, F. (2015). *The wild edge of sorrow*. North Atlantic Books.

Radio broadcasts/Podcasts

Damaged leaders rule the world. (2019). Under the Skin podcast. Russell Brand and Gabor Maté. July 28. https://youtu.be/C-mJnYmdVmQ

The Listening Project. (2020). First conversation. Mohini Patel (Dir.). BBC Radio 4; 16 February.

Films

Griefwalker. (2008). Tim Wilson (Dir.). National Film Board of Canada.

Webpages

The Forgiveness Project: www.theforgivenessproject.com

Resources – The shock of death

Books

Ferdinand, R. (2017). *Thinking out loud: Love, grief and being mum and dad*. Hodder & Stoughton.

Frederick, A. & Levine, P. (1997). *Waking the tiger: Healing trauma*. North Atlantic Books.

Prechtel, M. (2015). *The smell of rain on dust: Grief and praise*. North Atlantic Books.

Some, M.P. (1995). *Of water and the spirit*. Penguin.

Van der Kolk, B. (2014). *The body keeps the score: Mind, brain and body in the transformation of trauma*. Penguin.

Wertheimer, A. (2001). *A special scar: The experience of people bereaved by suicide*. Routledge.

Online articles

Harding, T. (2020, January 18). We keep him close, always: How I survived the loss of my teenage son. *The Guardian*. www.theguardian.com/lifeandstyle/2020/jan/18/keep-close-always-how-survived-loss-teenage-son-thomas-harding

Jensen, C. (2020). *The 'freeze response' when trauma energy is trapped: Symptoms of post-traumatic stress and how somatic experiencing works*. www.christine-jensen.co.uk/somaticexperiencing.php

Films

A Song for Jenny. (2015). Brian Percival (Dir.). BBC Northern Ireland Drama Productions.

Being Mum and Dad. (2017). Matt Smith (Dir.). OTB Productions Ltd.

Dead Poets Society. (1989). Peter Weir (Dir.). Touchstone Pictures.

Evelyn. (2018). Orlando von Einsiedel (Dir.). Grain Media/Violet Films Production.

Ordinary People. (1980). Ronald L. Schwary (Dir.). Wildwood Enterprises Inc.

Truly, Madly, Deeply. (1990). Anthony Minghella (Dir.). BBC Films.

What We Did On Our Holiday. (2014). Andy Hamilton (Dir.). BBC Films.

YouTube Videos

Nature's lessons in healing trauma: An introduction to somatic experiencing. (2014). Peter Levine. https://youtu.be/nmJDkzDMllc

Trauma, somatic experiencing and Peter A. Levine. (2009). https://youtu.be/ByalBx85iC8

Treating trauma: 2 ways to help clients feel safe. (2017). Peter Levine. https://youtu.be/G7zAseaIyFA

Websites

RoadPeace: www.roadpeace.org (Information, emotional and practical support to those bereaved or injured in a road crash)

SAMM: Support After Murder and Manslaughter: www.samm.org.uk (Supporting those who have been bereaved as a result of murder or manslaughter)

Somatic Experiencing: www.christine-jensen.co.uk/somaticexperiencing.php (A helpful description of what can happen when trauma energy is trapped; symptoms of post-traumatic stress, and how somatic experiencing works)

Support After Suicide: www.supportaftersuicide.org.uk (National partnership of organisations working across the UK to support people bereaved or affected by suicide)

Outside the Box

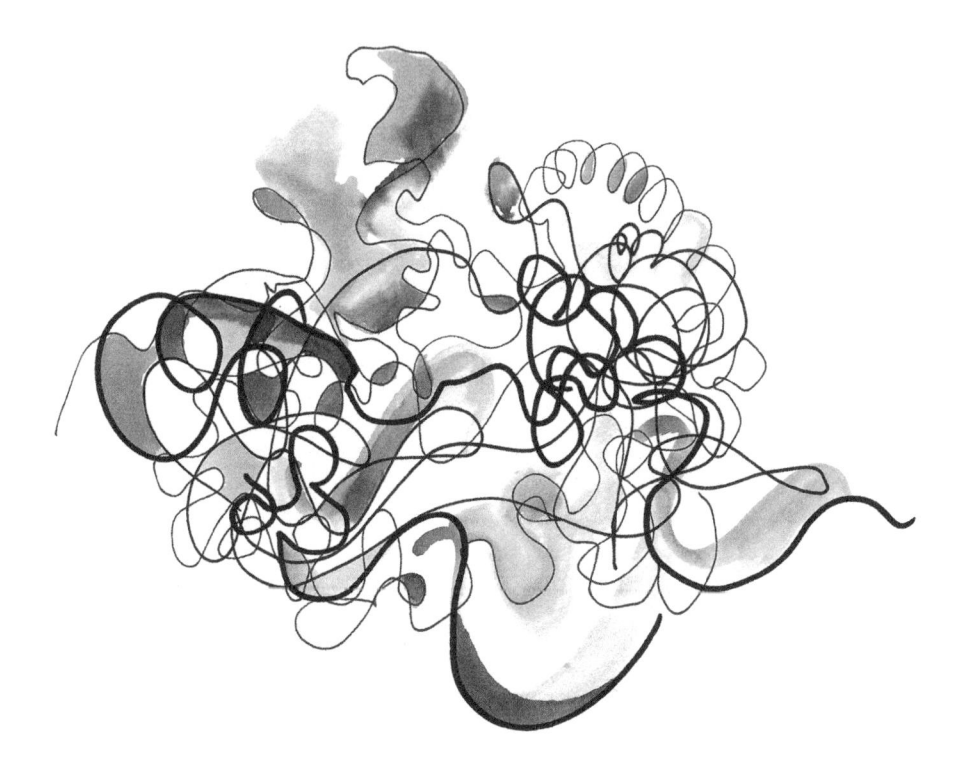

6 – Dementia

It felt important that dementia stories should be part of the weave of the whole book, and not confined only to one chapter. Other stories can be found in other chapters where the subject touches on the main chapter theme, and are referred to in Hazel May's commentary that follows.

Stranded

This woman who was my mother,
this woman who is my mother,
sits opposite me in the cafe,
her coffee untouched on the table between us.
Conversation sputters as she looks

past me.
To where?
Forgotten.

Silence settles like damp fog between us.
A warm tide of people flows around nearby.
Adults chat, children play, forks scrape on plates,
the door opens and closes.

But we are adrift.
I cast out my net of words.
It splashes back empty onto the water.

I weep silently. She does not notice.
I am still a little girl and she cannot pick me up anymore.
I must pay the bill and push the wheelchair home again.

We pass the lavender hedge as we have done before.
The ritual rubbing between finger and thumb,
snuffing the pungent purple.

We flare our nostrils and breathe in.
Our eyes meet.
I love you.
I love you too.

Rolling onwards together in the pale sunlight.

Hurry up, I'm dying

Some years ago I observed an interesting and thought-provoking scene involving a gentleman living with dementia, and a care worker. My role was to go to the care home every week to observe the residents before, during and after the music therapy sessions, as a way of evaluating the impact.

But, on this music therapy day, I got drawn into something not at all connected with the project. I found myself deeply engrossed in what was going on for another resident because of what he was saying and because of the response he got. He was a strongly spoken gentleman with a mesmerising, musical Welsh accent. 'I'm dying,' he said. 'Look at my hands, they are white, all the blood is draining out of them.' The young male care worker talked to him in a gentle voice: 'Your dinner will be here soon.' To which the gentleman replied, 'Well you better hurry up because I'm dying.'

The care worker was clearly caught on the hop; he didn't really know what to say. He wanted to be kind, and he was. He used a number of diversion tactics to try and change the subject and 'cheer up' the Welshman. They didn't work and, as the Welshman became more distressed and vocal, he was eventually escorted out of the dining room.

Waving

Dad had vascular dementia, kicked off by a stroke and then more random bleeds over time, affecting initially his visual perception, his orientation in time and his ability to initiate activity. Without help, he would frequently get lost in the house or in the community and he was unable to wash and dress himself or to look after his own diet and nutritional needs. A few weeks after moving into my family home, Dad was diagnosed with terminal bowel cancer. He would be dead within a year. Previously a strict, hands-off father with whom I argued, fell out with, fell back in with and loved unconditionally, he was now a vulnerable, dependant but much softer, humbler version of himself. He accepted care from me and my sister with good grace, always polite, appreciative and good company.

I believe that my dad's last year of life was a good one. We watched films together, did crosswords together, laughed a lot, talked a lot, he slept a lot. Previous grievances and injuries were soothed and resolved, not through words but through some kind of visceral mutual regard for each other, heightened by the fact that we knew he was dying and that this was his last lap. Sometimes he would tell me what he had just dreamt about while napping – very often, dreams of his mother. I remember I shared one of my dreams with him. 'Dad,' I said, 'I dreamt I was walking through the front room and you were sat at the end of the room smiling and waving to me.' 'I was,' he said.

Our gentleman ghost

Sometimes we have a ghost in our house. He glides from room to room and can suddenly appear behind you in a bedroom or the kitchen, making you jump out of your skin. But it's okay, he's always friendly. And polite. He's also dapper and unassuming: tall, slim, upright and handsome. Some days, he looks a little chunkier, but when I investigate I count three pullovers and five pairs of socks ('Where are my shoes? These aren't mine, they're much too small.') He tops off the ensemble with his tweed cap and my purple dressing gown. It seems he never gets too hot, only too cold.

Some days he likes to talk, though not much. And when I ask him what he'd like to do, he'll say, 'It's up to you' or 'Whatever you'd like me to do.' Always amenable.

On other days we find a dear, elderly gentleman living with us. Always spotlessly clean, using a full tank of hot water to wash (both taps left running, with gallons gushing straight down the plug).

Today we met up with old friends for lunch. Dad read, then re-read the menu (despite having already ordered). Next, he showed a passionate interest in the list of ingredients on the label of a bottle of sauce. I filled his glass, cut his pizza, and the circular conversation continued. He listened intently to everyone's words. He nodded and occasionally smiled, while pushing food around his plate, but ate very little.

As we left, I felt a sense of bitterness, not for the first time. Neither of our guests had directed a question or barely a glance in his direction. He's become invisible. A living, breathing, beautiful but invisible, man.

Our gentleman ghost.

Impact and truth

My mum died aged 86, after several years of ill health. She had dementia so I felt my 'real' mum had died five years earlier. I was determined to read an appropriate piece I had written about this at the crematorium. I did so, and was in floods of tears throughout, but so many of those there spoke to me and contacted me afterwards to acknowledge the impact and truth of what I said.

Commentary
Living and dying with dementia – Hazel May MA

Hazel is a state-registered occupational therapist and holds a Master's degree in philosophy and healthcare. She has more than 30 years' clinical experience working in health and social care settings directly with people living with dementia and their families. Hazel has designed and delivered dementia care training to a wide range of organisations including the College of Occupational Therapists, as well as headed up projects for the NHS using person-centred approaches in dementia care settings. She has also designed and delivered dementia-specific training programmes for formal carers and family carers within university settings and for charitable organisations. Hazel has published two books on person-centred dementia care and has travelled extensively in Europe, Hong Kong, India and Japan to teach and lecture.

It is important that there is a chapter focusing on dying and end of life for people living with dementia and their families and friends, because there are issues that are particular to dementia that can be misunderstood or overlooked. My own father (*Waving*, in this chapter) had dementia and came to live with me in my family home for the last year of his life. We had a good year and he died a 'good death' from cancer, largely because of the support that he and my family had from the health and social care professionals in our local GP practice and the cancer and palliative care team. Had he not had cancer, we would not have received much support at all and, without a doubt, the quality of our lives and of his death would not have been good.

There are reasons why the end-of-life care for people with dementia may be different to end-of-life care for other terminal conditions. The main one is that dementia is not widely recognised as a terminal condition. A bereaved carer I was involved with recently told me, 'When we got the diagnosis of dementia, I thought all we were facing were problems with his memory. I thought we could handle that. If I'd know that he would lose his mobility, his independence and become so frail and poorly, we would have crammed in so much more in the time we had when he was well.' Even where it is known that the condition is terminal, it can be difficult to predict when a person with dementia is nearing death, as they may present with signs that suggest they are very close to death for many months, or even years. Or they may seem near to death and then improve and live for many months longer. People with dementia often develop other medical conditions, as well as infections and minor illnesses on top of these ongoing conditions. Having these other conditions and illnesses may mean the person is cared for, or ultimately dies, in a hospital or a facility that does not specialise in dementia care, or in a dementia care facility without access to the specialist medical and nursing support that they need.

Many people who have dementia live well for several years; the average life expectancy is around 10 years after diagnosis. An estimated 850,000 people are living with dementia in the UK. This is set to rise to one million by 2025 and to two million by 2050 (Prince et al, 2014). With dementia now recognised as a leading cause of death in the UK (Public Health England, 2019), the end-of-life grief and loss issues that are particular to dementia need to be understood and recognised more widely so that living and dying with dementia is the best it can be for each individual.

There are many different types of dementia, each with different symptoms and different treatment and intervention options. For this reason, it is crucial to seek a diagnosis sooner rather than later. Initially, this will be with a GP. Early diagnosis means that you can access support, services and resources and, importantly, start to talk about how the person with dementia wants to live and how they want to die. Both the person with dementia and their main carer are likely to be entitled to certain benefits and exemption from some taxes. Age UK has years of expertise in helping families living with dementia to access what they are entitled to and sort out their affairs. Details are in the Resources section at the end of this chapter.

Four clear themes emerge for me from reading the opening poem and the dementia stories here and elsewhere in the book. The themes are:

- ambiguous loss
- the notion of a 'good' death
- when the bereaved spouse has dementia
- talking about dying.

Ambiguous loss

This is eloquently and movingly described in some of these stories. In the opening piece in this chapter, *Stranded*, a daughter describes how she and her mother 'are adrift' and how, when she (the daughter) casts her 'net of words, it splashes back empty onto the water'. In the later story, *Our Gentleman Ghost*, the father has 'become invisible. A living, breathing, beautiful but invisible man'. Similarly, in *Impact and Truth*, the story opens: 'My mum died aged 86 after several years of ill health. She had dementia so I felt my "real" mum had died five years earlier.' All three daughters are describing someone they love but barely recognise. This is hard to understand because the person is still there, but they do things they would never have done and are not there for you in ways they previously were. Despite seeming rather abstract, it is experienced as very concrete and real grief.

A good death

The notion of a 'good death' has its roots in the hospice movement and the view of death as natural thing. Tim Beanland (2015/16) proposes that 'for most of us a good death means being treated with compassion, being kept comfortable and free from distressing symptoms, and being somewhere we know with people who are close to us'.

There are some wonderful testimonies in this book bearing witness to this notion. In *Emanations of Love* (Chapter 8, p.147) the writer explains that s/he 'resolved to accompany my father on this journey and to be a spiritual anchor and a presence of love… It was a time when I knew I was exactly where I needed to be'. In *Finding our Way* (Chapter 2, p.26), a niece shares her observation that, in the last days of her aunt's life, 'she was peaceful, dozing quietly, ethereally already somewhere else until she died, having shared her final gift that a slow dying of old age and dilapidation, as she called it, can be a journey made with soul, as well as feistiness and humour'. And in *Waving* (this chapter), a daughter says, 'I believe that my dad's last year of life was a good one… Previous grievances and injuries were soothed and resolved, not through words but rather through some kind visceral mutual regard for each other, heightened by the fact that we knew he was dying and that this was his last lap'. But in another story we learn of the contrast in one family, where the mother died at home (*Home Death*, Chapter 9, p.166) 'with enormous humility and dignity' and her family around her, but her husband, who was living with dementia, died 'a quite different death, in a crowded hospital ward, separated only by thin curtains from all the goings-on in the ward around him'.

Despite the notion of a good death being widely accepted as both desirable and possible for people living with dementia in the UK, this group continues to receive undignified treatment. Many are ending their lives in pain (Kane, 2012; Health Service Ombudsman, 2011; Commission on Dignity in Care for Older People, 2012; Royal College of Psychiatrists, 2011) and partnership between dementia care and palliative care is undeveloped (Gibson, 2009). Yet dementia is currently the leading cause of death in the UK (Public Health England, 2019).

When the bereaved person has dementia

Extraordinary issues arise when the bereaved person has dementia. Again in *Home Death*, Leslie, the bereaved husband living with dementia, is unable to retain the news that his wife is dead. He keeps asking 'Where's Gertie?' and his family have to keep reminding him that she has died. In *Plan B* (Chapter 10, p.190), a family has to change their plans for laying to rest their father's ashes because their mother, who has dementia, has accidentally flushed them down the loo, believing them to be dust from the hoover. Dealing with our own grief in addition to trying to support a bereaved person with dementia is tough and, in my experience, families struggle to know what's right. Should they tell the truth, over and over again? Should they use avoidance and even explanations such as 'She's popped out' or 'He's away on holiday'?

For the person with dementia who does not have the cognitive capacity to retain new information, not even the death of person close and important to them, does this mean that the loss is not felt? Or is the loss felt in a different and more visceral way? It may be important to know that, although dementia affects cognition, people's emotions are often still intact, and the loss of somebody or something that is important can still have a strong emotional impact, which may be reflected in their behaviour and mood. Sources of advice about how to respond to these types of situation are listed in the Resources section.

There are no black-and-white answers, though; loss and grief are highly individual experiences and usually complex, influenced by cultural, social and individual factors. Dementia brings additional complexities to the table.

Talking about dying

In the UK, we are uncomfortable about talking about dying, probably even more so with a person who has dementia. Dementia is not recognised as a terminal condition and it is understandable that family and friends might not see the need to talk about dying. Furthermore, a discussion might be deemed futile with a person whose thinking processes, memory and grasp on reality may be compromised because of their condition. Talking about dying to a person living with dementia is not an option that many people would choose, as we see in *Hurry Up, I'm Dying* (this chapter). Here, the topic of dying was ignored, even though the resident was clearly inviting it and needing to talk about it. There could be several takes on what was happening here. Possibly, the Welsh gentleman was psychotic. Psychosis is a mental illness that can include delusions. A delusion is a false idea or belief held by the person who, when in a delusional (or psychotic) state, cannot be talked or reasoned out of it. So, maybe the Welsh gentleman's belief that he was dying was a delusion, a false one, brought on by mental illness. Another possibility is that he may have been delirious, a condition caused by drug toxicity, infection, dehydration or constipation, which causes the person to become acutely confused. Or, perhaps he was suffering from depression – this condition can cause nihilistic delusions, such as a fixed belief that you, or a part of your body, or the real world does not exist. But the much more likely possibility is that the gentleman really did, in saneness, believe that he was dying, and that he had good reason to believe that he was dying. It may also have been true that, as well as believing he was dying, he actually was. After all, he was elderly, he had dementia and elderly people living with dementia die; they are expected to die.

Talking about dying is a personal preference and this is also true for people living with dementia. Like any other dying person, they may want to talk about their own death, as was the case for the aunt in *Finding Our Way* (Chapter 2, p.26), who anticipated that death would mean that she would have to 'stand up and be counted'; who wanted some ideas from her niece about how to 'be released', and who, when the time came, was clear that she was ready to say goodbye and 'go to the river alone'. I would encourage more open discussion and a stepping towards, rather than away from, the topic of dying and loss for people living with dementia and their families. In my experience these conversations can be valuable, important and not at all difficult. If you have dementia or you are caring for a person who has dementia, bear in mind that support and healthcare workers may be waiting for you to signal that you are ready and able to cope with the conversation.

Anticipatory grief

An important theme arising from grief and loss for people living with dementia and their friends and families that is not represented in these stories is that of anticipatory grief, which can feel just as intense as the grief felt after the death of someone important to us. Anticipatory grief is a response to impending loss – of, for example, skills and abilities, roles and relationships – as opposed to grief following actual loss, such as the death of a person or the loss of a house. Family members and friends, as well the person with dementia, commonly experience this.

For family and friends and for the person living with dementia, anguish comes from a combination of losses that have already occurred, doubled by anticipation of more significant impending losses before physical death. Many losses are, as already described, ambiguous, such as losing the companionship, wit and problem-solving abilities that were so strongly valued throughout the relationship, or losing the opportunity for sexual intimacy. For friends and family, anticipatory grief is painfully experienced in knowing that the dementia will worsen and that, for example, at some point in the future, the person living with dementia may no longer be able to recognise friends and family members or participate in once-valued events and activities.

For the person living with dementia, anticipatory grief is common, especially in the early stages when symptoms may be mild and communication and thinking skills are still reasonably intact. Grief may be felt over the impending loss of their own abilities, skills and independence, and fear and anxiety may be felt about what's going to happen to them and to those they care about in the future. Talking about what the future may hold and making plans can help to reduce the feelings of anxiety and fear of the unknown for all concerned.

Advance decisions

A further theme that should not be overlooked is that of advance care planning, which offers people the opportunity to plan and request their preferred future care and support, including medical treatment, while they have the capacity to do so. This is especially relevant for people who are at risk of losing mental capacity through progressive conditions such as dementia. A person with advanced dementia may be unable to express their feelings, wishes and needs about end-of-life care. For this reason, it is important that anyone living with dementia should consider drawing up an advance care plan and/or a funeral plan in addition to sorting out wills, power of attorney, and finances sooner rather than later, while communication skills and mental capacity are intact (see Chapter 1).

The process of talking about and expressing wishes and preferences is just as important as the written plan for the person who has dementia and for family and friends involved in supporting them. There are a number of good templates that you can download online to guide you through these processes. Use a reputable source such as the NHS, Age UK, Dementia UK, Alzheimer's Society or any of the organisations in the list of Resources at the end of the chapter (see also Chapter 1).

> **Advice points**
> - Push for a diagnosis as soon as you suspect that dementia may be developing.
> - Try to step towards what's happening and what may be coming, rather than avoid it.
> - Get help to talk about and document what you want and don't want when you die – i.e. an advance care plan.
> - Get help to sort out your finances and legal affairs such as power of attorney as soon as possible while you have the mental capacity to do so.

References

Beanland, T. (2015/16). What might the idea of a 'good death' mean for a person with dementia? *Dementia Together*, December/January. www.alzheimers.org.uk/get-support/publications-and-factsheets/dementia-together-magazine/what-might-idea-good-death-mean-person-dementia

Commission on Dignity in Care for Older People. (2012). *Delivering dignity: Securing dignity in care for older people in hospitals and care homes*. NHS Confederation.

Gibson, L. (2009). *The power of partnership: Palliative care in dementia*. National Council for Palliative Care.

Health Service Ombudsman. (2011). *Care and compassion? Report of the Health Service Ombudsman on ten investigations into NHS care of older people*. The

Stationery Office. www.ombudsman.org.uk/sites/default/files/2016-10/Care%20 and%20Compassion.pdf

Kane, M. (2012). *My life until the end: Dying well with dementia*. Alzheimer's Society. www.alzheimers.org.uk/sites/default/files/migrate/downloads/my_life_ until_the_end_dying_well_with_dementia.pdf

Prince, M., Knapp, M., Guerchet, M., McCrone, P., Prina, M., Comas-Herrera, A., Wittenberg, R., Adelaja, B., Hu, B., King, D., Rehill, A. & Salimkumar, D. (2014). *Dementia UK: Update* (2nd ed.). Alzheimer's Society. www.alzheimers.org.uk/sites/ default/files/migrate/downloads/dementia_uk_update.pdf

Public Health England. (2019). *Death in people aged 75 years and older in England in 2017: Research and analysis*. Public Health England. www.gov.uk/government/ publications/death-in-people-aged-75-years-and-older-in-england-in-2017/ death-in-people-aged-75-years-and-older-in-england-in-2017

Royal College of Psychiatrists. (2011). *National audit of dementia*. Royal College of Psychiatrists.

Resources

Books

Anderson, E., May, H. & Perrin, T. (2008). *Wellbeing in dementia: An occupational approach for therapists and carers*. Churchill Livingstone.

Boss, P. (2011). *Loving someone who has dementia*. John Wiley and Sons Inc.

Brooker, D., Edwards, P. & May, H. (2009). *Enriched care planning for people with dementia: A good practice guide to delivering person-centred care*. Jessica Kingsley Publishers.

Online resources and websites

Age UK: www.ageuk.org.uk/information-advice (Free information and advice to help you on topics as diverse as claiming benefits and care homes)

Alzheimer's Research UK: www.alzheimersresearchuk.org (The UK's leading dementia research organisation)

Alzheimer's Society: www.alzheimers.org.uk/get-support/help-dementia-care/grief-loss-and-bereavement

Care Fit for VIPS: www.carefitforvips.co.uk (An easy-to-use online toolkit that gives you everything you need to get started on understanding and implementing person-centred dementia care)

Care Quality Commission (CQC): www.cqc.org.uk/sites/default/files/20160504_ ISL116_15_ER_What_you_can_expect_from_a_Care_Home_Low_Res_Final.pdf (What you can expect from a good care home)

Carers Trust: https://carers.org (Campaign organisation working to improve support, services and recognition for anyone living with the challenges of caring, unpaid, for a family member or friend who is ill, frail, disabled or has mental health or addiction problems)

Cruse Bereavement Care: www.cruse.org.uk and www.cruse.org.uk/sites/default/files/default_images/pdf/Areas/Waies/Dementia%20brochure%20English%20%282%29.pdf (Information about bereavement, loss and dementia)

(Dementia Just Ain't) Sexy: www.dementiajustaintsexy.blogspot.com (A place to share thoughts about the impact of dementia on those who live with it)

Dementia UK: www.dementiauk.org/wp-content/uploads/2019/05/Grief-Bereavement-and-Loss-R1-new-style-Web.pdf (Information about bereavement, loss and dementia for those caring for someone with dementia)

Independent Age: www.independentage.org (A charity providing free advice and support to older people)

Live Better with Dementia: https://dementia.livebetterwith.com (Information and advice to help make day-to-day living a bit better for people living with or caring for someone with dementia)

Marie Curie: www.mariecurie.org.uk/professionals/palliative-care-knowledge-zone/condition-specific-short-guides/dementia (Information on caring for someone with dementia towards the end of life)

NHS Care Homes: www.nhs.uk/conditions/social-care-and-support-guide/care-services-equipment-and-care-homes/care-homes (Information on choosing the right care home)

NHS Continuing Healthcare checklist: www.england.nhs.uk/healthcare

NHS Planning for your Future Care: www.england.nhs.uk/improvement-hub/publication/planning-for-your-future-care (Information and advice on future care planning)

Playlist for Life: www.playlistforlife.org.uk (How to create a personal playlist to support people living with dementia)

Social Care Institute (SCIE): www.scie.org.uk/dementia/advanced-dementia-and-end-of-life-care/end-of-life-care/last-days-hours.asp (Information about care in the last days and hours of someone with dementia)

Together in Dementia Every Day (TIDE): www.tide.uk.net (UK-wide network of carers, former carers and health and care professionals working together to build a better future for carers of people living with dementia)

Which magazine: www.which.co.uk/later-life-care (Guidance on making later-life choices)

YouTube video

Anticipatory Grief: The Songaminute Man, Alzheimer's & Dementia (2018, October 15). www.youtube.com/watch?v=0uArkK366Gc

Outside the Box

7 – It's not all about humans

Only a dog

'Oh it's only a dog,' and 'Well you can get another one' – I still remember those words said to us after our dog Annie died very suddenly, aged 13 years. Annie was a very important part of our lives, our family unit. My partner Gill and I adopted her from the Blue Cross when she was just a couple of months old. We both had waited all our working lives for the right moment to take on the responsibilty of adopting a dog, and changes in both our careers, combined with a move to the countryside, meant this long-held ambition was possible. Annie was lively, intelligent, obedient and very soft in nature. Our home felt complete as she settled into a companionship with us and our cat, Dusty.

In April 2014, just before we were to leave for a holiday in France, Annie suddenly became ill and our UK vet couldn't find anything seriously wrong. He said we should go. Just four days after we arrived, she had to be put to sleep, due to untreatable tumours. We buried her in a friend's allotment, here in the French village where we now live.

The shock is the biggest emotion. I can remember even now, the sense of disbelief, the absolute loss and finality. For weeks, I would wake up and look for her where her bed should have been. A few years before, someone had drawn her portrait for us, and I would look at it every day, unable to accept that she was gone. Over many years, I had experienced loss and bereavement with the deaths of friends, parents and Gill's mother, yet this felt so much more painful, more shocking, more destabilising. These feelings were then confused with a sense of guilt, of questioning… Why am I feeling like this? Why does this grief feel so different from all the other experiences of loss? I kept thinking I should get over it now, it has been weeks, months… Being someone who needs answers, I turned to the internet and found a book called *Losing a Pet*,[1] by Jane

---
1. Matthews, J. (2007). *Losing a pet: Coping with the death of your beloved animal.* Small Books.

Matthews. Reading this book gave me insight and restored my self-belief. This experience wasn't unnatural or 'over the top'. Subsequently, others have shared their experiences with us, and so many have had similar feelings of guilt and confusion about the strength of their grief following the death of a pet.

Buff Beauty

It was through Jacob, my first dog, that I met my current landlord, in a pub in town ('Can my dog buy your dog a packet of crisps?'), and so Jacob and I moved into our ninth address in the 10 years of our being together, for Jacob's last three years of life.

Jacob got old and ill, and his back legs were going. I had to prepare for his death. I'd already planted a Buff Beauty shrub rose for him when we'd moved in, calling it the Golden Labrador rose, and as October ebbed into November, and Jacob's legs were failing so much that he couldn't get up to pee without help, I knew I'd have to make that awful decision to have him put down soon. I had time to prepare – digging his grave one long golden autumn afternoon, watching the steam rise from the mound of dark earth as the low sun gleamed on it, fallen leaves all around on the still green fresh grass, sun slanting through apple and honeysuckle leaves; digging up Cotswold stones, one to be his headstone. The nice sympathetic lady vet came to the cottage to put him to sleep, there on the sofa between me and the then boyfriend. Jacob was dozing and hardly noticed her coming in and the needle going into his foreleg. I'd lined his grave with straw, then one of his sheepskins. We laid him on it, covered him with his favourite jumper, more straw, then the soft dark earth.

Twenty-three years later, the Buff Beauty, Jacob's rose, is a big, generous glossy-leaved, seven-foot-high-and-wide shrub, never failing every June to bear massive sprays of scented Golden Labrador-coloured blooms, and always again every September to October too. Ferns, hellebores, foxgloves, comfrey, yellow archangel and alkanet thrive there in the shade of the two apple trees; climbing rose, clematis and honeysuckle, with honesty, snowdrops, primroses and native daffodils in the spring.

I was bracing myself as I entered that unknown territory of life alone after Jacob's death. The loss of a best friend, a confidante, a companion, the first time I had to go through that depth of loss and grief – he was my partner. Living here alone in this little cottage with the elderly, ill Jacob was so like living with an old ill man – like living with Pa in his last months; his grunts and groans of pain, his shuffling around during the restless nights – except this time I was able to love and care for my old dog, with full, open-hearted compassion, patience and tenderness, instead of the irritation, impatience, out-of-my-depthness that I felt then, in the cramped family house full of isolated people.

And so, in looking after my old, dying dog when I was 40, I was, at last, on some level, able to let some tenderness and compassion in for my old dying

Pa, and for the locked-away self I was when I was 26, wanting but unable to connect.

Jacob's death gave me so much – the loving and the letting go. I've gone on to love and let go of two more dogs, and am with dog number 4, Buster. The garden's getting full!

> I had a dog called Jacob
> And now he's gone to ground
> But across the fields,
> Inside my heart,
> Still he roams around
> And on the sofa of my soul
> He's sleeping safe and sound.

Beloved cat

The biggest death I remember being affected by was my cat, Joe. He was three, and it came on so quickly that I didn't have time to come home and see him before he was gone. I was at university, more than five hours away, at the time. It seemed silly to travel home just because he was sick. Then he was gone, and I never had a chance to say goodbye. My last picture of him is him all wired up and sedated, far from the lively cat that brought in half a rabbit as a gift for me. One consolation I have is that he didn't die alone. He was loved, and I think he knew that.

Genuine grief

I know what genuine grief is because I felt it this year for the first time when my cat died. When both my parents died in quick succession at the end of 2017, I realised I had no idea what to do and I didn't feel much. My relationship with both of them was strained and my father was a nasty man, but people still reacted as if I should be in grief. The vicar did actually ask if I wanted him to say that my father was an arsehole – some do apparently! I declined, so he was euphemistic.

Chicken parade

When my daughters were aged four, six and seven, our chicken died. The youngest daughter placed her on a trolley, on a bed of grass, decorated her with flowers and took her down our street, 'parading her' and showing her to everyone she met, stopping at the café to show her to all of the interested customers (mainly pensioners). She was very chuffed with herself.

Farm life

We run a dairy farm. Our cows are fat and sleek. They are relaxed and easy to work with. Other farmers comment on this. They ask us what the secret is. It's simple – it's kindness. You won't hear shouting on our farm. Sometimes, despite our best efforts, a calf dies. And our children have seen that. The still body lying on the clean straw, the coat wet and slick. It sounds strange, I know, but I am glad. They know that death is a thing. They know there is no life without death and sometimes that means there is hardly any life at all. I feel sorry for the children growing up in the city who never get the chance to understand this so gently.

Chicken Frank

My nephew was five when Uncle Frank died. He was not allowed to the funeral. A few weeks later, when one of his chickens died, he held a funeral with his sister and me… for Chicken Frank!

A proper goodbye

I was an infant-school teacher in the days when pets were welcomed in schools. We had a delightful gentle little guinea pig called Rosie. She was adored by the children and we allowed her to wander about the classroom. When she died, the children insisted on a 'proper funeral' – what was that, I wondered? Well, they decided that we must sing her favourite song, write some special words and bury her in the Wildlife Garden. The caretaker solved the problem of the coffin by providing a Chivas Regal box. It was a lovely sunny day and the children were very happy to have said goodbye 'properly' to their lovely pet. I was the only one who cried!

My guinea pig

I am now older and wiser, still in my teens, and have since experienced the loss of my beloved Grandpa, but my first loss was Ron, my guinea pig. Ron was my first real pet. Up until then I had Splish and Splash, my goldfish, to whom I am ashamed to say I fed Smarties and crisps, leading to their demise when I was two.

I was five when I welcomed Ron into the hutch in the garage. He squeaked very loudly when I spoke to him and we had a special relationship, though I confess this didn't involve the cleaning of the hutch, which my mother did weekly, as I held the bag for the straw, the most important job! Ron was two years old when he died, we had gone to the hutch on Christmas Day, singing carols to him, and I gave him his Christmas stocking. We had moved him into the house, as I said it was cold in the utility room. I loved sneaking in, and he would squeak hello to me. Boxing Day, I rushed in, threw back the blanket and screamed. Ron lay there his, eyes staring at me, a little trickle of blood on the side of his mouth. Crying, I ran for my mother. My mother sorted everything and the next time I saw Ron he was in a little box, with bedding, and he looked asleep. My mother explained he had died and that he was safe now. I am not sure how or why he died. I put some toys and a letter in the box, and we held a special ceremony. My dad said a few words and I held my mother's hand and sobbed.

Every night for years I said my prayers and asked Ron if he was OK and that I missed him. This was my first experience of death and the realisation that we all die in the end. I am now 17 and still miss Ron. I have a dog, Chester, who I have had for nine years and all I do is worry about when he dies, as he is so loved. Every time I need him, he is here. My mother has explained to me about anticipatory grief. When my Grandpa died, I really understood what grief was, but the loss of Ron did help prepare me for the future losses. But as they say, everyone and every loss is different and I can tell you this is true, animal or human, it hurts and made me realise that every day and everything is important.

Baraka's story

Baraka came to me as a white Andalusian stallion. He was wild, traumatised by harsh treatment and determined attempts to break his spirit. We could not communicate in the early times and this problem led me to the path of natural horsemanship and my own training as an equine therapist. I work mostly with children. Through this work, he became my co-therapist and a blessing to the children with whom we worked. I think of him as a master of sorrow and of healing. He died very suddenly. The white shock, Baraka the Horse was gone. I remember the early September morning when I saw him and knew there was no help to give. His life-light was dimming but his deep dark eye was upon me. This was farewell, his heart breath to mine, mine to him in the shadows. It was strange to be so fully present in this death and I did not step away. Only years later, I am aware that when there is true heart connection there is no separation. On that day, standing by my horse, I received the gift and blessing of courage to continue without him. The pain of his passing was dark, violent, and I cried in the light of the full, blood-red moon and felt a total eclipse. The waves of grief engulfing, and my inner compass was in pieces. Time ceased for a while. Grief took its wild course.

Alongside my own grief, I had to tell the children about his sudden death. He had been such an anchor and we mourned and remembered him, together with his herd.

Healing balm came from many sources – the natural world at first and then my human clan, who gently and consistently held me in mind with all manner of kindness – talking, not talking, listening, no judgements on the tears, which did not ease for many moons, and so much more.

A year or more after Baraka passed and he had been cremated, I contacted Guy at the crematorium. The shame for leaving it so long to discuss collecting Baraka's ashes faded with Guy's warm response. 'It takes the time it takes.' He told me that they hold on to the ashes, some for years. Some are never collected and are placed in their own area, all together there, in his store. I arrive at the animal crematorium. There is a feeling of welcome and calm. Time to cry, time for a cuppa, time to look around and learn about this process of respectfully letting go of physical beings, to be free.

Guy showed me what he does. It was so clean and without horror. I was amazed at how much I wanted to know. This was an inspiring experience, so different from other end-of-life experiences for me and our animals.

Sometimes now, when I am at a loss in a session with a child, I ask for guidance and it always comes.

A hard day's work

I am a vet. Some years ago, I took a call from the RSPCA requesting my attendance, along with the police, at a local animal rescue centre. It was a dismal autumn day and I was shocked at the scene that greeted me – police officers, RSPCA officers, local people and, of course, the owner and her family, all milling around, heated voices, pleading. There had been reports of animal neglect and cruelty at the premises. It was my job, along with the RSPCA officers, to inspect the premises and document the conditions the animals were housed in. I witnessed a scene of the most dreadful squalor imaginable, so much so that I still struggle to adequately describe the scene.

Normally a dog kennel is a noisy place full of yappy, inquisitive creatures who bounce up to greet (or snarl) at anyone who gets near. Here, nothing, they barely turned their heads. These dogs had given up on humans. That really got to me.

We were able to move the majority of the animals off the premises to temporary new homes or to the vet clinic for ongoing assessment and treatment. I was having a final walk around before setting off back to the clinic when I thought I heard a noise by the back of the house and I spotted a small mesh cage, on top of a pile of rubbish and rubble. I took a closer look and was astonished to see a pair of eyes peering at me around a column of what I later ascertained was a stack of dried excrement reaching from the floor to the top of the cage. The eyes belonged to a small Staffordshire bull terrier. She was shivering and frightened but was unable to move much because she was paraplegic. Clearly this cage had been home to this disabled dog for some time.

Euthanasia is something I do on a daily basis and people often ask me how I can do it. Does it not affect me? I can honestly say that I see it as a treatment, as much as anything else I do, and it does not affect me, even when I am dealing with animals I have known from a very young age.

This little Staffi was different. I wanted to explain to her that not all humans are the same, that not all humans are cruel and uncaring, that not all humans are indifferent to the sufferings of others. I wanted to apologise on behalf of the human race, but, of course, I could not. This one got to me.

Even as I write this, I feel myself welling up; it still gets to me. I often revisit that day in my mind, and I struggle with the emotion of it all. I feel it is a form of post-traumatic stress disorder. I cannot talk about it without being swallowed up by raw emotion. Maybe writing this will help!

There was a successful prosecution for animal cruelty. However, I cannot think of a punishment adequate enough to assuage what those animals suffered under their 'care'.

I have grown

I lost my best friend in 2014, in the form of a beautiful rescue dog called Gromit, who I named lovingly after 'Wallace and Gromit', and yes, he loved a bit of cheese!

My life changed in an instant from the moment I knew I had to say my final goodbye. The first year of my bereavement was devastating, although I knew I had rescued him through love and let him go through that same love and had support from my mom. I was the most loneliest I had ever felt in my life.

I felt I had no purpose, no reason to get up, no need to take care of myself, no need to smile. I felt guilty for doing anything but couldn't bring myself to do anything either. I was in utter turmoil.

I made a memory box, I put a photo of Gromit in a locket I could wear at all times to give me inner strength, I had a photo of his face printed onto a cushion, pride of place on my bed, and I wrote a letter to him, telling him how much I loved and love him.

I believe there is no time limit to our grief, certainly no rules and we never 'get over' our loss; we just adapt and try to cope the best we can.

And that's what I did…

My loving mom pointed me in the direction of the Blue Cross pet bereavement service, to train to become a volunteer, to pass on my pet-loss experience, kind nature, understanding and my empathy.

My life has kept on changing, all from the love of Gromit. I have grown in confidence in all aspects of my life. Gromit's love gives and has given me the courage to cope with my long-term health condition. I still feel his support in a different way now. He has shown me the true meaning of love in its purest form and made me want to have a career in anything pet related.

The best thing I ever will have achieved is rescuing Gromit.

Dealing with death

When I was nine years old, my father taught me how to lay out the dead when one of the puppies born to our family dog died. As a midwife for many years, I then could draw from his teaching when I, on occasion, would help a family celebrate and say goodbye to their child. Now, years later, I'm a psychotherapist and, again, these lessons of death and laying out are used in our conversations.

First death

When I was a little boy, my goldfish died. It was still, in its bowl, lying with one eye up on top of the water. My mother told me it was dead but I didn't believe her. I put my finger in the water and stirred it. 'See,' I said as the goldfish rode the swirl. My mum just stroked my hair and gave me a settling glance. Then... I knew. I remember this very clearly, because it made me feel more grown up and a little stronger in myself.

Repeat performance

Mrs Reeves told me about burying her childhood pet stick insect. She organised the readings, decorated a matchbox lavishly for the occasion and roped all her siblings into the funeral procession. She came from a very religious family, so the stick insect was buried with due pomp and ceremony. Prayers were spoken when the hole had been carefully filled in, followed by a reverent silence around the diminutive grave. When they had finished, they all agreed it had been such fun that they dug it up and did it all again.

Such a hard decision

We knew we had to put our lovely dog to sleep. He was not yet seven. The vet was compassionate and kind, acknowledging that our dog was a part of our family and that this was a very difficult thing for us to be doing. We lifted Jasper onto his bed and all sat around him while the vet gave him the injections, stroking him and talking to him (I think – it's a bit of a blur), and then the vet left us. We covered Jasper with his own blanket and took it in turns to sit with him. It was an amazingly beautiful, crisply cold, clear night and my daughter and I spent some time looking up at the stars and looking for the ones we recognised – like Orion – trying to find some comfort in the sense of vastness.

I feel a little broken inside. My wonderful lively intelligent fun and loving companion has blinked out of my life (and all of our lives) so abruptly. I am so bereft without his presence. Particularly after the children left home, he was with me every day (I work from home), sleeping on my feet sometimes, pottering around the house with me and making me laugh. My husband is also grieving but he grieves in a solitary way, so I feel very alone with this. He is kind and sympathetic but wants to 'move on', as he puts it, while I just feel so stuck in the misery. I replay the progress of Jasper's condition and the decision we made and, even though I know we saved him from any more suffering, it hurts that it turned out the way it did.

Saying goodbye

When my young son Sam realised that his pet rat ('Mouser') was unwell, he promised her he'd take care of her properly if she died. When this happened, he was so gentle. It was winter. I lit the fire. He came in bearing Mouser's body and laid her in the flames. I hadn't realised his intention. We stilled, we watched. It felt like Sam had taken on the mantle of saying goodbye to his friend and seen it through. Oh, how we missed her.

The fox who came to our garden

Death is fascinating – the process of decay, what actually happens to the body – particularly if you are four years old. This story began when I walked down the garden of my terraced city house to hang the washing, and found a big, bright, furry wild animal in my flower bed. Fox. It was very still, but its presence was immense. I put down my washing basket, gingerly stepped closer to this surprise visitor. It was an honour to be so close, to see the perfect teeth, small paws, whiskers. An intimate encounter with a piece of the wild.

An honour that she had come to die in my garden. I was reminded of the story where Old Woman assembles the skeleton of a wolf and sings the life back into it.[2] I wished I could sing that song now and see this fox twitch her paws, stand up, shake and slink off back into her world. But no, this fox was dead, and staying dead.

What was one supposed to do with a dead fox? It was my husband who suggested we bury it in the garden. I don't know why I hadn't thought of this. 'Then, in a year or two, we can dig up the bones,' he said. Immediately our four-year-old was caught. We buried the fox good and deep, and whenever we were in that part of the garden, my daughter would ask if it was time yet to dig it up. It was nearly her seventh birthday when she suddenly said, 'You said we could dig up the fox when I was six and now I'm nearly seven!'

She had a point. So somehow digging up the fox became the main event of her seventh birthday party. She invited a bunch of friends. We had sandwiches and crisps and Pass the Parcel, and then the digging began, supervised by my husband. I was portioning jelly and ice cream into bowls when one of the boys raced up to the house, breathlessly announcing, 'We've found the skull!' Never have I found it harder to interest children in a bowl of pudding. It was the best kind of treasure hunt we could have invented. The children scrubbed the dirt off the bones, examined them thoroughly, tried to fit them together. Then the friends washed their hands thoroughly, went home, and I always wondered what their parents thought of it.

I am glad they had such a close encounter with these bones at a young age. In a society where death is mostly hidden away, it was an important childhood initiation. I am grateful to that fox for choosing our garden as her place to die.

---

2. Pinkola Estes, C. (1992). *Women who run with the wolves*. Rider.

Commentaries

When a pet dies – Diane James, Manager of the Pet Bereavement Support Service, Blue Cross

Diane has worked for Blue Cross animal charity since 2014. The pet bereavement support service is a free phone and email service for support for any type of pet loss. She also trains and presents to vets, animal organisations and other animal charities on the topic of pet loss. She has appeared on TV and radio and in podcasts, and contributes to magazines and newspapers regularly, as well as being involved in academic research in many areas that involve pet loss. It's not a job, it's a vocation.

For many of us, our first experience of death is at a young age; it is the loss of our beloved fur, feather or finned animal friend. With it comes the realisation that life comes to an end and that is a shock for all of us. I am firmly convinced that, if we got it right at this early stage in our development, it would pave the way for future losses – not that it would make it any easier but that understanding about death would be part of our development, questions would be answered honestly and there would be more openness, compassion and realisation that we should take nothing for granted and cherish every day.

I hope that, as you read the stories in this chapter, you began to understand that the death of an animal can, in some cases, be harder for some than a human death. I am usually greeted with a variety of responses to this, including people saying they are offended – they cannot imagine using the word 'bereavement' after an animal dies, and ask how I can compare a human loss to that of an animal.

I am simply trying not to make any death less important than another.

Often, we hear people say, it was only a dog, cat, rabbit... as the usual response to a pet's death. Usually this will have come from a non-animal-loving person, or someone who has never experienced the unconditional love that having an animal as part of your family unit can bring. For it really is unconditional; they are reliant on us for food, water and care, medically and emotionally; it is love like no other. As a mother, I can perhaps liken it to that of my child when a baby, though it continues for most pets for the whole of their life.

I am not immune to death; its impact on me has been both devastating and traumatic, but grief affects everyone differently and we need to understand that everyone is entitled to react how they want, over who or what they want. Some of these stories may have struck a chord; some people may find them unusual or strange, but remember, they are very personal to the writer.

One thing I do know is that talking about a death can be helpful, as can writing about it. If you have not had a chance to say those final good-byes, or there is no animal to say them to as they were never found, write down your thoughts and feelings. What you do then is your choice – burn it, bury it, place it behind a picture of the animal, or keep it in a memory box. No matter what you decide to do with the writings, they can really benefit you.

There are many different views and perspectives on the subject of whether animals grieve when another animal dies. I wonder why we think that the loss of a fellow animal will not affect the other animals in the household, stable or field? Do we think, only humans can feel loss and love? There is no clear evidence to support the long-held idea of elephant graveyards, but researchers have found that elephants will spend some time investigating the remains of a dead elephant, before moving on. So it may be that in future our understanding of these phenomena will be corroborated by clearer research. If possible, I would advise allowing animals to see the body of a dead fellow animal. I have heard from others who have witnessed horses bowing their heads in silence in the stables and dogs carefully sniffing the body of those with whom they used to share a home. It offers them the chance to understand what has happened. Then they often resume whatever they were doing, seemingly untroubled.

Guilt is a word that is often mentioned when the death of a pet comes up. It tends to be followed by the words 'if only' – 'If only I had done this sooner', 'If only I had got a second opinion'. I have to say, this is not unique to the loss of an animal, but it is something that appears more often, perhaps due to the fact that, as owners, our responsibility is total. Animals rely on our judgement and care, trusting us implicitly to make the right choice and decision for them. And this may also include the decision to end an animal's life. One thing that sticks in my mind is how often people liken signing the paperwork for the pet to be euthanised at the vet to signing its death warrant, making it so much harder to deal with. Home euthanasia is becoming more widely available, as more vets and home euthanasia companies have started to offer this service. For larger animals and animals who have a fear of going in the car or surgery, it's a good way to make a difficult task easier and ease the pressure on all concerned.

People often think they can make the loss easier or ease others' pain by straying from the truth. Usually it is when there is a younger person involved in the love and care of the animal. How many times have you heard or read that a child or young adult has been told the animal has 'gone to live on a farm', or run away? We think we are helping to reduce the pain, anger, hurt, grief, whatever it is we think they will feel. It doesn't, it just makes them imagine they may be in some way to blame. What did I do wrong, did I hurt it, upset it, why did it run away, who has it now, where is it? Honesty is the best policy.

When I was in my early 20s (so not a youngster), we had a large black-and-white cat, Smudge. I was working away from home. One weekend when I came home to visit, I was told he had run away. I couldn't understand why. Smudge was never found. Years later – and I mean more than 20 years later – my mother confessed he had been ill and the vet had advised he be euthanised. I am not sure how it made me feel but it made me realise that my mother thought it in my best interest not to know the truth, even at that age. She was a loving, wonderful person, but it stopped me having closure.

Having now worked with grief and loss, and particularly in the case of animals killed in tragic accidents or genuinely lost, stolen or never found, I know that being truthful is vital. As with any death, if it is sudden and unexpected, information and communication can be key to the owner. If possible (and not too traumatic), the return of the body can prove very important to the grieving process. Things are so much better than in years gone by, with more people understanding the need for owners to be made aware of tragic accidents. The development of microchipping, legal reporting, lost pet groups and social media is definitely moving us in the right direction. I look forward to a time when reporting of animal deaths in accidents becomes routine, because everyone is aware of the impact of the death of pets on their owners (in most cases).

Closure does not take away the pain of loss; it helps us to learn to live with it. Sometimes this is harder to achieve, due to the circumstances around their disappearance, but we can do things to support this. Adults and children can benefit from memorialising them. You can plant a bush, tree or flowers. You can make a scrap book or collage or create a memory box and fill it with the things that remind you of the special relationship you had. Write a letter or draw a picture, tell them all you wanted to say but never did. It's the same advice we would give for a human loss. Grief is grief, after all. It can help to hold a ceremony or memorial talk. It is entirely a personal choice that should be discussed with everyone, if the animal was part of a family unit or relationship, respecting everyone's points of view and, of course, taking into account any religious views or beliefs held by the family.

I have used the word 'euthanasia', as have some of the stories in this chapter. The word actually comes from the Greek, *eu thanatos*, which means 'good death'. People often find it easier to use phrases like 'put to sleep' (PTS), 'passed', 'lost' – anything but the actual word. It is important to remember that a young person may not understand that the phrase 'put to sleep' means the animal has died and will not wake up. If the young person does understand it, they may be fearful that the same will happen to them when they go to sleep.

We sometimes don't give children enough credit for their intelligence. If they do understand what it is about, they should be given the choice about whether to attend the euthanasia. This is where clear understanding and communication will be vital, from the vet as well as the parents. In many cases, it can be reassuring for the pet to be in familiar surroundings, with the people and smells that they know. But it is a very personal choice and many adults find it impossible to accompany their pet in this way. It can be a very different experience when a large animal like a horse is being euthanised. It is most definitely not something that all people can bear to witness. It really needs a lot of thought and heart searching.

It is wise to think about whether you do want to see the animal's body if they have been killed by a car. It may not be the last memory you want to have of them. Each person must decide what is best for them. Children can be fascinated by death, and they often have a need to ask questions, which is how they learn, of course. Why do the eyes not close? Can it feel pain? Will it be lonely? These are just a few of the questions I've heard asked at a euthanasia or death of an animal. Of course, no one really knows what happens when we or an animal dies. What is clear is that, if we can explain the death of an animal to a child and so help them process it more easily, we surely must make the future losses more understandable, but obviously no less painful.

The response to the death of an animal can depend on whether it was viewed as a pet or a working animal. The relationship between human and animal is very different, in many ways. It may be a more common occurrence or, indeed, part of the working life of a farm for animals to die and these animals would not be viewed as a member of the family. Sometimes, of course, that daily working relationship, such as between a sheepdog and its master, can be one of the closest of relationships between human and animal.

Sadly, not all animals are in safe and loving homes. Sometimes this makes the death harder for those tasked with dealing with the neglect and abuse. Some people seem to think, because of their role, professionals are immune to the grief, the horror that faces them. This clearly, is not the case. Time and time again, I speak with people working with animals – welfare assistants, vets, veterinary nurses, volunteers and workers with animal charities and other organisations – who face daily the subjection of animals to a human's cruelty. The most humane response and the kindest thing is to take away the animal's pain and suffering. If these people are lucky enough to have a good support network in place and effective coping strategies, they may just be able to retain their faith in people and avoid the worst impacts of these experiences, including compassion fatigue.

The response to the death of a pet mirrors the grief cycle we experience for humans, but one major difference is, as animal lovers, we can also make sure they don't suffer and that they are out of pain. I often feel that we treat our beloved animals much better with regard to quality at end of life than we do our fellow humans, but making that choice can also feel like a massive burden. Trust in your vet, communicate openly and take comfort from knowing you have done the best you could in the circumstances.

Advice points

1. Talk to people, family, friends or a pet bereavement support service. Talking will help.
2. When the loss involves having to tell a child or children, remember to be open and honest. Showing and normalising emotions is good.

3. If your animal must be euthanised, make sure you are fully aware of what will happen.
4. Make the choice that is right for you about after-death body care.
5. When and if you feel able to rehome or get another animal, make sure everyone in the family unit is involved.

When it's time: euthanasia – Sophie Stainer

Sophie trained as a vet at Cambridge University and has worked for 13 years as a GP vet in Oxfordshire, in a small, independent practice embedded in the community.

In the majority of cases where I have been involved in care through the pet's last months, I find that pet owners do know when the time is right to help their pet to die. I try to prepare them well ahead of time, often as soon as we have diagnosed a condition that I know will shorten life or seriously affect welfare. It helps if I am able to explain what to expect as their pet deteriorates, so that owners can recognise the stages of illness and understand better what their pet may be feeling. The death of a pet always feels premature to some extent; to most people, a pet feels like a member of the human family, but their life is, of course, significantly shorter. For some people, this can make the loss harder to accept than losing elderly members of their human family. Preparation really helps here.

It is often hard to know when to draw the line with elderly pets with chronic conditions who are gradually ageing and declining. People sometimes struggle with having that power in their hands, of making a decision over life or death, which of course we don't really have for humans. When the time does come that owners begin to question quality of life, we tend to have a conversation about the balance of pleasure in life versus pain or discomfort. I encourage them to draw up a list of things their pet has always valued, and whether they are still able to enjoy them – a walk, a cuddle on a lap, their food or treats, games or toys, company. I suggest that when the negatives outweigh the positives, that might be time, or when they refuse breakfast, or when they spend all their time on their own and no longer wish to socialise. Most often though, in the end, the owner will say to me , 'I just know it's time now.' There is rarely a case when I actually have to tell an owner their elderly pet needs to be euthanised without them really already knowing – but those cases certainly stick in the mind.

Then there are the cases where it is unexpected; when I have to ring an owner with bad news very shortly after the onset of symptoms and advise that we are already out of options other than euthanasia. When it comes as a shock, particularly in a younger animal, there are often accompanying feelings of guilt – that perhaps they have given the wrong food or somehow exposed the pet to risk. It is the effect of responsibility on the feelings of grief, and much like having an ill child, I think. I often wonder how doctors feel doing this kind of thing regularly, without even having euthanasia to offer.

Most of the time, I don't 'mind' performing euthanasia at all. Owners frequently say to me, 'This must be the worst part of your job', but it usually isn't. What I often find difficult is to witness the owner's grief, and especially when there is some deeper significance (the last link with a parent or spouse who has died, for example). But in terms of the animal itself, I don't usually feel sad; I feel as though I am giving a great gift. If we have got the timing right, I do feel it is a kindness and that I am offering a release. The only times when the act itself feels negative are when the euthanasia is not, in my opinion, for the benefit of the animal but for some other, possibly pragmatic reason. I try my best to avoid those, but have sometimes had to concede that the alternatives might be worse (they may find other ways to 'get rid' of the animal). On those occasions, it feels more like a betrayal of the animal's trust and an abuse of power. The animal itself knows no difference as I can at least ensure it is a death free from suffering.

I still remember the first time I was invited to be present at the euthanasia of a pet, when I was a teenage work-experience student at my local vets. I felt a bit afraid, not of the death itself but of the grief I might witness. Facing people at this raw moment in their lives was something I felt unprepared for, and to be honest this is still sort of true – vets don't get any training in grief counselling. We end up working out through experience what helps people. I often remind owners that their pet has no concept of the future but lives only in the moment, and that is why we must make the present as lovely for them as we can, and that when we know that tomorrow is going to be full of pain, we can make sure they don't have to walk through that door. The bit I can't help with is what comes next. I recently put to sleep the elderly dog of a friend, who said she found the death itself peaceful and calm, but what seemed unbearable was the thought of the future without her dog in it – a very human pain.

Resources

Books

Dean, E. (2012). *Everybody died so I got a dog.* Hodder & Stoughton.

Eastwood, L. (2012). *Soul comfort for cat lovers: Coping wisdom for heart and soul after the loss of a beloved feline.* Sparkletonic Books.

Friedman, R., James, C. & James, J. (2014). *The grief recovery handbook for pet loss.* Taylor Trade Publishing.

Lambert, A. (2006). *Missing my pets.* BGTF Ltd.

Lee, L. & Lee, M. (1992). *Absent friend: Coping with the loss of a treasured pet.* Ringpress Books Ltd.

Matthews, J. (2007). *Losing a pet: Coping with the death of your beloved animal.* Small Books.

For children

Kerr, J. (2003). *Goodbye Mog.* Harper Collins

Thomas, I. (D. Egnéus, Illus.). (2020). *Fox: A circle of life story.* Bloomsbury.

Wallace, S. (2019). *My pet memory book: To help a child through the loss of their pet.* Pinfold Publishing.

White, E.B. (1952). *Charlotte's web.* New York: Harper & Brothers.

Websites

Blue Cross Pet Bereavement Support Service: www.bluecross.org.uk/pet-bereavement-and-pet-loss

British Horse Society, Friends at the End: www.bhs.org.uk/our-work/welfare/our-campaigns/friends-at-the-end

The Association of Private Pet Cemeteries and Crematoria: www.appcc.org.uk

The Cinnamon Trust: https://cinnamon.org.uk (For people in their last years and the care of their much-needed, much-loved companion animals)

Outside the Box

8 — What is dying like?

A close shave
Gracie didn't want to be admitted to hospital for any reason at all and had been clear with everyone that she wanted to die at home. Her neighbour visited daily. Then Gracie got a chest infection and the paramedics found her unwell and confused. There was nothing written down to say what she wanted and she had no DNACPR form in the house (although she didn't want resuscitation). Her neighbour called the hospice, in distress, as they were taking Gracie into the local hospital for intravenous antibiotics. When I arrived (I am a palliative care nurse working in the community), Gracie was unable to join in the conversation, but luckily the paramedics were experienced, understood what was happening and gave me some time to call in extra care. The GP prescribed medication to help her breathing and she died peacefully at home two days later.

Death in Amsterdam
My energetic and eccentric aunt Charlotte had lived with leukaemia for many years, and lived well. She was 82, had just been to India and was now in Amsterdam. She had got up early to take a canal trip but had a massive bleed on the brain as she waited for the boat. Charlotte was taken to their university hospital where the doctors told us the bleed was so damaging nothing could be done. She was put into a coma and just given painkillers. From when I first heard of her collapse, I tuned into her in my mind and asked how she was and I always got this image of us dancing together. I knew her spirit was okay. I arrived at the hospital on day three. Charlotte was in her own room. At first, I was left alone with her. I sat by her side, stroking her hands and hair, talking about all that had just happened to her, where she was, what the doctors had said. I told her everything as it was, no bullshit. And I talked about the tender feelings.

    I thought about how Charlotte had told me people often need permission to die and how she herself had said to her father that it was time for him to let go. I said to her that I was off now, it was getting dark and I needed to find my hotel. I would be back tomorrow and the next day and the next. And I said: 'You have had the most wonderful life, we have loved you so much and we will never forget the fun and laughter and love we felt with you and from you, but this is it now, Charlotte, this is your time to let go. We will love you forever, but it is time for you to go now.'

At 4am I woke up. It was as if she woke me and was right there beside me. I checked my phone but nothing, so I went back to sleep, engulfed with thoughts of her. I imagined her surrounded by loved ones who had died, showing her the way, helping her move on. At 5am the hospital rang to say she had died an hour ago, at 4am.

When I got to the hospital, her door was closed. I walked in; the curtains were closed. The nurses had put a circle of nightlights all around Charlotte's bed. She was sitting up slightly, and on her face was the sweetest, most contented and loving smile. She had made it!

The arrangements and decisions after Charlotte died were confusing and it was difficult to know what to do for the best. As we walked among the canals, agonising about what to do, her brother and I noticed a fabulous doorway and went to investigate. Above the door was written in large script, '*It really does not matter*'. We fell about laughing: 'Thank you, Charlotte!' We had our instructions, but most importantly, a sense that she was still with us, helping us through.

You can never be fully prepared

My Dad is dying. I am ready. We have talked about what he wants. The staff at the home know. The GP knows. I know. Then he changes his mind, but is it his right mind? Which part of him should I be listening to? It is not peaceful and beautiful. It is uncharted and horribly familiar. We are together and deeply alone. We are still the same embattled people, even in this extraordinary moment. And we cannot find the safe shore.

I do not know everything I need to know. I cannot know everything I need to know. You cannot ever be completely prepared. But a few signposts could have helped.

Like a birth plan, a death plan should be made, and we should be ready to tear it up as the reality of the situation unfolds.

My mother had died the year before. A few days before he died, he said he had seen her. I was guarded. 'Really, Dad?' Trying to keep the doubt out of my voice. Failing. I thought, I must check on his medication. Now I know this experience is common in those close to death, whether they are believers or not. This comforting presence is an aid to the dying, and I could have embraced it, instead of thinking I had to remedy the situation. Sometimes there is nothing to do.

He tosses and turns in the bed, trying to get out of it. Too weak to stand but still fighting. I get in and hold him. I try to comfort him. Sometimes it feels more like restraint than an embrace. Now I know that terminal restlessness is a feature of dying. We sometimes have to wrestle our way out of our bodies. It is a normal feature of many deaths.

When the nurses came with the syringe driver and set it up, I was frightened he might hurt them. But they made him feel safer and he calmed almost immediately. They handed me a leaflet. I was too preoccupied to read it. They did not say, we only use this when we expect death to come within the next few days. They did not take me aside and make sure I really realised the significance of what was happening. My confident articulateness probably made this seem redundant to them. It wasn't.

I wet his mouth and offer him sips of chamomile tea with honey. He loves tisanes. 'You are trying to poison me.' A faint, failing voice, but still the words cut like blades and I am seven again and afraid of what he might say or do. Now I know that, towards end of life, our taste buds change and things taste odd to us. Knowing this comforts me.

So when I said, 'Dad, what is it you want that you are not getting?' and he said, 'Love', I was silent as Cordelia. I could not heave my heart into my mouth. And this silence has influenced my work for the last 10 years and I have determined that others shall not live and die in ignorance. This is the story I choose to pass on.

Remembering the transition

Irmgard Johanna Eva Pollack, born 20th January 1927, died 2nd February 1997.

In remembering my mum's death, my first feeling is the pain of loss, razor sharp, as in 'cutting-out-my-heart' sharp. I can still feel it if I let myself, still piercing me inside my chest, even after all this time.

Then, reflecting on the day of her death, I remember her soft skin, impossibly soft, receiving my last kiss on her forehead as she lay dying.

Then I recall my mum alive. I remember layer upon layer of her life and the lessons of faith she taught me. I only fully understood what faith meant and how it overpowers death itself as she received the news of her impending death with utmost serenity, like it was nothing much. Don't be afraid. Accept with magnanimity.

She had built her faith over a lifetime. Faith that was simple, unsung, unassuming, unostentatious. At the last, she was reconciled to leaving this world, but did so encompassed by a Love too overflowing to be contained in these words.

And at the end moment, a sense of the glorious, effervescent, lifting up, rising of her soul filled the room. It was a pure and good feeling and I was deeply overcome with thankful love.

A paramedic's point of view

We were called to this lady's house. She was clearly dying; her breathing was intermittent and laboured. The family were terrified and didn't understand what was happening and wanted us to take her to hospital. I knew from my training that it wouldn't be long until this lady died. Although the lady could hardly speak to us, I sensed she was afraid, possibly because of her family's anxiety. I was able to explain the situation to the family and give the lady some of her end-of life medication that was in the house to help with her symptoms. I stayed with her and her family in the bedroom and my colleague made everyone a cup of tea because they hadn't had anything to drink, they'd been so worried. The patient died about 30 minutes later. I was able to verify the death and tell the family what to do next. We all had a hug and a good cry. I've never hugged or cried with a family before but it felt absolutely right. Paramedics care very much but they don't like to show it. I think they're frightened of falling apart if they do. Actually, it helped a lot!

Parting gift

7.00 Christmas morning, 2005. My sister calls: 'Mum's back in hospital and they are recommending that we attend.' Mum greets us as though our visit was an everyday commonplace occurrence. 'Thank you all for coming,' she says in a just about audible voice. The only words that I now recall her speaking. We greet her with a 'Happy Christmas, Mum'. She is clear headed and present, much as she always was, but now she is struggling for each breath as her chronic obstructive pulmonary disorder and failing heart take a further nibble at her mortality. Affirmative nods of the head assist dialogue between us.

At 10.45, the ward is livened up by the arrival of Father Christmas, dressed in red and white, sporting a white beard, carrying a sack. He arrives at our bed but quickly drops his mask of jollity; he can see the seriousness of the situation. He draws himself together and we have a genuinely pleasant 'passing the time' sort of conversation. He then moves to leave, steps a few strides away from the bed before remembering his day job and turning back to us. 'Oh, I nearly forgot.' He pulls the sack off his back, reaches into it and pulls out a Christmas present. We open the present and the black humour invades us in a second. Mum can see what it is. It's a diary. Her expression says it all. 'I won't be needing that where I'm going,' her eyes tell me. By 11.00, Mum was dead.

We completed the death formalities in the hospital and left for my sister's home. My sister raised the matter of the diary and we let flow – both the bottled-up laughter and the tears of sadness.

If only we had known

Les had a massive stroke on Sunday 30th December last year. He couldn't speak or swallow food, was paralysed down the right side of his body. He couldn't do anything for himself. It was devastating for him as he had been fine up until the afternoon of the same day. He drove me to church that morning, collected me and we had a bowl of soup together afterwards.

Within three days I was told that, if Les didn't give the doctor his permission to have a tube inserted into his nose, he would die in a few days. After six weeks, the doctors decided (without consulting us) they would put in a grid peg so that he could carry on with the treatment. His daughter and I were very distressed. We could tell from his expressions and hand gestures that he didn't want to live. He wanted to die. He did not want to carry on having to depend on nurses washing, cleaning, dressing him etc. He was a very proud and private man. He did not want to end up living like that.

Then he had a very bad reaction to the peg, developed a severe infection that had to be treated with intravenous antibiotics. He had to endure five months in hospital. It didn't matter how much we implored the doctors to let him go. We were told they could not do anything as they had a duty of care and had to keep him alive until either his heart stopped or he couldn't respond to antibiotics when he had an infection. In the end, I had to put him into a care home, where he stayed for another three months. We implored his GP to let him go. It was terrible watching him – I wouldn't let a dog suffer like that. Finally, his doctor agreed. All nourishment, water and meds were stopped immediately. It took another 10 days for Les to leave us. If he had put in a 'do not resuscitate' form and instructions that he didn't want to be kept alive if he ever had such a devastating stroke, then he would never have had a nasal tube or peg. We were told this by his doctor. Since then, I have arranged to have a DNR and made out a living will so that I won't ever be kept alive against my will.

Eyes wide open

I had been with my grandfather as a teenager when he died in our house, after us nursing him over several weeks. I feel very blessed by this as I saw death as very natural and it held little fear for me. So when my mother-in-law was dying of cancer, I was happy to take the lead in the last few days while she died at home. I knew about Cheyne-Stokes breathing and could explain the pauses etc to everyone, so they didn't pre-guess the moment of death. She died with her eyes open and I calmly leant forward and shut them, only for them to pop open again. Luckily, I did not scream, but I wish I'd known!

Night shift

I nursed a lady on a hospital ward when I was working a night shift. This lady's wishes, which were expressed a week before her dying days, were told to her very large family – she didn't want them around her bedside while she died. The family were horrified but respected her wishes. Then, on my night shift, it was nearly time for her. She looked scared when I walked into her room and I held her hand. Her eyes opened and she said, 'It's you'. I had nursed her for many weeks. I reassured her she was fine and put the radio on. I stayed by her side all night, holding her hand, singing to her. This lady was at peace and pain free; she was no longer scared, holding my hand tight. At 6.50am that morning, she took her last breath. This will always be an emotional memory for me. Her family were informed she wasn't on her own or frightened.

Can you tell them?

A middle-aged man had been battling leukaemia for many years. He came into the ward for treatment. He waited until I came on duty and asked to talk. He told me he couldn't fight anymore and wished to stop the treatment. At this point his family came in and he said, 'Can you tell my family what I just told you.' I told his family, who were upset but understood. I told the doctors and they documented this. He died peacefully four hours later, surrounded by loved ones.

My ring

My grandad was dying from pneumonia. He was in a coma. I visited him in the hospital. He was peaceful and still. We talked for hours. I had just got married in another country and, as I left, I held his hand to say goodbye. With his fingers, he felt my ring finger, and I realised, although he hadn't shown any sign of response all day, he must've heard and was showing me he knew I had married. It was lovely. I left and he died the next day.

Far from Africa

My brother, who was born in Zimbabwe, died unexpectedly in the UK. To our joy, he had a Shona nurse (Shona being a tribe in Zimbabwe). She sang to him as he drifted away – he knew the language so well. Such a comfort to us all, far from Africa. God bless that NHS nurse.

Better than expected

I have worked as a Macmillan nurse in Edinburgh for many years. A 70-year-old woman who had never taken alcohol found that a modest dose of morphine produced an unpleasant sensation of dizziness etc, which was for her worse than the pain. I managed to persuade the GP to prescribe a homeopathic dosage and this enabled her to feel comfortable without blurring her mind. (She was a wee bird of a wife and the dose would have been minute even for a child!) On the day of her death, I made a second home visit at around 6pm. I went to adjust her pillows for a little more comfort. As I bent down to say farewell, she whispered a barely audible, 'I didn't know it was going to be like this…' and a beautiful smile lit up her face. I have no idea what she was experiencing, but whatever it was, 'it' was okay.

Lovely death

My mother-in-law's death was lovely. Her sons fought to have her brought home; we set her bed in the downstairs living area (kitchen at one end); a cat came in through the door and jumped on to the bed and stayed there for a bit; I made an apple crumble. At some point in the morning, she must have died, because one brother checked on her and said, 'I think she's gone.' When the undertaker arrived, I was very impressed that he bowed to her before touching her – it felt very right.

Not alone
My nan, who was in her 90s, kept saying before she died that Bill – her first husband – was in the corner of the room, waiting for her. She was happy to have conversations with him. She died in her sleep. She was perfectly happy.

It isn't always what you expect
My story isn't a particularly positive one. My father suffered a stroke and lost part of his abilities, including speech. The family were gathered round him in his nursing home and he looked very dishevelled and unhappy. We were probably making light of the situation and the grandchildren were playing about. My father mumbled something and I went across to see if I could understand what he was saying. He repeated the mumble several times, but I found it very difficult. In the end I realised he was trying to say, 'You f***ing wait!' This wasn't what I was expecting to hear, although perhaps summed up our difficult relationship.

Emanations of love
Over the past four years my father had been shedding bits of himself with a series of strokes and vascular dementia. He lost the ability to write, then his sight, mobility and much of his vocabulary. I never felt that he wasn't 'all there' though. His intelligence shone through as he navigated these losses painfully, with frustration but with some humour and immense grace too. His emotional wisdom, sensitivity and sense of timelessness increased and I felt very connected to him in this way.

Both my parents said they wanted to 'let nature take its course'. At the death bed, however, my father was emphatic he wanted to go to hospital, as the nursing home were not offering anything to relieve his suffering. There were some wonderful carers but only 50% of the staff had any training at all. My feeling was he was unlikely to survive the journey and the agitation of medical interventions, so he didn't go. The palliative care nurse arrived the day he died.

In the last few days, my father's body was restless, his left leg moving ceaselessly. For someone so skeletal, the movements looked energetic, as if he was shaking off his flesh. Cranio-sacral therapy became the best kind of touch I could offer him. Sometimes it felt like touch was too dense for his lightness of being, so we met heart to heart. Familiar sacred music seemed the closest form of communication for this subtle state, offering a flashback of his life and who he was.

Two days before he died, he would feel his face with tenderness and wonder, as if remembering and honouring who he'd been. Maybe saying good-bye.

His dear presence grew stronger and stronger. It felt palpable: his kindness, gentleness, a certainty about who he was, his intelligence, his soul. Most of all, though, and I recognise this as a gift from him, was sharing an 'ocean of peace' that saturates everything and holds Life. Sharing the 'silence of eternity', the 'still dews of quietness', the beauty of Peace; an emanation of Love.

Before we were ready

My mum was dying in a very good care home. It had all been agreed. Everyone knew what was happening. We were sitting with her the whole time. She had pneumonia and it was not being treated. Still, a member of staff came in, took a look at what was in fact a quite peaceful situation and said 'Ooh, isn't it awful.' This threw my confidence for a while and I had to remind myself why we were doing this. That mum was quite clear in her wishes; that she was comfortable and surrounded by love. Then when she died, without my knowing, the home contacted the funeral director. This meant they arrived before me or my father felt ready and I was too overwhelmed to ask the man to go away and come back later. She was whisked away in the hands of strangers. It was so unnecessary. My dad wisely asked for her body to be brought to my house the next day so we could sit with her for as long as we wanted. When my dad died in the same place, we were much more confident and clear about our wishes. We were going to take him home ourselves. We were told we could not move his body until late at night, when residents would not be around. They told us they did not want anyone seeing us. I guess they thought we would not be as expert as the funeral directors. They were right. No one told us a coffin would not fit in the lift. It was actually quite hilarious. We had to ring some friends to come out at 11 o'clock at night and help us carry him down the stairs. It deepened our friendship profoundly.

Asking for what you want

As my father was dying, we embraced ancient soul midwife skills to focus on witnessing him, supporting each other to understand the process as normal, and working with the care staff. Our quiet vigil was to be our final gift to him. In a letter, we invited the staff to join us in our holistic approach.

On the last night of his life, they were completely at ease that he had placed himself on the floor of his bedroom. Wearing a vest and woolly bed socks, wrapped in soft, fleecy blankets, and accompanied by only the dim light of a battery-operated candle, he chose to die alone. We honoured his choice.

Dignitas

Sandy, my mum, woke up in a lot of pain and convulsing. We went straight to the hospital. It was weird to see her so out of control – wide eyed with pain like a child. I phoned Norah, my aunt, and she came, and Sandy had a scan. A tumour. We met the specialist, a lovely guy, and when we asked how long he said, at most three months. Sandy said, 'Let's have a party and get out of here.' I said, 'You always told me to get more than one quote. I want a second opinion.' Sandy was checked out of hospital with the hugest amount of drugs and we went to see a London specialist. Same diagnosis and prognosis. I said, 'Is there anything I can say?' She said, 'I have always had a hairy bum.'

She did not want to stick around and deteriorate. The Terry Pratchett film about Dignitas helped. We knew what the place looked like. We laughed about the ugly bedcovers. It explained the process. That was when we began to try and get it organised in time. It is not easy. They are very careful. So they should be. Each illness requires different paperwork. It is very Swiss, very organised. When we finally got on the plane, we thought, why are we doing this? Spending all this money, leaving England, instead of being able to do it at home. It's not romantic there. It is in the middle of an industrial estate. They keep checking you know what you are doing and if you still want to proceed. The doctor from Dignitas came to the hotel twice to speak to Sandy and there was more paperwork to read and sign. After three days and several meetings with the doctor and lots of paperwork, we got in the taxi and Sandy was giggling that it said Ausfahrt on the satnav. She was still Sandy with a wicked sense of humour. The first phial of liquid lines the stomach; then you have to wait half an hour. We walked in the garden, made conversation. It was pretty strange. As soon as the time was up, she wanted to take the lethal dose. The awful bedcovers were still there, so we sat either side of her on the sofa, me and Norah. When she took the second phial, I said 'Byeeee', and she giggled and said it back.

We were lucky. We had time to say goodbye and we were very close, without any real complications; that made it easier. It's not true that you have these deathbed reconciliations. The relationship is the same when someone is dying. It doesn't change by magic. There was a lot of adrenaline through that time. It was the most colourful and clear spring and summer I have ever experienced. Vivid. Energising. Strangely, one of the best periods of my life. A chance to say thank you properly to someone who had been there for me all my life. And since then, I have had a lot of support from others who share the same unusual experience with me, because there aren't many other people I choose to talk to about this.

Martini Bianco

When Grandpa died, Grandma realised how devastating it is when death and funeral come without preparations. She took the decisions needed, mourned for two years and took life back into her hands!

As time went by, she became fed up with all of her friends dying away. And, having learned from Grandpa's death, she took death into her own hands... The funeral, the ceremony, the grave... She asked my aunt and me if we would 'help her go' if she wasn't able to. It took us years to make her believe that would end in prison for us. So, she turned to assisted suicide (legal in Switzerland) and fought for her right to decide the moment of her death. And she succeeded against all odds.

The day the doctor prepared the poison for her to drink, he asked if she wanted a drink with it, since it would taste bitter. As always, her choice of drink was a Martini Bianco. She washed the poison down with it, stretched out on the bed, and died within 20 minutes, peacefully. When asked what I'd like to drink, I'll always go for Martini Bianco now, and raise the glass to the sky and to my grandma.

No easy resolution

I stood there, not believing the situation I was in, wanting to pinch myself to realise it was only a bad dream. But it wasn't. I stood next to him in his bed, that man, my father, Dad. A man I have hated and loved. A man I have not seen for over ten years, a stranger, unrecognisable yet so familiar. A man who was once my hero, a man who had hurt me like no one else has, a man who had let me down. A realisation overwhelmed me that, even in dying, my dad could still hurt me; the answers would not come; closure was not coming. In dying, my dad was still the man he had been. I stood there, feeling alien, numb, yet filled with pity and regret. I could not say, 'I forgive you,' despite a part of me wanting to. 'It's okay.' Those were the words I could give that day. My dad's reaction, the look in his eyes, the holding of my hand, told me those words were enough. To this day, I still don't know what I meant with those words; I hope one day I will. I am left knowing that this is not how it should be, but it is how it is. I was, I am, grieving for the dad I loved, the man dying in front of me, the relationship we once had, the relationship it still should be. Death is a funny thing.

He wasn't hungry

My grandad was dying but my mum and my aunts kept trying to encourage him to 'keep going'. I remember them almost forcing him to try and eat something so that he could 'get stronger' and 'get better'.

Last wishes

My mum and I called an ambulance and got my dad to the hospice. When the doctor came, he asked my dad what he wanted. My dad said, 'Water, a cigarette and death!' The doctor said, 'We'll do our best.' He died three days later.

Commentaries
Dying in hospital – Dr Andrew Jenks

I was first drawn to a career in palliative care while working as a junior doctor in oncology. Since then, I have completed specialist training in London, during which time I've worked in a number of hospices, with community palliative care teams and with hospital palliative care teams. I am currently working as a consultant with a hospital palliative care team in Southampton. I enjoy the satisfaction of being able to support patients and their families through this phase of their illness and helping them achieve what was most important to them at that time. I am also passionate about the support that palliative and supportive care teams can give to patients with life-limiting illness and their families earlier on in their disease journey, particularly as they start to consider their options for treatment for the future and the importance of planning ahead.

Dying in hospital is not what many people would choose. However, the reality is that this is where most of us will die. In 2018, nearly 50% of deaths occurred in hospital, compared with 24% at home and less than 6% in hospices (Public Health England, 2018). In the first year of their working life, a newly qualified doctor will probably look after about 40 people who will die. It is important that we do all we can to achieve a comfortable and dignified death for a person, wherever they are, and provide the right support and information to families and loved ones.

It is crucial to have conversations with our families and those important to us, as well as health care professionals, ideally well in advance of the dying phase. The things we may wish to discuss could include where we would like to be looked after, our preferred place of death, who we would like to have around us and our preferences about treatments and interventions, such as artificial feeding and fluids. In the UK, any adult with capacity has the right to refuse any medical treatment or intervention that they do not wish to receive. If we wish, we can put this in writing, in a legally binding document called an advance decision (or directive) to refuse treatment (see Commentary, Chapter 1). It must be made when we have capacity, and only comes into force when we lack the capacity to make those around us aware of our wishes. The advance decision must be specific in terms of what is being refused and in what circumstances. I would always recommend discussing it with a healthcare professional if you wish to make one.

Although we can refuse any medical treatment or intervention we wish, we cannot demand that a treatment or intervention is continued or started if the medical team looking after us do not feel that it will be of benefit to us. This is important to remember, particularly if writing an advance statement. This is a statement of wishes about the sort of care we would like to receive and what is important to us. Although your medical team will take this into account and do their best to follow your wishes, it is not a legally binding document (see also Commentary, Chapter 1).

The importance of making our wishes known in advance is highlighted in the story *If Only We Had Known*. It is also important to remember that opinions and situations change and can do so quickly. Having a death plan is rather like a birth plan – it often needs to be adapted. This is not a failure of the plan; more a reflection of the need to adjust to an unpredictable and variable situation.

I have worked in hospital palliative care for a number of years. As a team, we will do all we can to help people and their families achieve their preferred place of death, be that home or hospice. However, for some people this is not possible, despite our very best efforts, and others will choose to remain in hospital to die. For a significant number of people and their families, particularly those who have had frequent admissions to hospital for treatment for a long-standing condition, their local hospital is a safe place. When people are in the last days or weeks of their life, they may, understandably, feel anxious or apprehensive. The knowledge that they are being cared for in a familiar environment, such as the hospital ward they have been admitted to several times before, by staff they know and trust, can be reassuring and make the process of dying seem less frightening.

Over the years, I have been involved in the care of many people who have experienced peaceful and dignified deaths in hospital surrounded by their loved ones. It is usually possible to create a calm and familiar environment around the bed-space or side room, with photographs of family and favourite places, possessions from home, a comfy pillow or blanket. I will always remember a patient I looked after a couple of years ago. She wished to remain in hospital for the dying phase of her illness because she felt safe and was familiar with the ward and the staff. I suggested to her family that they brought in some photos to make her side room less clinical. By the following morning every wall in her room was covered with photos of her family, friends and special places, all of which documented important memories and moments from their life. This was not only important for her and her family but also was hugely valuable for us, as the healthcare team. It gave us more insight into who they were and what was important, so that we were able to personalise the care and support we gave them. The importance of personalisation of care and familiarity is demonstrated in several of the stories in this chapter.

There is often an understandable fear of symptoms at the end of life, both for the person who is dying and their loved ones. In her inspiring book, *With the End in Mind*, Kathryn Mannix (2019) discusses her initial surprise when, as a junior doctor working in a hospice, she heard her consultant explain the process of dying in great detail to a patient. She later reflects how reassuring this was for the patient and that she found her own way of explaining the process to patients and families as her career progressed. As a health care professional caring for people who are facing death, I too have found that both patients and their families often want to know about the dying process. As a society, we are much less familiar with death than we once were. Most people have not witnessed a death, sat with someone as they die or seen a dead body; death has become alien to us.

In the majority of deaths, the process is similar and predictable. The person will become increasingly fatigued and tired and need to spend more time asleep and resting. In the last few days, the person who is dying is likely to spend most of the time asleep or 'unconscious'; they may still have times when they are awake and responsive and are able to engage in some conversation. Even though they may appear deeply asleep, 'unconscious' or 'in a coma', we cannot know for sure whether the person is aware of people around them or if they can hear or recognise familiar voices or touch. In many cases, it appears that a familiar voice or touch can provide comfort and reassurance and may prompt an unexpected response, as highlighted in *My Ring* and *It Isn't Always What You Expect*. I always advise families: 'Imagine they can hear you. This means you should say what you want to say to them and what feels important, but equally, if there are things you don't want them to hear, step away from the bedside.'

Some other possible changes include the hands and feet of the person becoming cool to the touch; sometimes their skin colour changes to grey or blue, perhaps with some blue tinge around the lips. It is common that the pattern of breathing will change in the last few hours or days. Breathing may become slower or more irregular. You may see pauses between 'catch-up' breaths, sometimes called Cheyne-Stokes breathing (as explained in *Eyes Wide Open*). The pauses then become longer until the next breath simply does not come. Usually death is as peaceful as that.

Sometimes people may experience other symptoms: for example, pain, nausea or vomiting, breathlessness or chest secretions (fluid in the air passages). Most of the time, these symptoms can be controlled well with medications that can be administered by mouth or via a pump called a syringe driver. Not all people who are dying will need medication, but it is usually helpful to have it available in case it is required. In the final days, some people will become agitated, distressed or confused (as *You Can Never Be Fully Prepared* explains). This may be because of pain, constipation or being unable to pass water or for no clear reason that we can ascertain. It may represent existential or spiritual distress at what is happening. Often, simple interventions such as trying to create a quiet and calm environment, administering bowel care or inserting a catheter to drain the bladder can help. Sometimes, medication is needed to help the person to become more settled.

It is a normal and expected part of the dying process for people to reduce, and usually stop, eating and drinking. However, it can cause distress, both to the dying person and to their loved ones. There is no clear evidence that giving artificial food or fluid, either by a drip or tube, to a person who is imminently dying will help with symptoms or prolong the time they will live. Indeed, giving fluids via a drip may increase the chest secretions that we sometimes see in dying people, and thereby add to the burden of symptoms. Giving sips of fluid or tastes of food to the person when they are awake is usually the most effective intervention. Good mouth-care with water on a sponge, lip balm or using a soft toothbrush to gently clean the teeth and gums is probably the best intervention we can do to help with a dry mouth. Don't feel that water is the only thing to use for mouth-care though; it is fine to use juice, tea or coffee – or wine, beer or whisky, even – whatever is the person's favourite tipple!

In my experience, the vast majority of people die comfortably and with dignity. Symptoms can usually be controlled with drugs and/or non-drug interventions. Being informed of what is likely to happen and what might be observed is often hugely valuable and reassuring to both the person who is dying and those with them.

It is vital that, as a society, we feel more able to talk about dying and that the process of dying is not 'over-medicalised' or shrouded in mystery. That way we can hopefully achieve more dignified deaths for people, in a place in which they and their families feel comfortable. As Dame Cicely Saunders, the founder of the modern hospice movement in the UK, said: 'How people die remains in the memory of those who live on.' We only have one chance to get it right for people and their loved ones.

> **Advice points**
>
> - Talk to your family and loved ones about your (and their) wishes and priorities at the end of life.
> - Think about writing a death plan – this could be a legal document (for example, an Advance Decision to refuse treatment) or a more informal statement of wishes. But be prepared for the plan to change as death approaches.
> - Try to make the place of death calm, comfortable and familiar – bring in photos, treasured possessions and so on.
> - Food and fluids in the last weeks or days of life are an emotive subject, but not wanting to eat or drink is a normal part of the dying process.
> - Most deaths are comfortable, and symptoms can be controlled. Talk to your healthcare professional about your fears – they can usually be allayed.

References

Mannix, K. (2019). *With the end in mind: How to live and die well.* Harper Collins.

Public Health England (2018). *Statistical commentary: End of life care profiles.* www.gov.uk/government/publications/end-of-life-care-profiles-february-2018-update/statistical-commentary-end-of-life-care-profiles-february-2018-update

What happens at death – Deb Wilkes

Working as a nurse in an Auckland Hospice 30 years ago taught me the delights of holistic person-centred care, where the chaplain and counsellor were just as important as the clinicians. As a clinical nurse specialist in two UK hospices, alongside other health and social care professionals, I have supported and advised patients/families, mainly in their own homes. I believe that openness and honesty, as well as a good sense of humour, are essential when doing this job. Outside of the realms of the health services, I have tapped into other networks that have given me a wider perspective on death and dying and helped me give patients more choices. I'm involved in putting on 'Dead Good' awareness events in Southampton to help people think and talk about death and dying before it happens. *www.facebook.com/deadgooddays*

These stories remind us that how someone dies will stay in our memory forever. Like the stories of birth, we need to share them with each other. How else do we learn what dying is like and what we could do to make it the most positive experience it can be? The stories here from those who have been present at deaths before and feel more prepared and able to prepare others and those who don't know what to expect are completely different.

It is so true that we 'do not know everything we need to know' and, at what can be a painful, confusing and tiring time, it is easy to feel too overwhelmed to ask.

Like birth, death can be short and painless or protracted and painful. Birth and death plans should both be 'flexiplans', and we, as health professionals, need to be honest. Sometimes we do need to call in the cavalry in death, just as we would if a caesarean section needed performing at birth.

The 'normal' dying process is that of a body slowly shutting down, and it can be hard to watch. It might come on over days, hours or minutes. The person who is dying will usually be unaware of this process and will not be suffering.

Breathing may become quicker or slower. Long gaps between breaths (Cheyne-Stokes breathing) can have everyone on the edge of their seat, waiting for the next one – this can last some time so it's best to sit back in a comfy chair and relax if you can. Skin changes, involuntary movements of facial muscles that can look like grimaces, sometimes audible grunts or gasps may all occur.

And what is that 'death rattle', as it is sometimes colloquially known? When someone is dying, they are weaker; it is hard to cough up the normal secretions in the air passages, and the accumulation of mucus makes a noise as the person breathes in and out.

The dying person is not affected by it, but if you are not warned, it can be a really distressing thing to hear. Sometimes repositioning the person or using medication to dry up the secretions can lessen the noise, but this is often done more to help staff and relatives than to ease the dying person.

You may not notice anything at all. One of my patients, Maggie, had motor neurone disease and was scared she would 'suffocate' when she was dying. One visit, I was sitting in the chair next to her, talking to her teenage son. I suddenly noticed something he hadn't. Maggie looked just the same but had stopped breathing. As simple as that.

Families can keep a bedside vigil for days only for the person to die when they've all just popped out of the room for a few minutes. Some people feel they have chosen that moment to die, but actually nobody knows. Don't beat yourself up about it if you aren't there at the precise moment of death. Maybe say a small precautionary goodbye each time you leave, if that is important to you. You do have to have loo breaks!

Most nurses have stories about dying people who dream about or are 'visited' by their dead relatives, and I have certainly heard very old people calling out for their mum a little while before their own death. This is often reassuring and calming to anyone who witnesses it.

Beware of paying too much attention to answers to your question, 'How long is it likely to be, nurse?' We will all have different answers, from 'How long is a piece of string?' to 'Ooooh, it'll definitely be tonight'. You won't thank them when you are knackered a week later because you haven't left the bedside. I suggest you only ask a couple of people – the ones who are the most experienced in end-of-life care and who have already met the person on several different occasions, and don't expect it to be exactly right. Try to eat and sleep and get out now and again, even just to sit in a garden. It is surprising how exhausting it is, when it feels like you are 'just waiting'. Think about what you can do in that time, whether that is singing quietly, reading a book, looking through old photos, playing some music or curling up on the bed alongside the person, holding hands and snoozing.

Not everyone who is dying acknowledges it. Some people will seem to be in denial about it completely but, in my experience, most dying people will know what is happening. On a couple of occasions I have been with a patient who really can't bear the thought of dying and this is difficult for everyone and they have been given some sedation to manage the situation. Mostly, people at the end of their life are tired and death comes easily to them.

Relationships don't fundamentally change when someone is dying. There can be last conversations and comforting words (perhaps we have seen too many of these moments in films?), but this isn't as common as people may think.

What about that feeling of relief when someone is dying? It can be hard to admit, but lots of relatives have cautiously mentioned it and are surprised when we say it is quite a common feeling. You may have seen so much suffering over years, you may be knackered and want to get on with your own life, or you may have hated the bastard and wish he had died years ago (the term 'loved one' is definitely not always the right one!).

How much does it matter where you are? Many people say they want to die in their own home, with the familiar sights, smells and sounds, family and friends popping in and out, everyone speaking your own language, the children playing and the dog curled up on the bed. It can present a nice, rosy picture and I have witnessed many a lovely home death, but there are drawbacks to everywhere. If you can't get hold of the prescribed morphine, then even a few minutes watching someone in pain feels like hours; if there is no other family member to help, it can feel isolating and lonely for the main caregiver, and all the medical equipment piling up can make you feel like you are more in a hospital than your own home anyway.

Honesty, good communication and careful planning are essential. One young mother I knew didn't want to be at home when she died as she thought her children wouldn't want to remember her there, but after a family chat they said they wanted her to be at home so they could be with her and know what was happening. So that was Plan A. They all came to look round the hospice and were happy that, if home wasn't working, then Plan B would be put in place. Plan A worked out well. Sometimes knowing there are options is what matters most.

Most people don't want to ever go into a nursing home. In reality, many do, for lots of different reasons. There are a lot of care homes and a lot of variability in their provision of end-of-life care. But always, the staff want it to be the best possible experience for their residents and are upset if it doesn't go well. The stories here reflect the big differences – the good (*Lovely Death*), the bad (*If Only We Had Known*) and the ugly (*It Isn't Always What You Expect*). I personally have seen plenty of deaths in care homes – they are often managed very well, with respect and dignity, and without the need for palliative care input. It is a good idea to ask for regular meetings with the nurse or doctor who has overall responsibility; then you can have an update on the situation, ask any questions and raise any concerns.

People who haven't visited a hospice think they are full of dying people and must be depressing places to be in. That is exactly what I thought before I did my first shift as a student nurse. I love the hospice story (*Last Wishes*) – a reminder that palliative care focuses on what is important for the person and family, rather than the disease. Visiting hours are more relaxed (usually for pets as well as humans), relatives can stay overnight, there is often more time for the team to explain what is happening and there are nurses present all the time to help manage a symptom if it arises.

If you get the opportunity to visit your local hospice, you can see that it isn't a depressing place and that more things happen there than dying. At any time, about half of the patients in the hospice will go home again, as they have come in for symptom control rather than end-of-life care.

The principles of hospice care can be used in any setting. A specialist team should only be needed for advice and support when a situation is more complex.

Talking to family and healthcare professionals about your wishes is important, but if they are not written down then there is a good chance they won't happen. A DNACPR (Do Not Attempt Cardio-Pulmonary Resuscitation) form basically means 'allow a natural death'; it is discussed with the patient and family, then signed by a clinician. It is meant as guidance for anyone attending who does not know the situation. If it is not in place, there is potential for a needless attempt to be made at CPR.

Keep information in one place. The national 'Message in a Bottle' scheme, managed by Lions Club International (see Resources), is designed for people who are disabled, ill or dying at home. All the person's details, medication list, DNACPR form, contact numbers and anything else you want to add are kept in a special bottle in the fridge (to make them easy to find) and that is where any of the emergency services will know to look if they are called out. You don't need to make a pile of ham sandwiches every night, as one chap did – he didn't want them going into his fridge and not having a snack to eat!

Euthanasia is not currently legally available in the UK. The stories *Dignitas* and *Martini Bianco* both paint reassuring pictures of the assistance offered in Switzerland by Dignitas. I am sure it goes through a lot of people's minds as an option, but it is not always spoken out loud, and probably not to healthcare professionals for fear of how they might respond. Indeed, we are only just getting better at talking about it among ourselves. But saying, 'Just shoot me now' – which I have heard quite a bit – and actively seeking euthanasia – which I have encountered only a few times – are very different, and both need supportive conversations. Sometimes, just explaining what is likely to happen and who is there to help is enough to alleviate people's fears about the process of dying.

It's sometimes hard to ask for help. Relatives tell me they 'don't want to bother anyone'. If you can't do it when someone is dying then when can you? Often people want to help: 'Let me know if I can do anything…' but in the absence of instructions, they may just not know what to do. So, don't be shy; ask them to take the dog out, mow the lawn, cook dinner… they'll be hugely relieved to have instructions.

Note things down when they come to mind and ask the healthcare professionals when they visit. They won't mind – in fact, it makes their job easier, and remember that no question is too trivial, ever.

Family dynamics are likely to be sky-high at the point of someone dying, so try to check in with each other. Someone will always feel that they are doing most of the work, resentments easily set in, often to be played out after death. Acknowledging each other's strengths and playing to them is great if you can do it. Everyone is dealing with this in their own way, has their own problems and is probably emotionally and physically tired.

Every person and their circumstances are unique, which means every death is unique. We keep learning by sharing our stories.

Resources

Books

Brayne, S. (2010). *The D-word: Talking about dying: a practical guide*. Continuum Books.

Callanan, M. (2009). *Final journeys: A practical guide for bringing care and comfort at the end of life*. Bantam Press.

Chast, R. (2014). *Can't we talk about something more pleasant?* Bloomsbury.

Kearney, M. (2016). *Mortally wounded: Stories of soul pain, death and healing*. Mercier.

Mannix, K. (2019). *With the end in mind: How to live and die well*. Harper Collins.

Nuland, S.B. (1998). *How we live*. Vintage Books.

Scott, R. (2019). *Between living and dying: Voices from the edge of experience*. Birlinn Ltd.

Warner, F. (2008). *Gentle dying: The simple guide to achieving a peaceful death*. Hay House.

Articles online

Heley, J. (2016, February 3). At my father's bedside, I learned what death looks like. *The Guardian*. www.theguardian.com/lifeandstyle/2016/feb/03/death-hospital-nhs-end-of-life-palliative-care-family

Letters (2020, January 31). What it takes to have a 'good death' at home. *The Guardian*. www.theguardian.com/society/2020/jan/31/what-it-takes-to-have-a-good-death-at-home

Price, K. (2020, January 24). Talking honestly about end-of-life care. *The Guardian*. www.theguardian.com/society/2020/jan/24/talking-honestly-about-end-of-life-care

Videos

A graceful dying: A journey at the end of life. (2015). www.youtube.com/watch?v=EckVDi1RxJM

Before I die: A day with terminally ill patients. Death land #2. (2019). www.youtube.com/watch?v=aZdDXNmD9wk

Dying in 21st century Australia, a new experience for all of us. Peter Saul. TEDxTalks (2011). www.youtube.com/watch?feature=player_embedded&v=03h0dNZoxr8

Making end of life care matter. (2018). Deb Wilkes. TEDxTalks. www.youtube.com/watch?v=Lr6gvVnuW-0

We're doing dying all wrong. (2016). Ken Hillman. TEDxTalks. www.youtube.com/watch?v=gQVC-8WEB7s

What really matters at the end of life. (2015). BJ Miller. TEDTalks. www.ted.com/talks/bj_miller_what_really_matters_at_the_end_of_life

Webpages

Conversation between Reverend Ruth Scott and Chris Evans. (2019). Chris Evans Breakfast Show. https://player.fm/series/the-best-of-the-chris-evans-breakfast-show/chris-evans-with-reverend-ruth-scott

Death and dying. (n.d.) Sue Brayne. Articles with guidance on how to be present with someone who is dying, what death looks like, and how to take care of yourself. https://suebrayne.co.uk/death-and-dying-2

Dying matters with Mountbatten. (2019). Nigel Hartley. www.mountbatten.podbean.com

Dying words aren't what I'd imagined. (2019). Nathan Gray. www.medium.com/spiralbound/dying-words-arent-what-i-imagined-60d0f7f90cc5

Final moments of life. (2018). Marie Curie. www.mariecurie.org.uk/help/support/terminal-illness/preparing/final-moments#momentofdeath

Mental Capacity Act. www.nhs.uk/conditions/social-care-and-support-guide/making-decisions-for-someone-else/mental-capacity-act

Message in a bottle. (n.d.) Lions Club International. https://lionsclubs.co/MemberArea/knowledge/lions-message-in-a-bottle

Syringe drivers. (2020). Marie Curie. www.mariecurie.org.uk/help/support/terminal-illness/medication-pain-relief/syringe-drivers#worries

What are palliative care and end of life care? (2020). Marie Curie. www.mariecurie.org.uk/help/support/diagnosed/recent-diagnosis/palliative-care-end-of-life-care

Your stories of being there when someone died. (2019). ABC Life. www.abc.net.au/life/your-stories-of-being-there-when-someone-died/10147482

Outside the Box

9 – Now what?

The scent of lavender

Who laid us out a while back? A woman in our street, our village. Calmly, methodically going about her business. Who was she? A woman who knew a thing or two. Perhaps the midwife. Who bore the coffin? Friends, family, neighbours. We were in the hands of those who knew us.

I washed my mother's body after she died. I did it with a care assistant who had done it many times before. Kirstie. She told me I was the first person ever to ask to assist her.

She brings the bowl and talks to me in a low, calm voice. The water is warm and the soap sweet-smelling. She tells me, when we turn my mother over, there might be a groan from the air escaping her lungs. So when I wash a friend's body another time, I could tell others to expect this too. Because fear is always waiting, and distaste.

We are talking to my mother the whole time. Calling her by her name. 'Alright, Pauline, we are just going to move your legs now.' Reassuring ourselves. Staying in connection. 'Here comes your lovely fresh nighty.' 'There, Mum. All done.'

When you do this, you sense deep in your bones the difference between the living and the dead. It is strangely comforting. I know an atheist who described washing her partner's body as sacramental. And it is not for everyone, I know that. When we had finished, I put a sprig of lavender in my mother's hands. We used to sniff the lavender together when I took her for a walk in her wheelchair.

No heels

My friend's mum insisted she had to be buried in her favourite four-inch heels, but then she couldn't fit in the coffin. Should they bend her knees? They decided on placing the shoes neatly next to her and she entered the afterlife barefoot.

Bearing witness

My husband died quite unexpectedly of a heart attack at 4.30am when it was still dark. I had got into bed next to him, as I had done so many times before in the last 30-plus years, and we had exchanged tender words before dropping off to sleep. Although it was so sudden, it also felt so normal: death happens, heart attacks happen. It had been such an ordinary evening. I knew I had to call 999, even though I knew he was dead. When we were officially informed there was nothing that could be done, I returned immediately to take my place by his side. I wanted to be a witness to everything that was unfolding from his death and to be at the heart of it: for myself as his wife, for my children as their mother and for our friends who had so enriched his life.

I watched the paramedics tidying away their debris and gratefully appreciated the way they caringly lifted his body back onto the bed. The house emptied, leaving only a policeman and us, his family. I was insistent that his body would stay at home until at the very least my two children, making their way up from Brighton, had arrived to say goodbye. Even though, in these circumstances, I was told it was usual for the body to be collected within an hour, it was arranged that we kept him until 9.30 pm.

It had been arranged for everybody to hold a lighted candle when his body left the house. So, as the undertakers carried Pete's body out of our room and down the stairs, I led the way, holding a candle. The hall was filled with people holding candles and, as we turned to walk out the front door, so too was the garden path, and a friend sang 'Hold your candle to the wind'. I watched them load his body into the van and close the doors and drive away, out of sight. And turning back towards the house, I was met by that sea of loving, candlelit faces.

Our final witnessing was at the end of the cremation service when we were allowed to go and witness his body being placed in the furnace. Contrary to expectation, it was actually very comforting, far more so than simply seeing his coffin disappear from sight. It felt like his body was an offering. It had served its purpose. The atmosphere was calm and respectful: the quiet industry of the technicians going about their job, who explained that the oven temperature had to be at just the right level. And then the door opened, the intensity of the heat hitting us. As it moved into the space, the bright orange flames leapt up towards the cardboard box, moving forward to envelope it, and the oven doors shut. And instead of loss and despair, we felt a sense of completion. And we returned to join the others in the crematorium chapel, smiling.

Pebbles and petals

I worked as a chaplain at Sir Michael Sobell House Hospice in Oxford. In this amazing, challenging place, there were times when a person died and the family and friends did not know what to say or what to do. Families were usually very aware that death was approaching, but when their loved one died, they were in a totally new place. Waiting, and sometimes it was long waiting, was over, but how should they respond now, and how could they take in the enormity of death? There were occasions when I offered a simple ritual, if people wished it. I would gather rose petals from the hospice garden, place them in a bowl and bring along some stones in another bowl. I would then invite the family and friends to take a stone and place it on the sheet around the body of their loved one. I asked if anyone wished to say something about the hardness and heaviness of accompanying their loved one to this point. Words and tears expressed the toughness of their experience. I then offered the soft, beautiful rose petals, which were placed and scattered on or around the body. As the family did so, they gave thanks for their loved one, sharing memories and stories. Often there was laughter in the midst of the tears. I believe we need simple rituals like this to help us in the liminal space that follows the death of someone close to us.

Nana
I didn't say goodbye. Do I regret it? No. I know who she is. I know my Nana. We went to the funeral home. I felt sick. She had all her going-out clothes on but I was stuck in the corner. My legs failed me. My mam was stroking her hair, but I was screaming in my head 'Get off her'. Why was I so scared? Eventually, my mam persuaded me. Why was I worried? Her skin was smooth like pearls and she looked calm. Mocking me with how stupid I'd been. She was my Nana. Still family. In death and life.

Last act of love
My mother-in-law died 29 years ago. She was very much loved by all her family and, together with her sons and grandchildren, we kept a constant presence by her hospital bed while her life slowly ebbed away. I remember these days as a time of tremendous love for her and for each other. When she breathed her last and suddenly practicality took over, I felt doubly bereaved. I did not want her removed from us; I wanted to keep on caring for her a bit longer, and this is when I found out about our Jewish burial rites and the work of the group of volunteers who carry them out. I joined this society, which we call 'Sisterhood/Brotherhood', soon after. Our work consists in preparing the bodies so that they are totally clean, purified and ready for burial. I am often asked, 'Are you not scared?' or 'Why do you do this?' The answer is that death is not scary; rather, I often feel awed by the total absence of life in someone who perhaps a few hours before was a living being. Why do I do it? We are told that to help without being thanked is a true *mitzvah* (good deed). It is an uplifting experience and everyone who performs it will tell you so.

Our duty is to care for this person with all the gentleness and reverence that is due. The washing is done by three or four volunteers, who work in silence and are always mindful to maintain the dignity of the deceased, keeping the face and body covered and cleaning it very gently. After the washing, all the bodies are dressed in shrouds of unbleached linen. The body is placed in a plain, simple coffin and the family is called in to say a last goodbye before the coffin is carried to the grave.

Before I joined this society, I was very cynical about death and burial rites and insisted that I wanted to be cremated (which is forbidden by our religion). Since witnessing and participating in many rituals, I have come to appreciate that the dead perhaps deserve these last acts of kindness given by people who care – sometimes people who have been their friends. I am comforted by the thought that, when my time comes, some of my old friends will be there to brush my hair and hold my hand.

Paw Patrol PJs

A wonderful way for a family of a five-year-old child who died – a chill room with bed at the funeral director. He was laid out in his Paw Patrol PJs – Mum dressed him – and his own duvet and pillows for the 10 days before the funeral. They sat with him every day and moved him from the chill bed into his Paw Patrol coffin. Mum was allowed to visit whenever she wished – no fixed hours. She was able to take friends and family members too. No restriction.

The transplant

When my sister died very suddenly (subarachnoid haemorrhage), I was able to spend her last 12 hours with her in the intensive care unit before her life support was 'switched off'. I found she had requested her organs be donated and I was so happy to know this. But I had no idea of the comfort this would give to me – to know she had extended the lives of six people through her death was so powerful, so meaningful; I felt her life had not been wasted or lost. Through the transplant coordinator, I eventually met the recipient of her liver and we have remained such friends for 21 years until his death this year. Each year we have met for lunch and I've loved this annual event, being close to a part of my sister, still living!

Home death

Our mother Gertie Holland (née Hortner) died on the 28th January 2005, aged 93, just a month away from her 94th birthday. She was diagnosed with advanced stomach cancer approximately six weeks before and, with enormous humility and dignity, accepted no treatment and was told she would probably die within weeks of diagnosis. We had the privilege of caring for her at home.

For me as a midwife, caring for Mum at home had so many similarities to caring for women giving birth at home.

At that time, our father, Leslie, was still very much alive. He was 97 and physically remarkably well but had moderately severe dementia. We included him in all the discussions, but after Mum's death it became clear to us it was difficult for him even to recall that she had died.

We built a very lovely coffin out of recycled wood. Eddie had the opportunity to discuss with local funeral directors useful details for a coffin that were essential to incorporate – shape, handles etc.

In her last weeks, our mother had been nursed in the small living room of the cottage and we had taken it in turns to sleep on the floor beside her each night. As it was the middle of winter, our father would light a fire each day and we would sit with her, then extinguish the embers at night before we settled down to sleep. After her death, our father would continue this tradition, but only light the fire in the evening, as she lay first on the bed on which she had died and then in the coffin that Eddie had made. We understood it was very important to keep the room as cold as possible. Each morning, when our Dad woke up, he would come down to breakfast in the very small kitchen and ask, 'Where's Gertie?' We would remind him that she had died, in response to which he would open the door to the living room and, from where he sat at the kitchen table, express astonishment, and then carry on eating his cereal.

It was a very special time. Many close friends and extended family members came, brought food and flowers and the whole living room – barely 12 feet by 12 feet – smelt fragrant, felt peaceful, and we appreciated the precious time we had with Mum after death. It enabled us to grieve together; to know with certainty that we had done the best we could for her in the final weeks of her life; that we honoured and respected her body and soul in life and death, fully and completely.

Such a contrast to the very brutal and undignified death her own parents and relatives suffered in Auschwitz. Our greatest regret is that we could not achieve it for her husband and our Dad, Leslie, who died just six weeks after Mum. He died a quite different death, in a crowded hospital ward, separated only by thin curtains from all the goings-on in the ward around him.

The wake

In the Netherlands, it is common for a person to be taken home and kept on a fridge bed for up to three days. This happened with my father and seemed creepy at first to me, but after a couple of hours the grandchildren were virtually clambering over him and including him in their games. It was definitely the right thing to do and a great way to say your good-byes.

Over the threshold

When my father died this year in a care home, I asked if his body could stay in his bed until the next morning. The home managers reacted very badly and said no, they had never been asked such a thing. They were completely shocked. I did, however, manage to get time for my friends to join me in singing him 'over the threshold'.

Last night together

A woman came to see me at my burial ground and she said, 'My husband died in the night. I tucked him up nice and warm and lay down beside him and went to sleep. The children were horrified I didn't call the undertakers straightaway. I rang them first thing the next morning. Do you think I did wrong? I was married to him for nearly 50 years and I nursed him for 10. I didn't think one more night would make any difference. They seem to think I have gone a little mad.'

My best friend

When my best friend died in a mountaineering accident, aged 24, his mother went to identify his body. She said all she wanted to do was hug him and hold him close. No one would let her.

Funny side, sad side

The funny side of my dad's death – my three sisters and I gathered at his bedside in hospital just as he died. We asked the nurse to send for the chaplain because my dad was a devout Catholic. When he arrived, we were sitting round the bed talking, crying and laughing and the chaplain came over to the bed (he was very young and nervous) and began to ask my dad questions. We all had trouble suppressing our giggles, because the priest obviously didn't realise he was already dead. Eventually, one of us managed to tell him and he blushed and began to pray. Dad would have loved this!

The upsetting part of my dad's death – because a doctor hadn't seen him in the previous two weeks, they insisted on a post-mortem to determine the cause of death. He suffered from emphysema, heart problems, had had two strokes and a heart attack and was one week off his 97th birthday.

Fling wide the window

My husband died of cancer two years ago and during his last few days he couldn't stand any light in the room. When he died, I immediately opened the window so he could listen to the birdsong that he had loved so much, and the sunlight flooded back into the room. A few weeks later, in a counselling session, I told my counsellor what I had done, and he smiled and told me that hospice nurses always open the window when their patients die, to let their souls out of the room– a custom that goes back centuries. Now, no matter what the weather, I open the window on waking and say good morning to my much-missed husband.

A quiet goodbye

As a former healthcare assistant, I always felt the need to care for the deceased as though they were still living. Talking to them and so on because there never seemed to be another way of caring for someone. It was our personal chance to go into a quiet room and say goodbye to our patient before having to go back into a loud, busy ward and continue as though nothing had happened. We can never know if someone who has died will be aware of our actions in some way. As a member of staff, this helped me to cope with the loss.

Not on duty

When my mother died, my sister and I were present. The GP who came out to verify her death was not her own GP. He had lots of questions for me and my sister. We are both registered nurses and it felt like we were under interrogation. At the time, we were not on duty as nurses; we were daughters who were supporting our mother to have a dignified death. The GP's attitude and manner were not nice at the time our mother had died. I will always remember this and would hope other people are not treated like this at a very vulnerable time for everyone involved.

Off the shelf

A very close friend of mine died, unexpectedly, of a brain clot, more than 20 years ago. A vigorous, lively and hugely popular paediatric doctor, she suddenly got an acute headache and was rushed to hospital. At her bedside, a small group of us. Her daughter and baby grandson, me with my infant daughter, friends. This death brought certain questions. Carol was gay and an atheist. We all knew there was nothing on the shelf to suit her. We had to do it ourselves. Over several days we gathered in someone's house – shared photographs, letters, food and stories. Drawing together, carefully circling around the dropped stitch. Late into the night and over breakfast. Glad of each other's faces in this newly dimmed and unreliable world. And I thought, this is how it should be. We are the ones who knew her. We are the ones who loved her. She would have approved, but she would have said, 'Where's the cava?' So we went out and bought a bottle. And we learnt a lot about what we didn't know. We decided to have her body in an open coffin in a friend's flat for those who could not believe this raunchy, radical woman had really died. The undertakers came bang on time and brought her in. When we lifted the lid of the coffin and looked inside, she had make-up all over her face. A woman who had not even put mascara on since she was 14 and going to the school disco. It was a travesty. As upsetting as seeing a woman pale and unmade-up who always punctiliously applied lipstick, powder and rouge. We did not dare remove the face paint because her body in death had become strange and private to us. So we had to look past it to see our friend.

I did it

I grew up in Wales – in the middle of the country. When my dad died, it was late at night. My stepmother needed to be in bed. With a nurse, we phoned the funeral directors and were told it would be several hours before he could get there. So – I was asked if I could help lay my dad out. I have no medical qualifications etc and would never have believed I could do this – but I did it and was so glad I did. It gave me the chance to do one last thing for my dad that was so special and helped me grieve in a very positive way.

100 final strokes

I brushed Mum's hair for half an hour after she died, just as I used to as a child. I felt incredibly blessed to have shared this time in her life and death.

Lock of hair

After my mum died, my dad and I went to see her in the chapel of rest. They had made her face look lovely, but her hairstyle was completely different. It took me aback as she looked so different, but I wasn't upset; I just valued the chance to see her again. However, I knew my mum would have been *very* upset about her hair. She was always so particular about it. Afterwards I was distressed that I'd never thought to keep a lock of her hair – it would have been a very special memento.

Finally the tears

My uncle was diagnosed with cancer in 2015, in August of that year, and by the end of August he had passed away. On that day in August, I was at work. I look across the shop floor – I see my family. I think nothing of it at first because I worked in Morrison's, where my parents do their weekly shop, and my sister also worked there. As they walk over, I say, 'What are you doing here?' Then I see their puffy, watered eyes. They tell me that Uncle Tovie's very unwell and is expected to pass away. I leave and we all go to my aunt and uncle's house, spending time with them and my cousins. My cousin brings down the PlayStation and we play for hours, much like when we were young. Tovie hangs on and we leave to go home. A few days later, I am at work again and I see my family and I know instantly. They say, 'Tovie's passed away.' I don't cry. I don't panic like I did a few days before. They ask if I want to come home and I say, 'No, I'll stay at work. There's nothing I can do now.' I finish work at 9.30pm and get a milkshake from MacDonald's before I cycle home. I rest it on the rack on the back of my bike and it falls to the floor, exploding into a pink mess. I laugh at first, then burst into tears, as I felt I should have hours ago.

Emotions

With death, what worries me is emotions. If I had to break bad news to one of my patients (I am a medical student), how would they respond and how would I respond to that?

Looking dead

My father lost half his weight in the last few years of his life. When he finally died and myself, my mother and brother went to the funeral director to organise the funeral, he offered, happily and enthusiastically, to put the weight back onto him. I said calmly and simply, 'We'd like him to look dead.' The funeral director was horrified. Clearly this had never been asked. Luckily my mum and brother were nodding, 'Yes, dead is good.' He squirmed – and was shocked again with my father's choice of music, which was New Orleans 'Coming Home Music'. He allowed this too – but made sure there were no other funerals at the same time so as not to horrify them and their sombre services.

Nine night

It depends where you are from what happens. Some islands, it starts the night of the funeral, others the night of the day the person dies. What happens is people come to your house. There's music, drinking. Everyone brings food. Everyone comes. Lots of people. They don't leave you day and night. They bring you provisions. You turn the bed around to make sure the ghost doesn't come and disturb you. You are not left alone.

Bognor Bobby

I was a young bobby. Just finished my first year at Bognor. I was 24. My sergeant told me to go down to the seafront because there was an old couple sitting there and had been there for hours and there was some concern about them. I headed down there and spotted them straightaway. He was sitting on the sea wall and next to him was his wife in her wheelchair. I introduced myself and immediately realised she was dead. It was obvious, even though this was the first dead person I had encountered. He was chatting away to her about the view, the weather, the seagulls and that. I sat down beside him and asked if everything was alright. He looked worried. 'You are not going to take her away, are you?' 'No,' I said. 'We'll do what's right together when the time comes. Shall I get you a cup of tea?' I rang my sarge. I said this could take a while. He said, 'You've got all the time you need,' and alerted an ambulance crew. I brought back the tea and cake. Three cups. Three slices of cake. We sat there and talked. He kept telling her to drink up her tea, not waste it. Turned out she had died early in the morning. He had got up, dressed her, put her in the wheelchair and for eight hours he walked around Bognor to all the places they always went together, ending up at the seafront. I sat and talked to him for four hours. The ambulance crew were around the corner, waiting. I knew them. They were our local Bognor crew. It just wouldn't work like that these days. Eventually, he and I agreed it was time to put her in the ambulance. They had arranged for her body to go straight to the Chapel of Rest. We got to the hospital and he said goodbye to her there and then I drove him home. Job done.

Commentary
After the death – Liz Rothschild

Liz trained at the Bristol Old Vic and has worked as a writer, performer and director around the country. She directed a theatre company of disabled actors for Reach Inclusive Arts for 17 years and created an intergenerational arts project in her local town. In 1993, she became a celebrant, and in 2000 opened Westmill Woodland Burial Ground (*www.woodlandburialwestmill.co.uk*) with her partner on the Oxfordshire/Wiltshire border, where she lives. In 2005 she toured her show, *Another Kind of Silence*, about the environmentalist Rachel Carson. In 2012, she launched her first 'Kicking the Bucket' festival in Oxford (*www.kickingthebucket.co.uk*) and since 2016 she has been touring nationally with *Outside the Box – A live show about death* (*www.fullcircleproductions.org.uk*). She won a Good Funeral Guide award for her work promoting the understanding of death. She has two children and is passionate about making marginal voices heard and the life-changing potential of nature and the arts. She is an active member of the Women in Power UK community.

Someone has just died. Maybe you expected it, maybe you didn't. Maybe you had made some plans, had conversations, maybe not. Whatever the period that led up to the death (if there was any preparation), nothing can fully prepare us. Normal life is suspended and it seems impossible that people continue to walk up and down the street outside, laughing and eating and talking on their mobile phones. We feel so far removed from it all and it feels wrong that life looks so strangely normal. We want the world to stop. It won't. But we can – to some extent at least. What I always advise is to give yourself time and don't allow expectations of others to drive you forwards before you are ready.

And that includes the suggestions you may feel emerging from these pages.

Keeping a body at home is comparatively unusual still, but I have chosen to include a number of stories featuring this choice. That is not because I frown on taking the usual route and using a funeral director. It is because in my work I often encounter a feeling in people that death is a complex matter best left to professionals. They simply don't understand what is legal and possible and do not feel empowered to ask or know who to turn to for advice. As is revealed in some of the stories, they can even encounter resistance or incredulity when they attempt to do something that would have been absolutely commonplace no more than 60 years ago in this country and that is still absolutely legal.

If the person has died in hospital, you can still ask for some time to sit with the body before it is taken to the morgue. It may be possible for it to be transferred to the hospital chapel, which these days usually reflects an interfaith approach, welcoming all. You can push back on any suggestions from a residential home that a funeral director is called before you are ready. Signs can be put on the door preventing anyone coming in and you can sit there until the people you need to come have arrived, until you have observed any religious practices that are important to you, until you know the time is right. What makes holding your ground in all these cases so much easier is if you have already had some kind of conversation with the key stakeholders involved. And, of course, sometimes this is not possible because of the nature of the death or the family dynamics.

Organ donation

The exception to all of this is in the case of organ and body and brain donation. Then time is of the essence. *The Transplant* gives us a very positive version of this experience. It can also be quite traumatic, since action has to be taken very quickly. When the system was voluntary, only a very small percentage of people ever completed a donor card and so, in 30% of cases, the families refused the procedure, for a wide variety of reasons, some religious (Robbins, 1996). In May 2020, the law in England changed to an opt-out system. Unless someone has chosen to opt out, it is now routine to take organs. In conversation with the organ donation helpline, I scrutinised the wording that suggests families will be consulted and was told that, should anyone strongly object, this right will not be insisted upon. The aim, of course, is to reduce the waiting list for a wide variety of transplants and help others in the way that so comforted the person in our story.

In the case of brain and body donation, it is important to know that you will not necessarily find the gift accepted. If there is no need for additional bodies for dissection at the time of death, or it is a bank holiday, or the cause of or period before death has altered the situation from a medical perspective, you may find that the long-imagined plan cannot happen. So always have a plan B up your sleeve. It is also important to understand that it will be some time before any physical remains get returned to you, and so you may wish to think about how to mark the death meaningfully in the meantime, since you will not know exactly how long the delay will be – quite possibly at least a year.

What to do with the body?

Imagine you are sitting with the body. There may be things that you did not manage to say while the person was alive that need saying. These may be dictated by your religious beliefs or be entirely personal – they can be very important and help your grieving. As in *Pebbles and Petals,* it is sometimes important to acknowledge what has been difficult in order to allow the love that is there to flow. Maybe, like the woman in *100 Final Strokes,* you want to offer one last act of love and care after many months or years of tending to that person's physical and emotional needs, or you want to open the window briefly to let the spirit leave. You may want to wash and dress the body. (This can also be done at a funeral directors'.) You may want to sit by the body, perhaps with a lit candle or with music playing, and take time to really understand that the body remains but the person you knew has died. Sometimes, if the relationship was fraught or the final stages of life very difficult, you can only feel glad and as if a life sentence has been lifted and you can begin to breathe again. You may just long to walk away as soon as you can and begin to resume your usual life. Hopefully, there are people with whom you can share your authentic response at this time.

When visiting an elderly widower soon after his wife had died, I noticed on his computer screen the search, 'What to do when someone has died'. I wish he had not had to do that as the light broke on that first lonely dawn.

So, let's just go through the legal essentials and required procedures. This starts with the body of the person who has died. It can remain at home for as long as feels appropriate to you. This can mean for several hours, days or weeks, with the appropriate care. You do not have to call 999. What is legally required is to get the death verified by a trained healthcare professional, such as a nurse or paramedic. Then you need the death to be certified, with a cause of death. This can only be done by a doctor. If the person died at home and their GP has not visited in the previous two weeks, then another doctor, not known to the patient, will also have to come, if the body is to be cremated. If the death is unexpected or unexplained, or there are suspicious circumstances, the coroner will become involved (in Scotland this is the procurator fiscal). This always slows the process down, while investigations are made – often there's a post-mortem. If the death is in hospital, the doctors there can complete the certificate. The death must then be registered with a register office. This must be done within five days (eight days in Scotland). If your religion requires immediate burial, you can fast-track this process. You will need a medical certificate confirming the cause of the death, or permission from the coroner. It is also very helpful to use the Tell Us Once system, which the registrar can help you with or give you the unique reference number to use yourself within 84 days of the death (see Resources). This will inform all relevant government departments, such as benefits and pensions, in one go about the death, saving you a lot of time and work.

It is wise to get several copies of the death certificate, even though it costs you more, because you will find that, when winding up the person's financial and other affairs, most organisations and agencies will require an original copy. Only having one can cause frustrating delays and become very stressful.

The Resources section lists the excellent, clear government website explaining all this and more in full detail. You can also ask for a free bereavement guide from the register office. This is usually given out at the time of death, but I recommend getting one long before and getting familiar with the routine so that, when the time comes, you feel calmer about what has to happen.

Once the death has been registered, you will receive a Certificate for Burial or Cremation, which is commonly called the Green Form because it is on green paper. You will give this to the funeral directors or to the burial ground or crematorium, or you will retain it yourself if the burial takes place on your own property. The funeral cannot take place without this certificate. Once the burial or cremation has taken place, the section at the bottom of the form must be filled in, torn off and returned to the register office. If the body is cremated, the crematorium will do this and you will receive a white form – the ashes certificate – for you to keep as proof of the cremation. This is important, especially if you are travelling abroad with the ashes. It means the register office concerned knows exactly what happened to the body of a person whose death they have registered, and the circle is complete.

Choosing the funeral director, if using one, is very important, and I advise visiting several so you can see the range of charges, attitudes and flexibility that is available to you. Strangely, most funeral directors assume that, once you have come though their door, you are automatically their customer, and for most families, this is what happens. People are distressed and they feel in a hurry. The message they often get from the way they are treated is, 'Everything is going to be alright now. We will handle this now. Leave it all to us. We are the professionals.' When we buy a house or a car or choose a holiday, we shop around and compare what is on offer. When there has been a death, we feel rushed and distressed, and if the body needs to be moved quickly, this may be true. So, if possible, do this research well ahead of time.

Sometimes, sadly, death does not allow us this luxury. If you are not satisfied, always remember you can change funeral directors. I know of a family who did just that. When they told their first funeral director they wished to decorate their father's cardboard coffin with the mathematical formulae with which he had grappled with all his life, the director replied he 'could not allow them to scribble on their father's coffin'. They realised they were with the wrong firm and arranged for their father's body to be moved elsewhere.

The realities of keeping a person at home after death are very practical as well as emotional. You need to consider what they died of, the temperature of the room and what means you have to keep them cool. All these factors will affect how long the body can stay in your home. In *Home Death*, the family chose to continue to light a fire because it was a soothing and familiar routine for their father, but generally any heat in a room would be discouraged, and keeping the window closed is recommended, to avoid any flies entering. But anyone can keep a body at home quite easily, with calm planning and good guidance. And, as we see in *The Wake*, in some countries there is even specialised equipment that can be routinely obtained to ease the process. And you can improvise. I have used freezer blocks to cool the core of the body down, having wrapped them in tea towels to avoid damaging the skin, and there are other products, like Techni Ice sheets, on the market now. If this level of detail makes you feel squeamish, then this approach is clearly not the right one for you. The Resources section lists organisations that work routinely with home funerals and can recommend useful, inexpensive equipment and offer support.

Sometimes it is simply not possible because, for example, you live in a block of flats that has centrally controlled heating and you cannot turn it off. Ask yourself, is this choice practical for you? Is it emotionally appropriate for you? Does it feel right for all concerned? Knowing it is possible is very important, but that does not mean you have to choose it. Some of this has not been possible, of course, in cases where Covid-19 is involved. The virus has already altered religious practice enshrined in both Jewish and Muslim law regarding the ritual washing of the body before burial. It is not clear if or when it will be possible to resume these practices.

The funeral arrangements

So, either the body has been taken to the mortuary or the funeral director, or you have decided to keep vigil at home. Now the next stages will unfold. This is another point at which to take a breath. There is no law about how soon a funeral should take place. People may be abroad, there may quite a lot of different opinions to negotiate around. There is no rush. You can ask the funeral director what their daily rate is for keeping a body in the mortuary if you want to know the financial impact of waiting a little longer. They may be surprised, but getting itemised costs is always wise, I think, unless the person has a funeral plan, which means they have already paid for a set package. You may decide on a swift burial or cremation, with only very close family there, and have a larger memorial after some time has elapsed, or you may just wait three or four weeks before having the funeral, so all the right people can be consulted and involved – or you may not want any kind of funeral.

So, you have all these arrangements to sort out and you are devastated, shocked and probably completely exhausted. You may also be profoundly relieved. All of these feelings are normal and common. You may still have young children who need to be looked after and given a sense of normality amidst all the emotional and practical upheaval. You may be unable to know what you are feeling or not ready to fully accept the death, like the husband in the *Bognor Bobby* story. What empathetic sensitivity that young policeman demonstrated when he brought three cups of tea and pieces of cake and did not try to impose his reality before the elderly widower could accept it. How slowly and carefully he enabled the elderly man to finally allow others to help him take care of his wife.

In many religious and cultural traditions, those who have been bereaved are not expected to do anything for a set period of time. This is captured in *Nine Night*. In traditional Jewish practice, food and drink are brought to the bereaved, the house is cleaned, the washing done and the mourners' job is to sit together and allow their grief to flow. I think we could learn much of benefit from the ancient wisdom of such approaches. The compassionate community model is one that might replicate them, if family and friends cannot do so. It came swiftly to the fore in various forms in the efforts to support those isolated and unsupported during the outbreak of Covid-19 in 2020, and may have longer-term benefits to offer all involved. Again, you will find details in the Resources section.

My experience is that a lot of people want to help in these moments, but often they don't know how because they have no formal structure imposed by tradition or contemporary culture. A young widow, after being constantly asked what she wanted people to do and finding the request exhausting, put up a list of jobs on her fridge and asked her visitors to tick off the task and write their name and a date against it when they'd done it. This could also be done online, so everyone can see what remains to do. Some of us are not very good at asking for help. Maybe we are more used to being the supporter for others. What might you need doing?

When we were expecting our first child, we attended National Childbirth Trust classes and one exercise I vividly remember was to go home and together think about our family and friends and create a little diagram of who we felt closest to (not who we thought we ought to feel closest to) and what particular qualities they offered. We arranged the names in concentric circles, with us at the centre, and imagined when we might want to call on help from each of them. Why not apply the same idea when bereaved? If we try to pour out our hearts to the wrong person, it will not work for either of us; nor might our closest confidante be much use when the washing machine breaks down.

You may belong to a faith community whose members would offer support, or people you have never considered close before will step forward because they have had a similar experience of bereavement and feel more confident about doing so. The danger here can sometimes be that people assume they know how you are feeling because of their own story. A word of caution to those offering help: ask people what they want, and don't assume you know.

Perhaps, because of the circumstances of your life or the great age you have lived to, you struggle to put many names on your list. Unexpected people can be pleased to be asked. Sometimes people do not rise to the occasion and do something far more devastating – they avoid us. Invitations dry up. We can feel further isolated by this and doubly bereaved, both of the person who died and the social life we used to lead. This is captured vividly in *Don't Leave Us Out*, in Chapter 11 on grieving and remembering. We may sometimes need to look beyond those we know, to key professionals and support organisations. The Resources section at the end of this chapter and of Chapter 11 list some helpful sources of external support.

Moving on

Our society expects us to battle an illness bravely and mourn circumspectly. We are not admired if perceived as indulging in our distress or distressing others with our grief. Those who quickly resume normal life again are often regarded as coping well. I would counsel against being too influenced by this. Just as a broken bone is often stronger than it was before the injury, so we can become stronger by allowing ourselves to be broken by our feelings for a while. A new workplace right was enshrined in law in 2020 to allow parents two weeks' paid leave after the death of a child. Two weeks is not very long, but it is a step in the right direction and at least offers public acknowledgement and financial support in recognition of the enormity of what has taken place. And, of course, for some the resuming of normal routines is a vital part of their recovery. They need to feel that something about life is normal – the journey to work, work colleagues' banter, the requirement to think about something other than their own pain. Like everything to do with death and life, each of us is the wisest arbiter of what we need. Take advice but always listen very carefully to your own counsel.

Professionals working in the field of death, dying and bereavement need to stay aware that, although the situation may feel very familiar, even routine, to them, those who have just been bereaved are in an altered state and every gesture and word will have huge impact and significance for them. A woman whose daughter was gravely ill said that what made all the difference was that the paediatrician cried when she told her there was nothing more the medical team could do. Some would strongly discourage this. I am not advocating artificially manufacturing emotion or becoming overwhelmed by feelings. The bereaved or dying person should never feel they have to look after those looking after them in a professional role. It simply means sharing the human reality of the situation. I am not surprised that the young medical student in *Emotions* had concerns about this when setting out on her career. *With the End in Mind,* by Kathryn Mannix (2019), reassuringly demonstrates what empathetic, experienced care can look like.

There are ways all of us can look after ourselves. Knowing what nourishes and soothes you best is a vital way to live at any time and it can really come to your aid at times of acute distress. Caring for ourselves well enables us to care better for others. Today is the time to start practising!

Advice points

1. Do not rush. Nothing has to be done *immediately*.
2. Take time to say what you need to say to the person who has died and offer last gestures of care or religious rituals.
3. Use your support network skilfully – family, friends, neighbours, professionals.

4. Make time for yourself and do what you find most nourishing.
5. And one to do before the death has occurred… Get a copy of the free bereavement guide from your local register office or visit it before there has been a death, so you are familiar with what is legally required.

References

Mannix, K. (2019). *With the end in mind: How to live and die well*. HarperCollins.

Robbins, M. (1996). The donation of organs for transplantation: The donor families. In P. Jupp & G. Howarth (Eds.), *Contemporary issues in the sociology of death, dying and disposal* (pp179–192). Palgrave Macmillan.

Resources

There is not much written specifically about this period straight after death but a lot of the resources listed in Chapter 10, The Funeral, and Chapter 11, Grieving and Remembering, will be relevant at this time.

Books

The books listed here offer guidance for some faith traditions but the organisations listed in the websites can offer support to non-religious families.

Diamant, A. (1999). *Saying Kaddish: How to comfort the dying, bury the dead and mourn as a Jew*. Random House Inc.

Ghazali, A.H.M. (1989). *Al-Ghazali on the remembrance of death and the afterlife*. The Islamic Texts Society.

Gordon, T. (2007). *New journeys now begin: Learning on the path of grief and loss*. Wild Goose Publications.

Rinpoche, S. (1992). *The Tibetan book of the dead*. Penguin.

Starhawk, M. & Macha NightMare, M. (1997). *The pagan book of living and dying*. Harper Collins.

Ward, T. (2007). *The Celtic wheel of the year – Celtic and Christian seasonal prayers*. John Hunt Publishing.

Webpages

Association of Independent Celebrants: https://independentcelebrants.com

British Humanist Society: https://humanism.org.uk

Home Funeral Network: www.homefuneralnetwork.org.uk

Natural Death Handbook: www.naturaldeath.org.uk/index.php?page=book-shop

Register the death: www.gov.uk/after-a-death

Tell us once: www.gov.uk/after-a-death/organisations-you-need-to-contact-and-tell-us-once

What to do when someone has died. (n.d.). Westmill Woodland Burial Ground: www.woodlandburialwestmill.co.uk/arranging-a-funeral/what-to-do-when-someone-has-died

Films

Dead Good Film. (2018). Rehana Rose (Dir.). Ponder Productions. (New approaches to undertaking and organising funerals)

Departures. (2008). Yôjirô Takita (Dir.). Tokyo Broadcasting System. (Japanese film following a young man who takes work as a *nōkanshi* - a traditional Japanese ritual mortician. Not to be viewed when just bereaved but as part of reflecting on/preparing for a death)

Outside the Box

10 – The funeral

Something missing
I went to a funeral of a childhood friend. He died aged 37 – a couple of months after a sudden cancer diagnosis. His wishes were for a celebration of his life, for the focus to be on positivity, and love of life to be at the heart of it. This was how he lived and how he wanted to be remembered. I kept having to remind myself that this was a funeral. Summer's day, white marquee, balloons, cakes, prosecco, bouncy castle, his two small boys running around playing with their friends, people taking selfies. It felt like a wedding. On the one hand, it felt progressive and wonderful to celebrate him in this way. On the other, I felt an uncomfortable sense that something was missing. That the positivity and celebration was overriding what really needed to be there as well. I think it was the grief. There was no space for it.

With laughter
Growing up, I had a real bleak outlook on death. I didn't like the idea of being cremated… it seemed so dramatic, and all that body smoke. Somebody is breathing that in. (I don't know much about the process of cremation, obviously!) Then the idea of being buried in a box in a row with all these strangers. For the longest time, these were the only two options I knew of. Then you have everyone in depressing clothes, carrying on in a sombre way; all this sadness, just so bleugh! But then my uncle passed very suddenly, and young. My aunt was so distraught. She didn't know what to do. The thought of having to relive all of this at a funeral weighed on her heavily! Then my uncle's bandmates (he was part of an old country band) insisted they played one last time for him. Long story short, we had this amazing party, potluck food, the band jamming out, people coming up, joining in, dancing, laughter, fun. That's when I realised, that's how I want to go out, with laughter and smiles.

With a JCB

When I was Head of Planning at Sedgemoor Council, I took a call from an irate lady. The farmer down the lane was burying his wife on his land at the end of the lane – with a JCB. Surely this was not permitted. I believed this was OK but promised to check. Sure enough, he was entirely within his rights, not needing any planning permission or other legal consent in that location. The caller was rather aghast to get this information – it just didn't seem right! I was never clear if the concern was religious, proprietorial or environmental – or simply the use of the JCB! I got a lot of strange calls when I was working there.

I wish I had known then what I know now

I don't remember anything about my mum's funeral, or my dad's for that matter, which is odd because I singlehandedly arranged both of them, followed a few years later by my sister's funeral. That's my whole immediate family gone, and I suppose, if I stop to think about any of it now, I am left with a lot of sadness that I didn't know back then what I know now. My mum died shockingly and suddenly of cancer. My dad, in his grief, disappeared for days on his motorbike. My sister was not helpful, so I arranged mum's funeral by myself. I had no idea. I was at the mercy of a funeral director, chosen because it was the only one I knew. The result was a perfectly respectable, 20 minutes down the local crem, all suited and booted, running like clockwork, with military precision. Everyone said how lovely it was, but the duty vicar didn't know Mum, none of us are church goers anyway, the eulogy was non-existent as no one told me I was supposed to write one, and the music was whatever the organist fancied playing on the day. My dad died a few years later and his funeral was a repeat of Mum's. This time the vicar didn't even bother to visit; he just chatted for 10 minutes on the phone. I remember even less about Dad's day. When my sister then died, I felt I just about had the wherewithal to put my foot down about one thing. NO duty vicar, I would do the service myself. It was still 20 minutes down the crematorium, and while it was better and more personal than my parents' funerals, it was still, to my mind, a completely inadequate way to mark the ending of a person's life on this planet.

As time and circumstances moved on, I found myself in a job I had outgrown and looking for a change in direction. As a mature woman of limited means, my options for retraining were few, but one thing leapt out. My experiences arranging funerals and how, with the benefit of hindsight, I would do it very differently now. The knowledge that there must be a better way to mark the ending of a life and manage the grief of those left behind. The conviction that no one in that time of complete post-death bewilderment should be cornered into just going with what a funeral director tells them to do, unless it suited them to do so. The growing awareness that, among other things, what a funeral should really be about is preparing those left behind for a life without someone important to them.

I spent three years learning the funeral industry as a regular funeral director and then made the jump across to working in a green burial ground. I was determined that the families I talked to would be held and supported through their grief, as much as they wanted; that they would be told of *all* the options available to them, and that they would be encouraged to take all the time they needed to create a funeral that would enable them to move on with their grief. I know that what we offer here is not right for everybody, but I do badly wish that back then someone had offered me a choice.

Caribbean style

Some say, if you want to keep a baby safe, you pass it over the coffin. There are many superstitions. After a death, wear red knickers or black. That stuff goes back to the days in Africa. We always have the children at the funeral. Why not?! The colours for a funeral are black, white and purple. Forty days after the death, it is Ascension Day and people will come to your house to sing and pray and that is when the burden is lifted and you give the person who died up to the Lord.

In Scotland

In Scotland it is expected that the family will bear and lower. That is what we do. My mother knew exactly how she wanted this to be done and told us who was to be at the head, the foot etc. Often family are given cards telling them their position as bearer when burying their relatives. Carrying a coffin is seen as an honour and a privilege.

Crossing borders

A German woman who had spent many years in India had cancer. She knew she was dying. She wanted to have her ashes scattered in India and Germany. Arrangements were made. Family and friends all clear about her wishes. But she died in Germany. In Germany, only the undertakers may take charge of the ashes. The family may not collect them from the crematorium. There is a set legal period by which the ashes must be interred. They cannot be scattered. The ashes do not leave the premises of the undertakers until they are to be interred. So, the body was cremated, the ashes were collected by the undertakers. They were driven by the undertakers to the German border and handed over to French undertakers in Alsace Lorraine, with due decorum. The German undertakers drove away. Their duty fulfilled. The laws in France are different. The French undertakers handed the woman's ashes to the family and they too drove away. The family stood quietly together on the slopes of a golden vineyard on the border. Then, when they were ready, they opened the urn and scattered the ashes quietly back onto German soil. A few days later, the rest of her ashes arrived in India. Witty. Determined. Most of us have no idea what is possible.

Buried in your own home

Years ago, I worked as a medical officer in Papua New Guinea. One of my jobs was to try to stop people burying their dead in the earth floor of their houses, which was considered a public health risk. I was a complete failure. The most I could ask was that maybe they move their houses, which were only made of bamboo and thatch, after the period of mourning. The provincial governor was not impressed. When someone had died, their clothes might be hung in a tree and the period of mourning did not end until the clothes rotted and fell down. This has been fine in the days of organic clothing but became a problem with man-made fibres. I'm not sure how they resolved this, but I think they climbed up at night and cut them down. It was considered essential that people were buried in their own earth, their own place. Everyone understood this and strangers would help move bodies from the hospital morgue back to the villages, using the bus if necessary. I was left with a great respect for a world where death was in the middle of life.

Shovel burial

My Dad was buried at a green burial ground. After discussion with the people there, we learnt so much about what we didn't have to do and what we could do ourselves!! We drove Dad in his cardboard coffin to the burial ground, lowered his coffin into the grave (the children helped too) and then filled the grave. It was described as a 'bring a shovel burial'. We sat and had a BBQ around the grave while sharing our memories and stories. It was the happiest, most relaxed burial anyone had ever attended, and that's the way he would have loved it to be remembered. So much learnt for all.

Thunderclap

My father was of the 'Just put me in a binbag' school re his funeral. At the undertaker, however, when I suggested we must at least have only the cheapest coffin, my brother baulked – couldn't face using 'cheap kitchen laminate'. I gave in and we agreed to go with the cheapest my brother could tolerate. The weather on the day was dreadful. On the way to the funeral in the family car, there was an enormous clap of thunder. 'Oh dear,' said my brother, 'Dad's just heard how much the coffin cost!' We all laughed so much, as this was Dad's sense of humour, that when we got out of the car we had to pretend to the other mourners that these were tears of sadness, not joy.

Everything went wrong

At my grandad's funeral (same crematorium for all grandparents), everything that could go wrong did… Phones going off during the ceremony, my stepmother farting during the prayers and a radiator leak on the way into the crematorium. But… it was the most honest and open we had been with each other and in a way the things going wrong helped smash through the awkwardness of the occasion.

Hilarious and perfect

My friend Jim and his partner Phil both died during the AIDS epidemic in the 1990s. My last view of Jim was when he was in agony in hospital, being manhandled by many medical professionals. His funeral was then arranged by his family on my birthday. It was a terrible and distancing experience, but I got to know his mother and sister. His last wish was for his friends and family to scatter his and Phil's ashes in a botanical garden. We didn't have permission, of course. We sneaked the ashes in in two large plastic carrier bags. They were heavy. We drank cold white wine, picnicked and told stories about them. We took it in turns to go into the trees and sprinkle the boys from holes in the corner of the bags. It was hilarious and perfect.

Bootfuls of ashes

My mum and dad were rock climbers. When Mum died in 1985, she requested her ashes be scattered from Stanage Edge, a popular climbing spot in the Peak District. My brother and I obliged, but the ashes blew back in the wind and we got bootfuls of ashes in the process. In 2016, my father died and made the same request. We took his ashes a mile further along the same edge; my mother and father were divorced and there was a lot of bad feeling between them. But now their ashes mingle in the wind, and in the stark beauty of the place. Now they have to work it out. In 2015, my uncle died. The local customs included a lot of heavy pancake make-up and a visit to his open coffin in the dining room. Turned out he wanted his ashes scattered alongside my mother. So my cousin (his oldest daughter) and I (his sister's eldest daughter) made the trek up to Stanage Edge together. My mum now has a family ally with her, and I another bootful of ashes. In loving memory of Joan Brown, Philip Brown and Ivan Tiplady.

(It should be noted, the trustees for a nearby area of Outstanding Natural Beauty have pointed out that these little pyramids of human ashes that regularly appear change the composition of the soil in our wildernesses and beauty spots, affecting the flora and fauna that naturally grow there – and not necessarily for the better.)

The Big Lebowski

We kept our father in his box for a while before taking him to scatter across Blackstone Edge. On the way, we stopped to go shopping, leaving him in the car. Which is what always happened when he was alive. It was a windy day and when I got home I noticed he was caught in the punched holes and seams of my boots. I didn't clean them until he had finally vanished.

Atheist's mass

A Catholic friend of mine told me her uncle, an atheist, had told the family not to have any Mass said, and she felt guilty because they did have a Mass. I pointed out, if he's right, he won't know, and if you're right, he will be grateful. I do think funerals are for the living.

Cattle salute

I was taking a service in a very rural small church. The deceased had been a dairyman on the neighbouring farm and his family had lived for 50 years in the cottage next to the church. After the service, we moved to the graveyard. As we lowered his coffin into the ground, all the cattle in the adjoining field nestled their heads on the stone wall and angled their heads to watch us – as if saluting an old farm worker. It was truly magical, and the family will remember that forever.

Sunset with a burger

Aunty Jo fought cancer for years so was able to share her wishes well with her two sisters she held so dear. When the wake came, she insisted we were all to go to the best burger van she had loved, which was at the top of a tall hill overlooking the city. Thirty of us gathered around picnic tables at sunset with a burger! It changed the wake from reverent quiet to boisterous storytelling.

Death of a countrywoman

We slipped into the familiar coolness of the village church. The pews respectfully full. With this death, we lost a certain kind of knowing. A woman who observed the seasons turn, remembered where to find the best hazelnuts or sloes, who could turn the most unwilling fruit into jam. A cottage loaf of a woman with pale blue eyes as clear as her jellies. She knew when a jam was ready without thermometer or saucer of water, watching the wrinkling ocean in the pan, deftly removing the sugary spume. We sat, well behaved, in our motley black, with the wooden coffin and her frail bent widower, listening to the vicar talking about Dorothy, when everyone of us knew she was always Dot. Making a stranger of someone we all knew better than him.

I began to imagine how it might have been. Entering the church to the smell of baking. Each of us quietly carrying a jar from our store cupboards. Curd or jelly, jam or pickles, and placing them on her coffin, staining the wood golden and red, dark magenta and purple. Then, at a certain moment, the vicar would cut a fresh loaf of bread on the altar and hand each of us a generously buttered slice. We would approach the coffin with love and tenderness and a spoon, and choosing a jar, open it and spread the contents on our slice. Tangy sweetness, memory of autumn and hidden bursts of fruit. We would remember her through our taste buds – that soft voice, those capable hands, the sense of safety that she embodied as she filled all our shelves with jars and wondered at our lack of skill. We would tell our stories and the roof beams would listen until all the jars were empty. Then we would bury her.

Walking back into life the Jewish way
On leaving the cemetery, we wash our hands, pouring water over them with a jug, leaving the world of death behind. On coming home, the mourners are given a hardboiled egg to eat, usually in a quiet space, before joining the funeral guests, who will usually have followed them to the house. This is not only to give them sustenance but to symbolise life.

The Shiva, when the community comes to the mourners' home to say the daily prayers and to be a support, is a time out of time. I remember how it felt to be in the middle of this intense and different emotional world, not doing any of the daily tasks, wearing a torn jacket and slippers, not seeing myself in the mirror (all mirrors covered) and being comforted by the endless kindness and solidarity shown by the community. The end of this period can feel like a jolt. When I and my brother sat Shiva for our mother, our friends told us that it was customary to accompany the mourners on their first exit from this enclosed and held space, by accompanying them on a walk round the block. We were a small group, walking quietly through the streets of East Oxford, the men wearing skullcaps. On the way, we met our local postman, who asked us what we were doing. When we told him, he wondered if we would allow him to join us. I was so touched and honoured as he walked beside us.

Woollen coffin
Lilian always felt cold, so we chose a woollen coffin for her to be 'cosy' in.

Her actual voice
Today we were at a funeral of a much loved old lady. And she was there! Someone played a recording of her reading a poem. It was such a treat – we all loved it hearing her actual voice.

No funeral
Following a friend's death (no funeral, at her request), we were invited to meet at the cliff overlooking the beach she loved so much in Cornwall – close to where she'd lived. A photo of her had been fixed to the fence, beside two huge buckets of flowers (Marguerites, like her name). Her son spoke of his mother and her husband invited us to take a flower and process with them to the cliff edge, where husband and children scattered the ashes and we all sent the flowers after them.

Hard ground

My partner doesn't really do 'feelings'. His childhood friend's dad fell off a roof three years ago. He was the dad they all grew up with. He used to drive them from Wales to Bristol so they could go to drum and bass nights when they were teenagers. There had been plenty of parties at his house. He wanted to be buried on their land, in the area where all the Welsh rock and slate was. The guys all dug the graves with pickaxes; it was very fitting and a way for them to show their love and express their grief.

Plan B

My great friend's father died after illness in old age. His mother was fragile with, if not actual dementia, a developing confusion. They were great cruisers and so they booked everyone onto a 'final cruise'. They would all be together, they could celebrate their father's life, they could leave him doing what he had so loved doing… bobbing about on the sea. However, the cruise companies frown upon people flapping ashes about as they don't always go overboard on those huge ships and the wind can be a problem So they popped the ashes into a more disguised supermarket carrier bag. They picked a quiet time to meet when the decks would be clear. They had decided just to say a few words if they wanted to but nothing formal was arranged. They waited for a while. No one opted to speak. Eventually my friend gently asked his mother if she had brought the ashes as perhaps it was time. She looked puzzled. Eventually they understood from her that she had found lots of dust in a bag in her suitcase. Worried that she had lost her mind completely, she had assumed that she had brought the contents of the vacuum by accident and had flushed it all down the loo. Plan B, they adjourned to the bar.

The king reborn

My friend and father of our children died this year. He always said he wanted to go up in a rocket – that was one thing we know for sure. So, in the summer, I bought a big rocket (called the King Reborn) and had some ashes attached. Friends and family, including three children, gathered and we sent him up. It was a joyful evening! He studied martial arts many years ago in Hong Kong, so I'm going back next year with some ashes to scatter in Victoria Park where he trained with his Sifu – so many hours of dedication. We're also going as a family to Portugal to scatter a bit of him there, where we had a house. The rest of him will rest behind his house in Arnos Green burial woods. His funeral was a joyful celebration at the memorial woodlands. Rest in peace, my love.

All buried together

My great grandad's first wife died. He then re-married at 70. When he died, he was buried with his first wife. Then his second wife died, and she had no family apart from us. My great grandad had written that she could be buried with him. Now they're all buried together in one plot and share one headstone.

Itching to write

I am Jewish and have been brought up in the religion, though I am not at all religious. When my mother died 13 years ago, she couldn't be buried for four days due to the Sabbath and a post-mortem. I was determined to read at the funeral, but the Rabbi was unsure, as women don't usually speak. The night before the funeral, I awoke at about 3am, my hands itching to write. I have never been a poet but my mother was, and in the following hour I wrote a beautiful poem from my mother to all of her family and friends, many of whom still have it on their wall to this day. The Rabbi told me he was honoured to have me read it, and even translated it into Hebrew! I have no fear of death or the dead, it is another stage of life and, as my 94-year-old grandfather said to me, 'What would be the point of fear? If I'm right and there's no after-life, I'll not know anything about it anyway. If I'm wrong and there is, I'll be bloody relieved there's more to come!'

Flexible tradition

Our friend Xen tragically died aged 39. She had been a practising Muslim, identified as Queer, was a mother, a doctor, an activist and much, much more. The first part of the funeral was in a Mosque, where her body was washed and prepared according to Islamic practice by friends during Friday prayers. The mosque was open to trans people going to the women's section and the trans people accepted that. It felt so Xen to find a mosque open to our needs and her Queer friends finding a way to accept the gendered set up in the mosque.

Perfectly imperfect

I went to the funeral of a young girl. The daughter of friends. A coffin, small and white. Each of us given a rose bud to place upon it. My first time in my local Catholic church. The church was bursting, filled with the sounds and movements of children. There were readings from children's stories, poems, prayers and hymns. At a certain point, the older priest was overcome with grief and could not continue. A younger deacon gently stepped in and conducted the service while he sat and slowly composed himself. Between them, I felt all that needed to be expressed had been – perfectly.

Red admiral

My sister-in-law was buried in a woven casket. During the service, a butterfly was fluttering at the stained-glass west window, trying to get out. The next day, I phoned my brother to see how he was getting on. He said fine, but he'd been busy trying to catch a butterfly (the same species, a Red Admiral) that had come in the house, in order to let it out.

A fiasco

Last year I lost a good friend who had no kin, lived in rented accommodation, on benefits. The police took his mobile phone (and still have it!), the housing associating refused us (his friends) access to his flat – claimed they could not find his will. I know he had one as I witnessed it but have no idea where it was. We wanted only his music – he was a songwriter. It was all thrown away – his instruments and studio gear 'vanished'. His other possessions were offered us in a sale, bidding against professional dealers. He was buried in a churchyard. He was definitely not a Christian. The money we collected for a headstone had to be given to Blue Cross because it was nowhere near enough to pay the full costs. Fiasco. I wish to avoid my closest family, who are religious Jews, burying me according to their rites. They will not even recognise my differently gendered life and identity, let alone my religious apostasy and funeral wishes. I have to put a plan in place somehow in advance.

All sorted

I supported a young family, dad, mum, three daughters aged 15 and twins of eight. Dad and mum worked together in their own construction company. Dad was diagnosed with a cancer that could not be cured. The first thing that they had to do was to sell their home, as they could no longer afford the mortgage. They moved into a private rental, which was still a large home to accommodate their family. They were living on the money from the sale of their home. His wife was unaware of this. When he knew he was dying, he insisted that he arrange his funeral and spoke with a funeral director, laying out all that he wished. His wife was not present as she found this all very distressing. This gentleman came to the hospice for his end-of-life care, and this was when I first met his wife. A young woman in her 40s, feeling completely overwhelmed by the situation. I did ask if everything was in place and she was able to say her husband had it 'all sorted'.

She then came back for support following his death. The funeral bill had been over £7000, which she had paid, but this left less in the bank to pay for the home she could now no longer afford. She had to leave the house and found herself homeless with her three children. While the funeral cost only played one part in this situation, no one asked how the funeral would be funded, and he had chosen a coffin that cost £1,200 as he had liked the carvings on the side of it, and flowers at £300. Pity that it was going to be put into a cremator and the flowers put round the back of the crematorium! She was eventually rehoused, which was a small piece of security following living for three years with so much uncertainty.

Nothing to spare

I worked with a lady whose husband had died following a long illness. He was in his early 60s, a man who had worked as a self-employed window cleaner all his life. Following his death his widow, who I will call Sally, came for bereavement support. She did not have many people around her to speak with about how sad she was. Week after week, Sally attended, and I started to notice she was getting thinner. Not unusual for someone left on their own. As a counsellor, I will always work with what is in the room. But on this occasion I felt I needed to acknowledge the change. I gently asked about how she was managing to cook for herself, as I had noticed her weight loss. Sally looked at me and then looked down, 'It's not that I don't want to cook for me. I am struggling to buy the food to cook.'

She then explained that, once her husband had died, she had been asked for a deposit from the funeral director of over £600. Her husband had a life insurance policy, but it wasn't enough. All the savings they had had were gone in attending her husband's hospital appointments and the additional cost of heating their home. Sally had given up work to care for her husband, so they had been living on a very reduced income. She had taken out a very high interest loan to help with some of the funeral cost. She had borrowed from a friend who she was paying back. She was also now paying up the rest of the funeral to the funeral director. By the time she paid the funeral debt, rent, heating and council tax, there was very little left for food. This situation left me feeling horrified that, in this day and age (around 2009), I was bearing witness to this poverty created through paying for a funeral. I am pleased to say I was able to find some funding to relieve this lady of the debt.

Prejudice

When we go to the funeral directors we get pressure. They try to persuade us to have a really expensive coffin. 'So and so had this one. Wouldn't you like one like that? Or even better this one? You people always have this kind of thing.' You people.

Crowdfunding

Jacquie couldn't get state support for her partner's funeral. She was not recognised as next of kin, despite the fact the coroner had accepted she was. 'Get the council to dispose of the body,' the Department for Work and Pensions told her. She decided to raise the money online. Crowdfunding for a coffin. She raised over £2,000 and she shopped around. One funeral director quoted over £2,000. Another provided the same service plus a bit for £700.

Commentaries

A good funeral – Fran Hall, Chief Executive, The Good Funeral Guide

Fran is an award-winning former funeral director who trained and worked in North London. She has been involved with the world of funerals for more than two decades, moving into the world of natural burials and working at three green burial grounds. Currently she is CEO of the Good Funeral Guide CIC, dedicated to supporting, empowering and representing the interests of dying and bereaved people in the UK, ensuring they receive the best impartial advice about their rights and options.

It is said that, on average, most of us will only organise one or two funerals in our lifetime, although we are likely to attend rather more than that as a mourner. The two roles are very different, though, and from the stories in this chapter, we can see some of the different levels of involvement, and some of the feelings that were evoked from decisions that were made. Funerals are for the dead, but more so for the living, and a good funeral, I believe, is one that is designed to connect both – a bridge over the chasm of what was and what now is.

Funerals are complex – as complex and varied as the people involved with them. Every person, every family is different, and these differences and the dynamics in relationships will always have a bearing on the type and shape – the kind of funeral that is created. And funerals need to work on many different levels in order to do their job of providing a public acknowledgement of the impact of a death.

Throughout human history, funerary rites and rituals have evolved to mark the threshold moment where a human life ends, with customs and ceremonies varying with culture and religious influence. In our Western world, right up until the end of the 19th century, death was a constant presence, with infant and child mortality contributing to an average life expectancy of around 40 years. Death was visible, funerals were frequent, and the Victorian way of mourning evolved and became increasingly structured. Families could call on the support of undertakers to assist with funeral requirements, and the Church was involved in almost all of these rites of passage.

The 20th century brought huge change. The trauma of two world wars, with their millions of dead, meant that public displays of personal grief were less acceptable. The influence of the Church waned. Huge advances in medicine and healthcare and improvements in housing and social care led to prolonged life – and less familiarity with death. As a consequence, we seem to have forgotten that our dead belong to us. We've forgotten what to do, how to be, how to have our dead amidst us. The automatic assumption in 2020 is that, when somebody dies, the first call is to a funeral director, who will come and take over. We look to strangers to help us deal with our dead.

We've got used to immediately handing responsibility for our dead to people we've never met, to making appointments to 'view' them in a room in the funeral director's premises, to not knowing exactly where they are or who's been in contact with them, who's brushed their hair or dressed them in the clothes we provided, who lifted them into the coffin we chose for them. Our dead relative has become something other; they have become 'the deceased', and we have little or no agency over them.

For many people, employing a funeral director brings both comfort and relief. Having someone there to support you, to advise you and to steer you through the unfamiliar world of decision-making and form-filling can be enormously helpful, and there are many exceptionally good funeral directors who dedicate themselves to the families they support. The challenge for bereaved people is knowing whether the funeral director in their local high street is one of these.

Few people carry out in-depth research before appointing a funeral director; reportedly, only 14% of people compare more than one funeral director (Competition and Markets Authority [CMA], 2019), and in the many years I spent working in the funeral industry, nobody ever asked to be shown where their dead relative would be cared for or asked what would be done to them. Often, people engage a funeral director's services without knowing what the final bill will amount to, as the funeral industry as a whole has been reluctant to publicise prices online. Arranging a funeral is described in the CMA report as 'the ultimate distress purchase… made infrequently by inexpert, emotionally vulnerable clients under time pressure'.

It is possible to do things differently, if this is what you want. Everything involved with organising a funeral can be done without involving funeral directors. You can do as much or as little as you feel able to. The only legal requirement for funerals in the UK is that the death must be certified and registered, and the body must be disposed of. The official definition of 'disposed of' is laid down in the Births and Deaths Registration Act, 1926: 'Disposal means disposal by burial, cremation or any other means, and "disposed of" has a corresponding meaning.' In other words, as long as a death is registered in the area where it occurred, and as long as the body of the person who has died is not exposed in a public place, and as long as the body is disposed of, then nothing else is mandatory.

You or your family will be helped enormously at this time if you have managed to talk about the funeral while everyone is healthy and compos mentis. Talk to those closest to you about the kind of funeral you or they would like. Don't be too proscriptive, but give them an idea, a starting point. Start the conversation and, in turn, ask them what they would like. This will really help ensure that, when the time comes, those responsible for making the funeral arrangements will know where to begin.

When someone reaches the end of their life at home, and if the death has been expected, it's perfectly ok to keep the person at home, if this is what you want. You can truly, deeply, be in the presence of death, in all its fierce beauty and its sacred mystery. And in doing so, you can face your own fragile mortality. Being with our dead is a profound, ancient human experience. It is precious time unlike any other, where memories and emotions flood together, washing us onto strange shores of newness where we have never walked before. This is the new reality, our life after this death, and it takes time to adjust to where we find ourselves. If we deny ourselves this time, how difficult will it be to walk in a world without the person we loved?

If the death occurs in a hospital or care setting, then it's likely the body will either be moved to a mortuary or collected by a funeral director under a contract of convenience. It can feel challenging to take over the care of that person yourself, reclaiming their body from what feels like an expected process, but it can be done if this is what feels right for you. All you need is determination and an understanding of what the law permits. Don't be put off by bereavement officers, mortuary staff or care home managers looking surprised or disapproving if you tell them you will be collecting your relative yourself (or that you won't be paying a funeral director that they appointed), if that's what you decide. You are entirely within your rights to assert yourself as the person in control of what happens next.

Irrespective of whether or not you employ a funeral director to help you, there are many decisions that need to be made about a funeral. Decisions about where and when and how and who, and how much to spend, the tone of the ceremony, the reflection of the faith or beliefs of the person who died, a consideration of what other people will think, whether the ceremony should be held with the body present or whether a memorial ceremony or a celebration of life without a coffin would be preferred. Do you even want to have any type of ceremony at all? Your budget may dictate the type of funeral you choose, or the person who has died may have pre-arranged and paid for a particular funeral package (despite everything that daytime TV adverts tell you, it's not always helpful to pre-arrange your own funeral by buying a funeral plan, as this leaves family and friends with little choice about the kind of funeral that meets their particular needs).

Consider whether you want to be directly involved with the funeral in any way. There are so many ways you can do this. You can take charge of planning and shaping the funeral (with or without a celebrant or faith leader), and design and lay out the order of service. On the day, you can contribute by reading, lighting a candle, doing the flowers, singing, playing music or baking their favourite cake. You can also help carry the coffin. It doesn't have to go on your shoulders; you can carry it by the handles if you make sure the coffin you choose has load-bearing handles. Even small children can help carry their relative.

That physical connection to the weight of the person's body helps your body to recognise the reality of their death. Bear witness to the enormity of it. Literally. You can lower the coffin into a grave, fill in a grave or request to go around the back of the crematorium to witness the coffin going into the cremator. If you feel you can, then do it. Be involved in the final act. It will help.

It would be so helpful to have had a chance to talk about the funeral long before the person dies, but sometimes this just won't have happened, and the person making the arrangements will have to try to do their best to get it right. And what does 'right' mean? Right for whom? We're back to the question of who a funeral is for. You may feel you need the funeral to be wholly reflective of the person who has died; you may have the needs of all of their family to take into consideration, or you may have strong feelings about what you want and need to happen. Or you may just be working things out as you go along.

Every death is different. Every funeral is different.

Ultimately, the mystery of death will touch all of our lives. We owe it to ourselves and our families to face it as best we can, to talk about how we'd like to be remembered, and to acknowledge that a good funeral isn't about how much you spend or how many cars you have in a cortège; it's about what's right for you, what you say and do, about giving voice to love and loss.

And sometimes, if we're very lucky, there will be a slant of light, a clap of thunder, the fluttering of a butterfly or a gathering of cows looking over a wall at just the right moment to remind us that life is beautiful, that we don't know everything, and that we should be grateful for every moment we have while we still live.

Advice points

- Don't rush into making any decisions.
- If you employ a funeral director, shop around.
- When you go to meet the funeral director, take a friend (or family member) along with you for support.
- Get involved as much as feels right for you and your family and friends. Whatever you contribute will help your grieving process.

References

Competition & Markets Authority. (2019). *Funerals market study: Final report and decision on a market investigation reference.* https://assets.publishing.service.gov.uk/media/5c9ba9bf40f0b633f6c52a7e/funerals_market_study_-_final_report.pdf

Funeral poverty – Rosie Inman-Cook

Rosie manages the Natural Death Centre Charity (founded in 1991), staffing its funeral helpline and running its Association of Natural Burial Grounds. She established three of the busiest award-winning natural burial sites in the country, one of which has more than 2,000 residents. She helps individuals up and down the country create an expanding network of woodland and natural burial sites. She frequently talks to the press on any death-, dying- and funeral-related topic, hoping that empowerment through information will create change. She is a self-builder (now an excellent thin-joint block layer), allotment appreciator, carer for a 92-year-old mum (aka Lady Gaga) and has two teenagers still in education.

When asked to write this, I was reminded not to forget the normal – the everyday person organising a funeral. I don't meet many of those. However, the charity's helpline has been operating for nearly 30 years and I have been in 'the trade' for 20, so have probably come across most scenarios.

To help me understand this challenge, I recalled my pre-death work days – a time when I knew nothing about funerals, and I do mean nothing. This is how most people are, I suppose – inexperienced and potentially 'vulnerable consumers'. All I knew back then was that everyone loathed the 'conveyor-belt process' at the crematoria and moaned about costs.

So who is at risk? Who are the people falling into 'funeral poverty'? Often the families contacting me will have reasons for hardship: dependency problems, unemployment, immigrants on basic wage, pensioners only just managing, students, bereaved carers with no savings, people with mental health issues and those on the minimum wage who are just keeping their heads above the water. In recent years, there has been a steep rise in enquiries to our helpline about funeral poverty.

The starting price for a basic, traditional cremation package across the UK (what the majority sign up for) is around £4,417 (SunLife, 2020).Could you rustle up that much money within a week, or three? Could your neighbour? The person opposite you on the park-and-ride bus or in front of you at the supermarket checkout?

Burial usually costs even more, especially for those living in urban areas, where cemetery space is at a premium. Most London boroughs, for example, charge more than £3,000 pounds just for the grave space. Last time I investigated these costs, one borough was charging more than £8,000. For these communities, and especially those for whom burial is an essential part of their tradition or faith, this can cause huge financial problems.

A survey in 2019 found that 12% of people would struggle to find this sort of money at a moment's notice, and that funeral poverty is rising – up 12% on the previous year (Royal London, 2019).

I have access to normal credit facilities, should I need them, but this is not the case for everyone. Some 14 million people live in poverty in the UK (Joseph Rowntree Foundation, 2020) – more than one in five of the population – and the unfolding economic downturn due to Covid-19 will make these figures dramatically worse. The average debt resulting from a funeral in 2019 was £1,490, up 14% since 2018. Between 2015 and 2018, there was a 70% increase in those turning to public health funerals (House of Commons Work and Pensions Committee, 2016).

The Department for Work and Pensions (DWP) offers a benefit, but the SF200 form is 23 pages long with 12 pages of advice and no payment is made before a bill has been presented, so families do not know if they will qualify for a grant until after the funeral has happened. There is a DWP helpline that you can call for advice (on 0800 731 0469). For some communities, like Muslims and Jews, with a religious requirement to bury within 24–48 hours, it is even harder. What is frequently misunderstood is that the eligibility relates to those paying for the funeral, not the status of the deceased. The 2016 Work and Pensions Committee review found that nine per cent of deaths led to claims for payment, of which six per cent got some level of payment.

Funeral costs have risen significantly above the rate of inflation. In 2020, the overall 'cost of dying' was £9,493 – up £289 since 2018, according to the 2020 SunLife report. Currently, there is a postcode lottery and higher prices in areas with less choice of funeral directors and consistently higher prices from the larger chains compared with independent funeral directors. This is a longstanding problem and led the 2016 Work and Pensions Committee review to recommend more scrutiny of funeral industry pricing.

I am firmly of the opinion that the first reason many people get into trouble with funeral costs is that they are ill advised and misled by an industry that knows full well their ignorance and vulnerability. I believe that many funeral directors are not placing all options on the table when families who need clear guidance walk through their doors.

The second reason is the taboo nature of the topic. The public are their own worst enemy by not researching or discussing death, dying and funerals. Consequently, too many bereaved folk fall into a cycle of following family 'tradition', choosing the formulaic, usual, standard funeral beloved by many undertakers. Fear of criticism and conflict within the community or family are common issues, but mostly it comes back to a lack of basic communication.

Sometimes relatives have a sense of, or are made to feel that, if they choose a more affordable option, they are in some way being disrespectful to the dead or cheapening the send-off; that they are being uncaring and unloving. You need to give permission to your family to do what they feel is best and can afford, so that they are strong enough to ignore these pressures, whether real or imagined. Just tell them: 'When I die don't you dare waste money on [fill in the space] and, while I'm on the subject and have your attention, I would like [fill in the space]. All the information you need and the funds are located [fill in the space]. Oh, and I have already bought my plot.'

Tell everyone, not just one relative, who will possibly be challenged and doubted by others when the time comes. By announcing your wishes to anyone who will listen, not only are you helping your family organise what is right for you but, importantly, having the discussion will reveal if your choice is right for them too. You will also be spreading knowledge of options and helping to break down this taboo situation.

The industry has relied on ignorance and silence for a long time. That, and the comforting ease with which folk can easily fall, exhausted, into a Stockholm Syndrome-like torpor. Understandable in the situation, I grant you. In shock, sleep-deprived and floundering in the unknown; unquestioningly trusting the empathetic, suited 'professional' on the other side of the desk. They are your new best friend, the expert; you can trust what they say, they know the facts, they know the law and what they are doing; this is their thing.

Funeral directors are not all bad or self-serving. However, these are the people who should be helping families avoid getting into debt. Instead, some are steering them straight into it. The good news is that things are so much better than they were when I entered the arena in 2000. For many, though, adequate guidance is still, unfortunately, pot luck. The natural burial grounds, the celebrants and the boutique/progressive undertakers are generally fabulous, but they still only enter the lives of a few – a fraction of the half a million-plus folk who die in the UK each year. We have a lot to do.

There is nothing worse for someone than to try to guess what the dead person wanted. On top of everything else, they have the added pressure of not knowing if they are choosing the right things at the right price. Actually, there is one thing worse than not knowing what to arrange; it's hearing people say, after the event, 'Why did no one tell me?' or 'If only I had known'. Finding out they have not done what was wanted or have arranged something inappropriate can mean that, on top of grief, they have to live with guilt. This is especially lamentable when it transpires that they have got themselves into financial difficulty unnecessarily.

However, there are situations where the dead's instructions may be either inappropriate for the family or beyond their means. In *All Sorted*, we can see how the husband's no doubt well-meaning plans, made directly with the funeral director, but not paid for before he died, ended up costing his wife £7,000 and sent her into a downward spiral of debt and eventual homelessness. And in *Nothing to Spare*, the poor wife was literally starving herself in order to pay the funeral director when her husband's life insurance policy fell short. Did either funeral director or anyone else tell these women that there were alternatives before they went through with these expensive funerals?

When families get in touch saying that they are struggling to find the funds to honour someone's wishes, my first response is always, 'This is not your fault. If they didn't leave sufficient funds to meet their wishes, you can only do your best. Find a compromise.'

Choices that help avoid trouble – if you find out about them in time
More affordable options and alternatives are increasingly available. You can arrange the following.

1. Direct, unattended funeral
These have really taken off in recent years. They cost between £850 and £1,700, cremation or burial, for an all-inclusive package, payable upfront. Families and friends (if there are any) can hold a separate ceremony/party/memorial service at a nicer venue another time, without the funeral director in tow. How about at the weekend, when more folk are free, you can have a time-rich experience at a lovely or more appropriate venue? No conveyor-belt slot with this option, and you'll save a couple of thousand pounds at least. (See Resources.)

2. Do-it-yourself
Cut out the funeral director and do the paperwork, coffin purchase, booking, fetching and carrying yourself. Same price as the direct option above, but you get to hold a ceremony with the deceased present. (See Resources.) If this is out of the question for practical reasons (you do need others to help carry the coffin), and you will need an undertaker's help, shop around. Another misapprehension is that a funeral director is a funeral director, that they are much of a muchness – they are not. Yet only five per cent of families shop around (Royal London, 2019).

3. Donate your body
This has to be organised by the deceased directly with the relevant authority before they die. Sometimes the donation is declined at the last minute, so it is important to have a Plan B. If accepted, the receiving organisation (often a teaching hospital, for example) will cover the cost of a cremation once they have finished with the body – which can be up to three years later.

4. Private land burial
Free and easy if you, or a friend, have land and aren't too concerned about future ownership and access. Surprisingly, you do not need anyone's permission. (See Resources.)

5. Mix and match
Any of the above with a flexible, package-free undertaker you have found by shopping around.

The last resort is to walk away and not take any responsibility for the funeral. You can hand the disposal (with registration, the only essential bit) over to the authorities. Different local authorities have different policies about attendance, communal graves, memorialisation and return of ashes. But they will be top of the list of creditors for any money that is available and will try to recoup what they've spent.

There are some benevolent funds – for ex-service personnel, for example – and some employers have a death-in-service package. Crowdfunding is another option for some but could be unreliable. More and more people are raising money for funerals through such online platforms as Crowdfunder or Just Giving.

Is funeral poverty the fault of those who have made no provision? Possibly, but then the funeral planning market can be a nightmare to navigate and it is all too easy to put off organising something. The Natural Death Centre is not a fan of plans and policies (see *Bad Advice*). There are a lot of rotten products about.

Much better to squirrel away the necessary amount, if you can, fill in a funeral wishes form (see Resources), and let your next of kin and executor know where these can be found, what the details are and what's covered.

Now you know how to avoid leaving a mess behind, please spread the word. The bottom line is: You don't need to spend £4,000 to have a fine funeral.

Advice points

1. Research and investigate your options.
2. Shop around.
3. Don't allow yourself to be bullied.
4. Communicate your wishes to those close to you while you are able to understand one another.

References

House of Commons Work and Pensions Committee. (2016). *Support for the bereaved*. House of Commons. https://publications.parliament.uk/pa/cm201516/cmselect/cmworpen/551/551.pdf

Joseph Rowntree Foundation. (2020). *UK Poverty 2019/20*. Joseph Rowntree Foundation. www.jrf.org.uk/report/uk-poverty-2019-20

Royal London. (2019). *Change on the horizon? National funeral cost index report 2019*. Royal London. www.royallondon.com/siteassets/site-docs/funeral-plans/national-funeral-report-2019.pdf

SunLife. (2020). *Cost of dying report 2020*. SunLife. www.sunlife.co.uk/siteassets/documents/cost-of-dying/sl-cost-of-dying-report-2020.pdf

Resources – A good funeral

Websites

Life. Death. Whatever: www.lifedeathwhatever.com (An initiative to re-design the dialogue around death and dying)

Scattering Ashes: https://scattering-ashes.co.uk (A useful website with lots of information about what to do with cremation ashes)

The Good Funeral Guide: www.goodfuneralguide.co.uk (Supporting, empowering and representing the interests of dying and bereaved people living in the UK)

The Natural Death Society: www.naturaldeath.org.uk/uploads/Forms/Questions%20to%20ask%20a%20funeral%20director.pdf (Questions to ask a funeral director)

Videos/films

A very natural DIY (dig-it-yourself) funeral. (2012, April 28). Wendii Miller. www.youtube.com/watch?v=BOXMa10WEXY

Dead good (2019). https://deadgoodfilm.com (An intimate documentary film about giving death back to the people)

Death, grief, ritual and radical funerals. (2015, November 5). Claire and Rupert Callender. TEDxTotnes. www.youtube.com/watch?v=GWBfWD2qGk0

This could be the last time. (2017, November 28). Louise Miller. TEDxKings CollegeLondon. www.youtube.com/watch?v=Iyakrq12AYc

What is natural burial? (2013, October 15). James Leedham. www.youtube.com/watch?v=oUQWh_3hgjs

Resources – Funeral poverty

Books

Astley, N. (Ed.) (2003). *Do not go gentle: Poems for funerals*. Bloodaxe Books.

Collins, N. (2000). *Seasons of life: Prose and poetry for secular ceremonies and private reflection*. Rationalist Press Association Ltd.

Doughty, C. (2014). *Smoke gets in your eyes: And other lessons from the crematorium*. Canongate.

Fox, J. & Gill, S. (1996). *The dead good funerals book*. Engineers of the Imagination.

Morrell, J. & Smith, S. (2006). *We need to talk about the funeral: 101 practical ways to commemorate and celebrate a life.* Alphabet and Image Ltd.

Toolis, K. (2017). *My father's wake.* Weidenfeld & Nicolson.

Ward, T. (2012). *Alternative pastoral prayers: Liturgies and blessings for health and healing, beginnings and endings!!!* SCM Press.

Watson, J. (Ed.). (2004). *Poems and readings for funerals.* Penguin Random House.

Wynne Willson, J. (1989). *Funerals without God.* The British Humanist Society.

Websites/blogs

Cremated Remains Information Bureau: www.crib-ndc.org

Fair Funerals Campaign: www. fairfuneralscampaign.org.uk

Incandescence Photos: www.maeveberry.com (Photos taken by Maeve Berry through the aperture of a cremator)

Natural Death Centre Charity: www.naturaldeath.org.uk (Provides a large range of free downloadable pdfs offering advice on funerals and funeral planning)

The Funeral Discourse. John Birrell: www.johnbirrell.com/blog.asp

Outside the Box

In the Wilds

11 – Grieving and remembering

Grief is selfish
I was a palliative care nurse for a hospital for many years. I went to all the courses and knew all the right things to say. Then my father died, and I realised I knew nothing. Grief is selfish – I grieved for myself, I was angry that he had gone and left me. That it was a 'good end' was irrelevant.

Saucepans
A lady whose husband had died after several years of being cared for by her at home phoned up three months after his death. There was only a wail at the end of the phone and then she managed to get out the words: 'My saucepans are too big.'

Crossed the road
My father died when I was 21. He had cancer but the death was sudden. I lived in London, and someone I knew well crossed the road so she did not need to speak to me. This was destroying at the time, but since that moment I have always approached friends, colleagues, relatives to acknowledge the death and their emotions.

What not to say
In the beginning I avoided others as I didn't want to engage with anyone but close friends. Some people also avoided me, but one acquaintance came to me and said, 'Oh my god,' and gave me a hug. That was okay because I am a hugger but people need to take care and read cues from someone bereaved. Saying 'How are you?' can be a loaded question as people often expect you to feel better. They're not prepared to hear that you're feeling terrible today. Asking 'How are you doing today?' is better, because every day is different. Questions and comments can be hurtful: e.g. 'I expect you're getting over it now'; 'I know

how you feel' (NO, you don't!); 'Would you ever think about meeting someone else?' (NO, NO, NO!); 'It isn't the end of the world'; 'Take some Prozac.' People I trusted, family and the bereavement group I attended were very important to be able to express myself safely. Being really understood and listened to.

Icy plunge

I am very much still married to my soulmate – it just so happens that my husband is physically dead. That doesn't make him any less my husband. I am, and will always be, his wife. It was only death, not divorce, after all! Grizzly died incredibly suddenly at 3:06pm on Tuesday 12th February 2019. We, along with our daughter, were at the gym, all training together. He had just finished his workout, slightly ahead of me. He gave me a huge grin, his gorgeous blue eyes twinkling. I grinned back. Then Grizzly, my huge, strong bear of a man was staggering backwards. He hit the floor and I was there in an instant. Despite the overwhelmingly fantastic efforts from the gym members and staff, ambulance crew and the Air Ambulance, who were all working furiously on the assumption he had suffered some kind of heart attack or cardiac arrest, Grizzly died right there in my arms on the gym floor. The post-mortem revealed that he had actually died from a massive brain haemorrhage. Nothing on earth could have been done to save him. Grieving my husband has been like being plunged into the middle of the Atlantic from a great height. First, breath-taking cold-water shock. Then frantic survival mode. Then numbness. Getting right to the very edge of wanting to quietly slip under. Hopeless. No sense of direction or purpose anymore, just relentlessly swimming and drifting in circles. I'm 43 – the wrong age to be a widow. He wasn't ill – there were absolutely no warning signs. It wasn't anyone or anything's 'fault' – I have nothing to rage against.

For the first few months, I felt like I had become a spare part in my own life. Going through the motions. It would have been so much less painful for me to simply check out. The thing that massively helped at the time was keeping track of exactly how many days, hours and minutes had passed since Grizzly died. It was a concrete reminder that I *could* keep going, as I had already got X amount of time under my belt and I was still hanging in there. At the time of writing, I have got through eight months, four weeks, one day, 22 hours and 56 minutes without my husband physically by my side. I'm bloody proud of that.

Please remember, I haven't just lost my husband, I've also lost a huge chunk of *me* – my sense of identity and all my hopes and dreams for the future. Every part of our personal and working lives were completely entwined.

Finally, please don't assume I'm somewhere in the 'five stages of grief' – it's only a model, it's not something that feels particularly relevant or useful to me. So no, I won't be 'moving on from' or 'accepting' Grizzly's death – but I am bending my life to accommodate it.

Don't leave us out

I'll be honest, whatever we felt deep down, Mike and I spent most of our last months together in denial. Behaving as though, if we just carried on 'as normal', life would follow suit.

In some ways, I'm glad that's how we coped. It was as helpful a reaction as any, meant we lived the life we loved to the fullest to the very last second – Mike was a European Election candidate the month before he died, and finished writing a book.

In the months (and years) immediately after his death, I was in a state of shock and disbelief. But it didn't show because I am very strong and able and never once collapsed in a puddle on the floor or couldn't get out of bed – though I occasionally wished I was the kind of person who did. I cried and had much support immediately after – there were many, many people in shock at his death.

But the grief and loss continued for me – obviously and subtly – whereas those around me were mostly off the hook.

I remember talking to two local dads who knew us and our children quite well – they also had small children we knew well. I asked them quite specifically to please remember our two-year-old when they were going to the park or the swimming pool or bike riding, to occasionally invite him along too. It never happened. I pointed out to a group of friends who used to get together to watch sport, rugby mostly (as we didn't have a TV), that I used to come along in my own right, not just because Mike enjoyed the game, and to please remember me. It never happened. I was told by one mum, when I asked directly why I didn't seem to be included any more, it was because 'I didn't have a mobile phone, so they couldn't text me'.

My guess is, it was all too painful, too raw, too much to deal with and we have no guidelines, no experience, nothing to tell us how to be supportive and 'get it right' when someone dies in a society that simply doesn't talk about death or acknowledge its existence and inevitability in any way.

Embodied grief

'Get the first flight home that you can,' said my father down the crackly line of my boss's mobile phone. Aged 22, standing in the South African sun, in the plant nursery where I worked, I didn't clock the finality of his words, even though they were plain as day. Denial comes all too easily to the inexperienced.

She died the night I got back. She was so drugged up on morphine when I got there, she was barely conscious, but she did see me, knew I was there with her. I felt so foolish; I'd brought photographs to show her. The next morning, standing there with my two older brothers and father, I couldn't even approach the bed, her body. I stood, back against the wall, in a state of disbelief: 'This can't be real, my mother can't be dead.'

She'd elected to donate her body to medical science, so that really was that, for over a year. We had a memorial lunch in the garden, but then nothing until the letter arrived informing us where and when her cremation would take place. Fourteen months had passed and there we were, just us close family, standing in a crematorium in a strange town, and a coffin, supposedly her coffin, was brought in.

It took me years to even realise I had not grieved for my mother. With no idea how to grieve, I had stuffed all the pain behind a door somewhere. But years later, when I went looking for that door, I couldn't find it. The tragedy, I realised, was that I had stuffed not just my grief behind that door but all of her, not able to separate out the pain from her memory. My dreams spoke of this – she would be there but would not talk or interact with me.

Years on, I went to a funeral of a friend, a new friend, one of those people you meet and know a firm friendship is in the making, but very soon after she was gone. I stood by her grave, her little wicker coffin in the mud. Most people, including the family, had left; just a small group of close friends were there, getting anything they could find, bits of wood, slates or simply using their bare hands to fill in the grave. I stood transfixed. Grief, it seems, is like a well within us; all mixed in together. I was feeling the loss of my mother and my friend.

One of the group, a lovely woman, came and put her arm around me and asked if I was okay. She was Irish, they were mostly Irish. She said, 'We think it's important that your friends tuck you in.' So I joined in, and in doing that, I learned how the body needs to be involved in grief. The doing of things around death is what helps us understand that the person isn't their body anymore. They have let go, and in our doing around death, we too let go, into grief.

Letters to heaven

Shakila was 40 when she died. I was 33. It was 1998. My world shattered. We were two women of south Asian Muslim heritage whose lives were completely intertwined. We lived together, worked together and moved in the same social circles. We had been together for six years and – unbeknown to our friends and families – were about to try to start a family with a gay male couple. Gay men did not have an equal age of consent. There were no civil partnerships. Equal marriage was still a dream. Gay Muslim and south Asian groups and networks existed, but (with one or two exceptions) mostly hidden from the common gaze. I was not Shakila's legal next of kin. I started my life as a widow with no route map for my journey.

We had both been embraced by each other's families, but our relationship had enjoyed a strange, indeterminate status that, under the impact of sudden bereavement, broke open to reveal its true character. Fortunately for me, my own family and a few close friends proved to be incredibly supportive. Her family was afflicted by the overwhelming distress of her mother, which was channelled in my direction (though, over time, I realised the injuries I sustained because of her must have been minor compared with those she had inflicted on herself). I found myself unable to share with those around me the layered anatomy of my grief in the aftermath of this double catastrophe: Shakila's death and the loss of my family out-of-law.

So I wrote a one woman play, *Letters to Heaven*. The play was a simple device to convey complex realities with an attention to very particular experiences that somehow point to universal themes. The spoken monologue, some of it in verse, interspersed with lines from songs, is mostly in the form of seven letters from me to Shakila, wherever she might be.

This is from the last letter.

'Well, it happened just like you said. But you left out a few minor details. You never told me I would keep getting letters addressed to you… that I would have to tell a thousand and one people that you had died – people who needed to know that you were there for them… that I would have to live knowing that you might still be alive if the doctors had just done a fucking brain scan… that people would phone me looking for you – an Urdu-speaking counsellor for some wretched woman whose in-laws had driven her nearly mad… that your mother would tell me that I had no right to your jewellery because it was for *your* nieces and nephews and not *mine*. You never told me how clearing out your bedroom would feel like evicting you from the house, how your clothes wouldn't fit anyone else, how big and bloody cold the bed would be without you… and how a box of out-of-date frozen frigging Yorkshire puddings would reduce me to a blubbering wreck. Listen to me! Don't pay any attention to all of this. I'll write again soon. Your own Razia'

Deeply felt

I was born in Norway and lived with my family on the edge of Molde Fjord, in the middle of that beautiful country, with a view from our house to some of the highest mountains in Europe.

When I was aged five, my father (Papa) died. We didn't go to his funeral. Nothing was explained, other than he had 'gone to a better place'. I didn't have any words for any of my confusion and within a few months we (Mum and three children) had uprooted to live in Dartmouth, South Devon. This harbour felt like a goldfish bowl after the vast expansive landscape of Molde Fjord.

I spent most of the next 15 years feeling lonely and sad, without understanding that this was grief. We just had to get on with life, without the tool of the words for the emotions that we all felt.

In my 30s, my career in textiles was beginning to establish itself at the same time as I was having a family.

One day I was asked to take part in an exhibition called 'Treading Lightly', the theme of which was to demonstrate the sustainable aspect of my craft practice. Thinking about the Cycle of Life and our disconnect with it as humans, I decided to make a wool-felt shroud for burial, which also came from a desire to reflect our heritage and ancient law around burial in wool.

The traditional process of making felt is very physical, rolling wetted raw wool fibres in an energetic way to make them felt together and shrink, similar to the actions of a washing machine on your best wool jumper! I had been making big pieces of felt for years and I loved my work, although it was very physically taxing and tiring.

I put the weight of my body into rolling the huge wet roll that was to become the shroud; back and forth for hours and days, because of course the first shroud was not right, nor the second. I sang songs in time with the rolling. The effort released physical energy that I didn't know was there; it was a catharsis!

I was thinking about death, really thinking about a body; *my* body perhaps, or that of someone I love, decomposing. And for the first time in my life, it wasn't scaring me. I can only describe it as an awakening. This was perhaps a Universal Shroud, indicating something gentler for our beaten-up planet, and my added grief for the Earth. I was aware that the grief I had held since the death of my father was being teased out from its deep seat within my psyche through the rhythmic, repetitive exertion of rolling the felt. It was the equivalent of bashing big cushions in a therapy session, but with a tangible end result; a woolly cocoon-like shroud.

I could at last admit that yes, one day I will die, and perhaps someone very lovely will tenderly tuck me into this woolly cocoon and put me in the earth, to be gently transformed by a billion tiny mouths into nourishing soil that gives rise to brilliant and abundant life.

Over the following years my career gradually took a turn in a different direction from artsy wall-hangings and one-off felt pieces to a shroud-making business, now in its 15th year.

What I have learnt is that grief can be helped by acknowledgement and engagement – engagement with the process and acknowledgement that you are grief stricken. We all have different ways of grieving; we just need to acknowledge them. Checking in with it will probably be a lifelong process. I have my father to thank for this Life lesson.

We will always remember you

My daughter Sharon died of breast cancer when she was 34. She was kind, generous, loving. She liked to make people happy.

I remember holding her when she was a tiny baby and feeling so much love, but also fear. How could I look after this small person, this new life? So many memories: her first tooth, her first steps, her first words, her lovely smile.

When Sharon was 32, she found a lump in her breast. She had two operations and chemo and radiotherapy, and after 18 months she was given the 'All clear'. But then, in the autumn, the cancer came back. She died the following June. It was so hot that year. I was beside her, holding her hand and feeling so helpless because I couldn't make her well.

And afterwards she was gone, and nothing would ever be the same.

So sad for all those things that she never got to do: holidays, new jobs, new friends... and having children; she would have been a lovely mum.

For me, life seemed lonely, grey and empty. In September, I went back to work, putting on a face and pretending I was fine. It was hard to talk to people about it. No one seemed to understand.

Eventually I started seeing a music therapist. The songs that I wrote helped me to start making sense of a life that seemed so meaningless without Sharon. My grief felt validated. Bob Heath helped me to get in touch with my good memories of Sharon. The songs held some of the sadness, so I didn't need to carry it. I would always feel the awfulness of losing her, but I was ready to go on with my life too.

I wrote a song for Sharon's 40th birthday. It's called, 'We will always remember you.'

Catharsis

My friend's dad died when we were both 17 and her mum's very alternative friend organised an evening where she and her sister sat in a circle while all their friends sat around singing and playing music. I thought it was a bad idea as they were being forced to grieve but it was, in fact, beautiful. We all cried until we were empty and then we laughed and shared stories and hot chocolate. I would love to be able to do that when I am grieving but don't want to force people to support me like that in such a naked sharing of emotion.

Grief

Silence.
It was over.
I was alone.
Orphaned.

I made a cover from one of her old cardigans,
put it round my hot water bottle.
In the morning, it was always cold again.

Then one day, a wall I had not known was there
fell down inside me.
I wandered amid the rubble of my grief
and found my mother.

No one had told me.
Perhaps we cannot be told.
We have to stumble across it for ourselves.
I did not know I could still talk to her.
I am not talking about spirits or ethereal presences.
I mean she is inside me.

Our conversations can continue.
I carry her in every cell of my body and in my heart.
And when I get out of bed in the morning now and look down,
I see her feet,
which makes me laugh.
I am sure they were not there before on the end of my legs.

Walking

My husband died in November 2015. I had been walking Offa's Dyke in stages with a local rambling group, so, in April 2016, I continued with them on the next stage. Although I was feeling raw and found it difficult to socialise – just wanting to cry as I walked – I shall always be grateful to my fellow Ramblers, who would gently ask me how I was doing. They listened to me unloading my grief and my anger and my need to recall events surrounding my loss. Nearly four years later, I am in a better place and currently walking the Coleridge Way with this group. It was interesting to compare notes with other widows and find we all agreed that walking and being among nature are lifesavers.

The value of group support

Death is so isolating. You draw back because you don't want the floodgates to open. Because people can't deal with you. And you end up saying, 'Oh don't worry, I'm fine.'

A few close friends, widows, could deal with it.

At the funeral I didn't cry; I didn't cry for six weeks. But I remember somebody saying afterwards, 'Well done, you did so well, and I would have expected nothing less – no tears.' I thought, 'Oh well, I've obviously achieved something.'

People didn't mention Archie so I would bring him into the conversation and some didn't know what to say. And the physical symptoms, the palpitations, the anxiety were really getting to me.

I lost my faith at first. I do remember spending several evenings on the floor of my bedroom, unable to move. Just in a heap on the floor, sobbing. Because it was unendurable. And sort of not wanting to go to sleep because I knew that when I woke up it would all start again, or I really wanted to go to sleep and not wake up. Facing another day was what I dreaded most, along with the fear of being totally vulnerable and exposed to the world, completely alone. That feeling comes over me every so often and still can reduce me to a heap of jelly when I want to run and hide.

But I didn't expect the depth of the anger. I think I suppressed it. I was fairly desperate by the time I came to a local bereavement group. It had been seven years.

And that wonderful group of ours has held all of us in different ways. It was frightening in the group at first, but a huge relief when I did open up. One feels out of control and I don't like feeling that. But the facilitators had this uncanny ability to make it feel a safe and secure place and that it was okay. I think I have hope now and the group gave me that. Meeting up with the other participants is something we all look forward to; we have a special bond because of what we have shared.

I don't know if the pain has changed or if I just have a greater degree of acceptance. It's here but it's part of the fabric of everyday life. You carry it around like a weight strapped to you. And I accept that it's there and weave it into every day. I talk to Archie quite a bit and say, 'Why aren't you here?' or 'I had such a lovely time with the grandchildren.'

It's like snakes and ladders and hopefully one day it will go more in favour of the ladders.

60 postcards

It was a chilly, December day in Paris. 2012 was the year. I was there for a long weekend with a group of friends. Fuelled with coffee and croissants, we strolled through the streets of Montmartre on our first morning. I clutched 60 postcards tightly to my chest. As I saw the Amelie café up ahead, I knew that it was the perfect spot to leave my first card. I remember smiling for the first time in a long while. There was magic in the air.

Earlier that year, our family's life was thrown completely upside down. My mum, Vivienne, after a very short period of feeling unwell, was diagnosed with secondary bowel cancer. It was aggressive. It was too late. Just 16 days after her diagnosis, my mother passed away in our family home. I had experienced grief before, but nothing like this. At times I felt numb, at others I felt in a state of complete disbelief. Waves of unrecognisable anger would crash over me. I was reduced to a sobbing mess every time I went to bed, with images of Mum's last two weeks haunting me in my sleep. I tried, with everything I had, to be strong. In my day-to-day life, I attempted to put my 'game face' on. 'I'm okay. Everything will be okay.' But my facade was fading fast.

What would have been Mum's 60th birthday was on the horizon, and I was desperate to find a new way of approaching another heart-breaking anniversary. Knowing my love for Paris – a city I had only ever adored from afar – Mum had bought me Eurostar vouchers for my birthday a few months before she died. This was the moment – this is what I would use those vouchers for. I would mark her birthday weekend with a trip to Paris. I emailed a group of friends and I was overwhelmed with love, as the confirmations rolled in.

My mum was a creative soul with an artistic flair. Rather than simply visit Paris in her memory, I wanted to create a fitting tribute for her that she would adore. And so, I bought 60 postcards – one for every year of her life – and handwrote the same message on each – a personal note about why we were visiting, that we were there to celebrate my mum's life. We would scatter these notes all around the city for strangers to find. Grief is universal. It may be felt and managed in unique ways, but it is an experience that unites us. And so, I left my email address on the postcards, asking the finders to get in touch with me. With a passion for writing, I would document the tales of the cards in a blog, using the creative postcard project to open up a conversation around grief.

On that first morning in Paris, I slipped the first postcard – message-side-up – on the table next to me, and almost skipped up the hill to catch up with my friends. I felt something I hadn't in so long. I was smiling, I was excited. I was doing something not only to remember my mum by but something that I knew she would love so much. Creativity had saved me. It had given me a sense of purpose and hope. It had given me something to keep going for and to keep her memory alive.

Just three days after my return to London, my phone buzzed. It was an email: 'Postcard found...'

Continuing bonds

My son Joshua died in a road accident while on holiday in Vietnam. This was in 2011 and he was 22. At the time of writing, 8½ years later, it could have been yesterday. And yet at the same time it feels an age ago. Grief seems to be timeless. It is also boundless. It has no frontiers. It has no colour and it makes no sound. Yet it creeps into every aspect of my life… of my new life without and with Josh.

In the early days, I know I felt abandoned by normality. I lost confidence in myself and trust in the world. My home, my family, my life were no longer safe. If Josh could die then… shit, anything could happen. I didn't care too much whether I died too except for the impact that would have for the rest of the family, but our mortality and the fragility of all our lives was certainly put into perspective.

How to mend the wound? How to heal our brokenness? At first it was just going through the motions. His mum and I don't hold to any particular faith tradition and our culture hadn't prepared us for any meaningful way of dealing with all the necessary things you have to do when someone dies. So 'going through the motions' inevitably meant trying to find or to create a funeral ritual that would honour our boy's life and his death in the best and most memorable way possible. Something different, something special, something that we could all (his family and all his many friends) look back on and say, 'Yes, Josh, we did you proud.'

In a way I think we were responding to a singular idea – that life is made up of the stories we tell each other. And it's by telling stories (the memories we have and the new things we have done since he died) that we have begun to repair that all-important relationship we still have with our dead son.

The tree planted on a farm where Josh and his friends would often gather has now become a Mecca for those same friends and family alike. Josh's friends continue to send him postcards when they go away somewhere interesting. That way they stay connected to him and we stay connected to them. It has brought us all closer. And these are all shared and communicative experiences. On Josh's still active Facebook page, we talk to him (Josh, we talk to *you*), and in speaking of Josh in these varied ways, we acknowledge that new relationship not only with him but with each other.

The drive to understand experience and make sense of the world is as vital as the need to breathe, to eat. 'Grief,' they say, 'is the form love takes when someone dies.' For us that is what grief is about. Our stories have turned into books, films and workshops for other bereaved parents and led us to create a new charity, The Good Grief Project (*www.thegoodgriefproject.co.uk*), that has taken us on a journey of discovery about how other parents grieve for their children.

The isolation of grief

When I was 21, I was involved in a road accident. I was on holiday with my girlfriend in the former Yugoslavia when the car we were traveling in was hit by another, ran off the road and fell into a deep and fast-flowing river. My girlfriend, Gillian, could not swim. She died. I survived. Totally unfamiliar with very unexpected feelings (particularly guilt and shame), and without the necessary understanding from friends or family (and without professional help), I understand now that I was unable to process my grief in a healthy way. Much of this really was the isolation that I experienced. Returning to London, I felt shunned by many of my friends, who had their own fears of how to behave, as well as my parents' need to protect me from extremes of emotions. This left me in a place where I felt completely disconnected both from Gillian and from my environment. The thing to do was to make the best out of a shit situation and to move on. I had the rest of my life to get on with and to allow a tragedy such as this to mark me felt like failure. But I had been marked and I had been changed. And without the adequate means, both personal and social, to express my feelings, and with no acknowledgement of the importance of the grieving journey, I think I became quite introspective, learning how to cope on my own, actively avoiding close emotional involvement. I lost contact with Gillian's family and to a degree I lost my way in life.

Unfuneral

When my mother died in 1998, we thought it would be good to bury her ashes and create a memorial in the garden of our family home. By then, however, the only person living at the house was my father, and we quickly realised our error – he felt tied to memories when he wanted to move on with his life. The 'unfuneral' in 1999 was actually a time of much laughter and we were all sure Mum would have seen the funny side of it. Dad sold the house soon afterwards and had a very happy second marriage. Mum's ashes were scattered, and my brothers and I don't need a memorial to remember her.

People can't cope

On my first day of university, my best friend died. Spending my time around entirely new friends who didn't know him was hard. I constantly wanted to bring him to the surface of my mind and would talk of him very often. Sadly, this made people uncomfortable; they really had no clue what to say or how to even just be present around it. I had a new girlfriend at the time and one day I couldn't hold it in in front of her. I released a lot of emotion – anger, sadness, shock, confusion – but she had no idea what to do, and she just looked at me, shocked. This kind of non-reaction and avoidance was, I think, the worst way to be around someone. It's just so sad – people are afraid to get human around each other.

Long enough

Being told, 'Look, it's three months now. That's long enough' was not helpful. How long is long enough? I will never be able to get back to 'normal' life. What is that anyway?

The curlew's cry

The first I heard about David's death was through a telex sent to work. A few words on a piece of flimsy paper announced utter finality. He died falling into an icy crevasse on a mountain at the age of 23 – a dramatic, horrible death in the cold and loneliness of a glacier. All the laughter and warm skin, the brown eyes and thoughtfulness – gone in a clipped sentence using a handful of economical words.

David loved wild places, but mountains in particular. Where else to go but to the hills to find him and try to hold his spirit as it drifted through the heather and floated over tarns. It's where he always wanted to be. Maybe death was a welcome gift that allowed him to stay wild forever, freed from the concerns that always accompany the living. He now inhabits every wild corner of this earth. But that is cold comfort to those of us who loved him as a living, breathing, loving embodiment of humanity.

Then I heard it, an unearthly aria from a different reality. A piercing, heartfelt cry, a 'love weep', as W.S. Graham called the call of the curlew. Was there ever a lonelier sound to a distressed soul?

Legend tells us that six curlews are constantly flying around the earth, calling, calling, trying to find the seventh. When they do, it will be the end of the world.

I watched a lone curlew soar over the ridge and disappear, calling as it went. I was glad to see it, even more so to hear its song, a bird that seemed to understand what this human was going through. It didn't try to pacify with awkward words, it simply gave voice to pain, and I was so grateful.

Today, the curlew is singing its own lament as it quietly but swiftly slips away from the marshlands, meadows and moors of Britain. If you hear it, treasure it, because life is so precious and so very vulnerable.

Now I am married to myself

After my husband had been dead about two years, I felt I had to take off my engagement and wedding rings. It was quite a thing and felt hugely important, relieving, sad and tearful all at the same time. I didn't know why it was so important to take the rings off; it just didn't feel right anymore to have them on.

I had a little ceremony in the woods at the back of the house, all by myself, where I took off both rings. What felt right was to have bare hands.

After a few weeks I realised, in a flash of inspiration, that I needed to buy a new ring and marry myself.

I found a ring in the local high street jewellers.

A few days later, the perfect place for the ceremony presented itself into my mind. A spot on the Findhorn river where I had gone skinny-dipping in the heat of the previous summer. It was important as a symbol of emerging to the world from the caves of grief.

So, having decked myself out in some new pretty lingerie, just like a bride would, and before I met with my women's group (who I knew would love to witness me having been married), I went off to the river, via a visit to a favourite café. Over a cup of coffee, I wrote in my journal some of my vows to myself.

Down by the rushing river, much higher than in the summer, I had a private little ceremony, with Philip's energy in the air, quietly and lovingly approving, and I put the ring on the finger of my right hand.

A change into a beautiful dress at home, then to the women's group and a celebration with them, with a special bottle of wine.

It was a beautiful ritual, it felt so good to just trust that whatever was right would come to mind. I still have the ring on today, even though I have now met a new man and we are building a new life together, because I will always now be married to myself.

Dia de Muertos

My name is Noe Orozco, I was born in Mexico and now live in the UK. I moved to Oxford with my British partner, Dawn, in 2006. We met in the Mexican state of Oaxaca (pronounced Wahaca), where the festivities of the Day of the Dead are a huge collective act, as well as a deeply family-oriented tradition, rooted in ancient indigenous rituals and Catholic beliefs brought by Spaniards. Dawn and I, as does almost everybody in Oaxaca during the festivities, used to set up a private altar in honour of the departed loved ones in a prominent place in our house. Every 31st October, we would go to the central market to join other thousands of people, selecting carefully the best marigolds, the brightest burgundy local flowers, special bread, candles, seasonal fruit, copal, elaborate colourful paper-cuts and sugar skulls to decorate our altar.

The process of buying all these goods, putting the altar together in the house, adding the pictures of the departed ones to our altar, and placing some of the favourite food and drinks that our friends and family used to like is for me an act of remembrance, profound love, deep respect, a reminder that one day we as well will not be in the flesh in this realm of existence, and a celebration of being alive. As Dawn said the other day, the 31st October, 1st and 2nd of November, it's a time when the grieving process is not carried alone or only with the family but shared with a few other millions of people who are doing the same as us and any emotion is welcome: sadness, anger, acceptance, love, joy, fear etc.

Since we moved to the UK, every year since 2006, Dawn and I have done our best to put an altar in the houses we've lived in to keep alive this tradition, which fills our hearts and spirits with love, joy and gratitude. Moreover, we began to invite close friends during those days to spend time contemplating the altar, light a candle in memory of someone and speak their name if they feel drawn to. They tell us they have got a lot from being given the opportunity and the safe space they needed to grieve and to remember those who are no longer with us.

Tending the graves

Growing up in Germany I have distinct memories about the whole cemetery culture.

Looking after the grave of the deceased is a big thing, from buying the stone to having the inscription to the actual care-taking of the grave.

Most relatives keep plants and/or flowers on the grave, whether they've chosen a marble slab or left the soil exposed. Then the weeding, watering and general upkeep of the grave begins. And you better not forget or the neighbours will gossip.

When the husband of our next-door neighbour died, Frau Seng went every evening with her watering can to the cemetery, often accompanied by her daughter and son-in-law. A meaningful ritual that helped her deal with her loss. On the way, she invariably met other mourners with their watering cans and little rakes, which must have provided an invaluable sense of comfort during a time of grief – a time where community is especially important.

Whenever I go back to Germany, I also visit my parents' grave, wash the marble slab, make sure the gardener who I pay looks after the grave and that the flowers look healthy. It is like an anchor that logs me into them and one of the ways to honour my parents and show my love and respect.

Traditionally, fresh flowers or pot plants are placed at Easter, birthdays and at Christmas. The most important one is advent, where everyone lays advent wreaths, fir branches and lights a candle in one of the red see-through candleholders. One meets others from the community and sees which grave belongs to who. A whole pile of fresh flowers, wreaths and ribbons means that someone has recently died. Seeing relatives around such a grave engenders extra respect and empathy. A shared silence, a respectful nod or a chat connects and can have immeasurable value, particularly to those who live alone.

Washed away

My sister lived alone. In July, we had planned for me to drive across to her house late on that Sunday night, to do a few days of building work. I had thought it strange that she hadn't contacted me during that weekend, but maybe her phone was out of order. When I arrived at midnight, the lights were on, but there was no answer to her doorbell. Walking round the house, her door was open and her dog came running out to see me. As I walked into the lounge, I found her lying dead, crumpled on the floor.

Looking back on that time, I now realise what a state of shock I was in and how I was 'ambushed' by the image of her body lying there.

That September, my partner and I took our campervan on a drive up the West coast of Scotland. We headed across to the far west coast, past Fionnphort, to a wild piece of coast. We had arrived late on a sunny afternoon, in that flat landscape with wide open skies, just as the tide was turning. We were parked 30 yards from a small sandy cove on which nobody had walked. I sat on a rock, watching the setting sun, thinking of my sister and how I had never had the chance to say goodbye. So I drew her name in the sand and watched while the tide gently carried her away.

In mourning

In Guyana, back in the day, the wife and children wore black for three months, then grey for three months and then bright colours again. The young ones don't do that any more, but you see that the older ones still do.

Meeting my Japanese in-laws

Nearly 40 years ago, when I was a young English teacher working in Japan, I was invited to the family home of the man I was later to marry. We both lived in Tokyo at the time, and his family home was some six hours away by bullet train. I had already met his mother, when she was visiting Tokyo, but not the rest of his family.

The first person we greeted when we got to the house was my boyfriend's father. Unsurprising, you might think, except that his father had been dead since my boyfriend was 13. Dominating the main room of the small house was a large, elaborately carved Buddhist altar, rather like a carved wooden box on a platform with legs, with its doors open. This was the place that enshrined my boyfriend's father's memorial tablet, with his posthumous Buddhist name, a small container with some of his cremated remains (the remainder were kept at the temple to which the family belonged) and a large photograph of a smiling man in early middle age. He looked welcoming. My future husband introduced me to his father and spoke to him briefly.

After all these years, my memory of the other details has faded. But what I recall most vividly, as an English person new to Japan, was my surprise at being introduced to someone who at that point had already been dead for eight years, and also a sense of discomfort at a memorial to the dead being at the centre of a space inhabited by the living – this was very unfamiliar to me, coming from a background where there was a much clearer spatial separation between the living and dead.

However, in the years that followed, I came to take these interactions with my father-in-law increasingly for granted. And when our children were born, we introduced them to him too. As they got older, they also learned to greet their grandfather, placing their hands together and bowing to the altar and offering incense.

For ordinary Japanese lay people, like my in-laws, the family Buddhist altar is a focus for remembering dead family members. And through this, the dead continue to be important members of the family, even as the family grows to include new members.

Cheers!

When my grandmother died, I was away, in Germany, and when I heard about her death, I bought a beer and drank a toast to her. My mother will never forgive me for this. She thinks it was disrespectful, but the fact is that I was celebrating my grandmother's life, and I don't regret it. She is always with me and I feel her near me. And I'll always celebrate her life.

How do I remember them?

Nearly three years ago, my brother was killed on his motorcycle when a car pulled out in front of him. Also, my father died this December, fairly quickly and suddenly of cancer. What seems to perplex my family is my lack of interest in their possessions. I just don't want or need things to remember them by. This seems to cause some form of disquiet or upset for my family. I just think we all need to respond in the way we feel comfortable.

History lesson

Queen Victoria commanded that Prince Albert's clothes were laid out on his bed every single day after he died, until she herself died. The stranglehold of rigid mourning. We turned our back on all of that. Black is almost banished. No mourning rings or lockets of hair for us. We live without custom or comfort in a society where kind, well-intentioned people still cross the road to avoid meeting a bereaved friend. That has to change. Bring back mourning tokens. Nothing fancy. Something we all recognise for what it is. A token to say I am grieving. I want you to know this. Don't ask me to keep my chin up and get over it quickly to avoid upsetting you. Celebrating is celebrated in our society – sadness is much harder to tolerate.

Commentary

Life after a death – Dr Marilyn Relf, Chair, National Bereavement Alliance

Marilyn has more than 30 years' experience working in palliative and bereavement care. She set up one of the first hospice bereavement services, at Sir Michael Sobell House, Oxford, and has been widely involved in research, writing and education in relation to bereavement. She is a founder trustee of SeeSaw, a bereavement service for bereaved young people in Oxfordshire, and is a member of the International Working Group on Death, Dying and Bereavement. She chairs the National Bereavement Alliance, which provides a national voice for bereavement services. In 2017, Hospice UK presented her with a lifetime achievement award for her contribution to palliative care.

In this chapter we hear the voices of bereaved people and their experiences of grief and mourning. Descriptions of bereavement often give the impression that there is a 'grief process' that is more or less the same for everyone. We read that we will 'work through' a number of 'stages' in order to come to a point of 'acceptance' or – awful word – 'closure'. The moving stories in this chapter reveal that, although grief is universal, it is an individual experience. As one person says (*Continuing Bonds*), grief 'is the form love takes when someone dies'.

When a central person in our lives dies, we grieve, even if the relationship was complex and not always warm and loving. How we mourn varies widely and reflects our relationship with the deceased, how they died and the expectations and responses of the people we meet in daily life – our family, friends and colleagues. Reading the stories in this chapter reveals the depth and breadth of reactions, the sorrow and, maybe surprisingly, the joys that we can find in celebrating and remembering, in the continuing importance of our relationships with those who are no longer physically present, and in discovering new positives about ourselves that may emerge from loss.

The accounts here are full of the challenges of mourning. Has it always been so difficult to grieve? In the UK, as in many other countries in the Western world, it is common not to experience bereavement until late middle age. We live longer, healthier lives, child mortality rates are low, health care has improved; so, although we are no strangers to loss, we often feel unprepared for the depth of our reactions following a significant bereavement. Sadly, there is a general lack of understanding about grief and our society avoids sadness and suffering. Those around us may not know what to say and may feel perplexed and helpless when our grief doesn't 'resolve' easily. It's not surprising that bereaved people often feel misunderstood, isolated or abandoned.

A lack of understanding is a key theme in this chapter. In many of the stories, we read of a longing to feel heard and understood. We are social beings and other people's reactions can be helpful, but they may also be extremely hurtful. One study suggests that this lack of support is related to an existential anxiety in the face of the reality of mortality (Davidowitz & Myrick, 1984). In the study, ordinary people were asked, hypothetically, what they thought the bereaved would find helpful. The majority said that listening and empathy would be paramount but, in the same study, when bereaved people were asked about how others had reacted to them, they described experiencing the opposite. Inappropriate advice was the most frequent response encountered; empathy was only experienced by a minority. It would appear that, when faced with grief, we find it difficult to draw on our innate understanding and respond helpfully. As the young man comments in *People Can't Cope*, 'It's just so sad – people are afraid to get human around each other.'

Another factor that can limit support is the dominant cultural expectation in societies like ours in the UK that prize stoicism and emotional control above expressing feelings. Although this may be becoming weaker, with more permission, for example, for men to show emotion, it is still influential. We internalise expectations about how we should behave and express grief. Walter (1999) describes how, despite regional, religious and ethnic variations, both men and women are encouraged to keep grief private and avoid expressing undue sadness in public. He writes that the acceptable face of grief in the UK is to indicate that we are mourning while maintaining emotional control. As the widow in *The Value of Group Support* describes, she was praised for not showing emotion at her husband's funeral: 'Well done, you did so well... no tears.' She thought, 'Oh well, I've obviously achieved something.'

Studies of bereaved people provide insights that can help us to understand our reactions and how to help others. Traditional theories are widely known. These include 'stage theory', which was actually developed by Kubler-Ross (1969) to describe the grief of a dying person, not a bereaved one. More useful are the 'phases' or 'tasks of grief' (Parkes, 1986; Worden, 1983). In this chapter, we see evidence to support this broad understanding. There are descriptions of initial reactions of shock, numbness and disbelief, followed by 'unendurable', overwhelming feelings, such as deep sorrow, yearning for the deceased, unexpected anger and despair, as the grieving widow describes in *Icy Plunge*:

> Grieving my husband, has been like being plunged into the middle of the Atlantic from a great height. First breath-taking cold-water shock. Then frantic survival mode. Then numbness. Getting right to the very edge of wanting to quietly slip under. Hopeless. No sense of direction or purpose anymore, just relentless swimming and drifting in circles.

These theories have their limits, however, and more recent research (see Hall (2014) for an overview) has added much-needed depth to the way we understand grief. Unfortunately, these insights have not yet permeated everyday thinking. As the people in this chapter tell us, grief is multi-layered, it is more than an emotional experience and it is not linear. Grief does not flow from one recognisable stage to another. The final phase of 'acceptance', with its implications of 'forgetting' in order to 'move on', has proved to be a particularly controversial concept. As we read in this chapter, in reality we maintain a relationship with the deceased: 'I am very much still married to my soulmate – it just so happens that my husband is physically dead' (*Icy Plunge*).

The reality that people continue to be important to us even though they are not physically present is emphasised by 'continuing bonds' theory (Klass et al, 1996). Useful insights have also been provided by Tonkin (1996), based on her work with many bereaved people. She describes how grief does not disappear; rather, it remains part of us and we find a way of living with it. As one person writes here, grief became part of the fabric of her everyday life: 'I accept that it's there and weave it into every day' (*The Value of Group Support*). Another talks of 'bending my life to accommodate it' (*Icy Plunge*). Nowadays, social media bonds, such as maintaining Facebook pages, can allow us to continue to talk to the deceased, although this is not always problem-free. Reading other peoples' perspectives can bring pain as well as comfort and fresh grief can be triggered if the pages are taken down without warning (Kasket, 2019).

Often we read about linear timeframes associated with stages or phases of grief. This was not part of the original theory, but seems to have sunk into our collective way of thinking. In these pages, we hear how others expect grief to be time-limited: 'It's three months now. That's long enough.' We should be reluctant to place a timeframe on grief. Some people will adjust to life without the deceased within months, but others will find the second year harder than the first. Bereavement is a life-changing event. Our friends and family may want us to return to 'normal' as soon as possible and may be reluctant to accompany us on our journey towards finding a new 'normal', with its stops and starts and reversals.

Stroebe and Schut's 'dual process model' (1999) is particularly helpful in understanding grief. They found that bereaved people do not grieve all the time; rather, grieving behaviour oscillates between expressing and controlling emotions. Avoiding emotion means that grieving people are more able to cope with living in a changed world, rebuild their lives and manage the demands of work, parenting etc. Both aspects of grief can be stressful but seem to be a necessary part of making sense of our loss and building a future without the deceased. However, doing so can be tough, and this chapter is replete with descriptions of the stress of trying to appear strong.

Stroebe and Schut (1999) describe how grief can change over time, with perhaps more focus on emotional responses in the early months. Women may find it easier to express emotion and men may focus on problem-solving, but this is not always the case. Women may also cope by problem-solving and neither pattern of coping is likely to be helpful if allowed to be dominant. People who strive to strictly control their emotions may find their efforts defeated and that strong feelings break through their defences. This can be overwhelming and lead to a greater sense of vulnerability, particularly if accompanied by guilt or shame about 'giving in' to emotion.

Recognising that grief is multidimensional also helps us to understand how challenging it can be. Grief may affect our physical and mental wellbeing, our ability to think, focus and concentrate, and our sense of who we are and how we find meaning in our lives. It is not surprising that we can also find it hard to cope with work and everyday tasks, and that our relationships with others are affected.

Bereavement has been rated as the most stressful experience that we will encounter in our lifetimes. It is not surprising that it is associated with physical and psychological health problems. Bereaved people may experience physical symptoms such as palpitations, muscle tension and sleep disturbance, which are linked to stress. We may self-medicate by drinking more alcohol. Our sleep patterns may be disturbed and we may suffer nightmares. It is not surprising that our immune systems and general health may be affected. Up to a third of bereaved people experience mild to severe depression or debilitating anxiety, particularly after an unanticipated death. Sometimes it can be hard to go on. As one person describes in this chapter, she wanted to go to sleep and not wake up: 'It would have been so much less painful for me to simply check out' (*Icy*

Plunge). These feelings usually accompany deep despair rather than indicating that the person is intending to end their life. As one man writes here: 'I didn't care too much whether I died too except for the impact that would have for the rest of the family' (*Continuing Bonds*). If someone is talking about not wanting to go on, we should always ask, 'Is it so bad, you've thought of ending it all?' This can help people to tell us more about how they are managing. If they do describe concrete ideas about suicide, it's important to urge them to contact their GP.

Grief also affects our sense of self. Parkes (1971) calls grief a psycho-social transition from 'life as it was meant to be' to the new world without the deceased. It may feel as if everything has been thrown up in the air and come down in the wrong place. As one person writes here: 'I've lost a huge chunk of *me*, my sense of identity and all of my hopes and dreams for the future' (*Icy Plunge*). It can feel as if we have lost our compass, are unable to find our way, and that life lacks meaning and purpose.

Research into emotional wellbeing and resilience suggests that being able to talk openly and honestly to others and feeling supported by them is of great importance. Walter (1996) argues that talking about the deceased with our friends and family helps us to grieve. By sharing memories, we can explore who and what we have lost, their role in our lives and how we can carry on. This approach is summed up in this chapter by a grieving father (*Continuing Bonds*):

> ... life is made up of the stories we tell each other. And it's by telling stories (the memories and the new things we have done since he died) that we have begun to repair that all important relationship that we still have with our dead son.

This can be difficult, however, and it may be easier to pull back socially. As described in this chapter, some people want to run and hide. Sharing memories and our loss with family and friends can be daunting as well as helpful. Withdrawal from mainstream life is accepted in some cultures, and it was a feature of Victorian female mourning behaviour (but not if you were poor, when you were expected to stiffen your lip and get on with it). It can provide safety and a time to reflect, grieve and remember. Nowadays, however, such behaviour can be baffling for friends and colleagues.

Walter (1999) describes differences in mourning by comparing cultural norms using the dimensions of expression/non-expression of feelings and formal and informal rituals. Examples may suggest stereotyping, but this is not meant; rather, these dimensions can be used to consider how culture may influence grief. For example, as a generalisation, Catholic Irish, Orthodox Jews, Hindus and Muslims have clear funeral and mourning customs that ritualise the expression of emotion in a way that would be embarrassing for many

English people. Parts of England, Scotland and Ulster also have formal rituals, but the expression of grief is more reserved or discouraged. In California, and some parts of the UK, emotional expressiveness is encouraged and traditional rituals have largely been abandoned. In other parts of these countries, the norm is to be more reserved and traditional rituals are distrusted. Walter suggests that grieving people who distrust ritual and are reserved may feel particularly isolated.

Using this framework with people from varying cultural backgrounds can lead to rich discussions. For example, I witnessed a discussion between a woman with a Caribbean family heritage and another from Uganda, which revealed marked differences. The former valued reserve and the latter emotional expression. The latter felt that she was not understood by English colleagues, whereas the former found healthcare professionals' encouragement to express emotion was misguided and out of step with her cultural values.

Sharing with family and friends can also be difficult if people are grieving in very different ways. We read here how one storyteller caused a rift with their mother by toasting their grandmother with a bottle of beer (*Cheers!*). In *How do I remember them?*, the writer finds themselves considered somehow lacking because they don't want material tokens to remind them of the dead.

Ritual can help to legitimise and provide a framework for grief. In this chapter, we hear descriptions of helpful Japanese, German and Mexican rituals. These create continuing bonds, community and understanding. In Japan, 'the family Buddhist altar is a focus for remembering dead family members. And through this, the dead continue to be important members of the family' (*Meeting my Japanese In-Laws*). In Germany, marking advent by taking wreaths and candles to graves brings people together (*Tending the Graves*): 'A shared silence, a respectful nod or a chat connects and can have immeasurable value.' In the UK, sharing elements of the Mexican Day of the Dead with friends has provided others with 'the opportunity and the safe space… to grieve and to remember those who are no longer with us' (*Dia de Muertos*) As well as these moving accounts, in this chapter we also hear how rising secularity and a lack of consensus around ritual may cause problems: '… our culture hadn't prepared us for any meaningful way of dealing with all the necessary things you have to do when someone dies' (*Continuing Bonds*). One person describes how we 'live without custom or comfort, where kind, well-intentioned people still cross the road to avoid meeting a bereaved friend' (*History Lesson*), and describes how helpful it would be to bring back some of the Victorian tokens that signalled to others that someone is grieving: 'I want you to know this. Don't ask me to keep my chin up and get over it quickly to avoid upsetting you.'

These pages also reveal how people are using remarkable creativity to develop new rituals to honour the dead. Examples include scattering postcards around Paris, planting a tree to create a place to meet and remember, planting roses in favourite pub gardens, pounding out a felt shroud (and moving thence into a new, more meaningful career path), and developing resources for others who are sharing the same type of loss. In these accounts, we sense the transformative power of creativity. As a grieving daughter writes: 'Creativity had saved me. It had given me purpose and hope. It had given me something to keep going for and to keep her memory alive' (*60 Postcards*).

As described earlier, grief is highly individual. Some people do not experience high levels of distress, or do so over a relatively short period. This is more likely if there is time to prepare for loss and if the death is timely. There is a great difference between the impact of an untimely death of a young mother cut off in her prime and the expected death of an elderly person following a fulfilled life. A minority of bereaved people do experience enduring high distress, and we read here of one person experiencing seven difficult years before finding a way through by attending a bereavement group (*The Value of Group Support*). Studies suggest that levels of grief reflect the degree of distress caused by the illness and/or death, our relationship with the deceased (e.g. very close or very ambivalent), a lack of helpful support, and simultaneous stressful events such as multiple bereavements, redundancy and housing or financial problems (Stroebe et al, 2006).

Many of the people whose voices we hear in this chapter have experienced unexpected or untimely bereavements. Bereavement following a distressing illness can leave traumatic memories: 'I was reduced to a sobbing mess every time I went to bed, with images of Mum's last two weeks haunting me in my sleep' (*60 Postcards*). We also hear about the long-term impact of bereavement in childhood, when the child is not helped to understand what is happening and their grief is not acknowledged.

How can we help?

Human beings seem to be primed to care for each other but, as this chapter reveals, this seems particularly difficult in relation to bereavement. We cannot remove the pain of loss but we can do much to ease the loneliness of mourning. In order to be helpful, we need to recognise that the majority of bereaved people want to talk about the deceased and about their grief. We need to overcome our anxiety about saying the wrong thing and making it worse. As we read here, we should not underestimate the healing power of listening attentively and showing empathy. We need to be willing to do this long term, not just for a few weeks. We need to let people tell the story of the death in detail so that it may become more manageable. If we knew the deceased personally, we can share memories and stories; if not, we can ask what the person was like, how they met, what their lives were like together and what they miss most (and least!).

This does not need to be an intense encounter; it can be built into shared activities. As we read here, walking and talking (and listening!) in natural surroundings can be particularly helpful. Practical help is often welcome, especially if it is offered beyond the immediate crisis of the death, when the business of the funeral and the intensity of support have passed. We should remember that grieving is long term and that birthdays, anniversaries and special days such as Christmas and Mother's and Father's Days can trigger fresh waves. Above all, we need to be sensitive to what the bereaved person wants. Remembering Stroebe and Schut's (1999) model of oscillation between different ways of coping, we should recognise that sometimes people may not want to talk. As one person in this chapter points out: 'People need to take care and read cues from someone who is bereaved' (*What Not to Say*). It can be daunting to offer support, and at times it can feel like treading on eggshells, but being brave enough to overcome our anxieties is likely to deepen our relationship and be rewarding both for the bereaved person and for us. Dodie Graves' book *Talking with Bereaved People* (2009) offers further insight into how to help bereaved people (see Resources).

People often feel particularly anxious about supporting bereaved children. Above all, it is important not to overprotect children, to involve them so that they understand what is happening, and to give age-appropriate explanations about death and grief. (See Chapter 4, 'The Wisdom of Children', for more about this.)

As a friend, we can do much to help. However, some people may need additional support. Signs that indicate that additional support may be helpful include:

- persistent suicidal thoughts, especially if combined with concrete plans to end life
- feeling overwhelmed by persistent distress and sadness, especially if enduring for months
- feeling continually disturbed by traumatic memories or flashbacks relating to the illness or death
- grief affecting the ability to cope with everyday life
- a lack of support and feelings of isolation
- needing to talk about topics that are difficult to share with family or friends.

Nowadays, there are many services for bereaved adults and children. These range from mutual-help groups to specialist bereavement services (see Resources). Local services may be available from Cruse Bereavement Care, hospices/palliative care services, the Compassionate Friends, Age UK, Maggie's and faith groups. Meeting other bereaved people by attending drop-in sessions or support groups may be enough. One-to-one bereavement support and counselling is provided by Cruse Bereavement Care and by many hospice/palliative care services. GPs can refer people to psychological services that provide cognitive behavioural therapy (CBT) and to mental health services, if needed. National organisations such as Cruse Bereavement Care, the Compassionate Friends, Child Bereavement UK, Macmillan and Sue Ryder provide information about bereavement on their websites and may also host chat rooms. National organisations have been set up to help people affected by specific types of death, such as road accidents or suicide. A central directory of services to help people locate support is available from 'At A Loss'. You can find details of this and a list of key national websites in the Resources section at the end of this chapter.

In this chapter, we read that grieving and remembering can be hard work. Bereavement may cause us to re-evaluate our lives and who we are, as we learn to live without the deceased. We also read that loss can lead to personal growth and bring a greater sense of self-reliance and resilience. People describe how grief can be liberating. We are also reminded that the deceased are not lost to us. We carry them with us, as they have helped to make us who we are and influence who we will become.

Advice points

- Grief is universal but individual; it does not follow a linear path or timeframe.
- It is multidimensional and may affect our health, concentration and thinking, our sense of self, our beliefs, our relationships and our ability to cope with everyday life, as well as our emotions.
- We absorb and build our lives around our loss as we adjust to life without the physical presence of the deceased.
- Our relationships with the dead continue to influence who we are – we do not forget.
- Supportive, empathic listening is a powerful way of helping, but some bereaved people may benefit from additional support beyond that available from family and friends.

References

Davidowitz, M. & Myrick, R.D. (1984). Responding to the bereaved: An analysis of 'helping' statements. *Journal of Death Education*, 8(1), 1–10.

Graves, D. (2009). *Talking with bereaved people: An approach for structured and sensitive communication.* Jessica Kingsley.

Hall, C. (2014). Bereavement theory: Recent developments in our understanding of grief and bereavement. *Journal of Bereavement Care, 33*(1), 7–12.

Kasket, E. (2019). *All the ghosts in the machine: The digital afterlife of your personal data*. Robinson.

Klass, D., Silverman, P.R. & Nickman, S.L. (Eds.). (1996). *Continuing bonds: New understandings of grief*. Taylor & Francis.

Kubler-Ross, E. (1969). *On death and dying*. Routledge.

Parkes, C.M. (1971). Psycho-social transitions: A field for study. *Social Science and Medicine, 5*(2), 101–115.

Parkes, C.M. (1986). *Bereavement: Studies of grief in adult life (2nd ed.)*. Tavistock Publications.

Stroebe, M. & Schut, H. (1999). The dual process model of coping with bereavement: Rationale and description. *Death Studies, 23*(3), 197–224.

Stroebe, M., Schut, H. & Stroebe, W. (2006). Who benefits from disclosure? Exploration of attachment style differences in the effects of expressing emotions. *Clinical Psychology Review, 26*(1), 66–85.

Tonkin, L. (1996). Growing around grief – another way of looking at grief and recovery. *Bereavement Care, 15*(1), 10.

Walter, T. (1996). A new model of grief: Bereavement and biography. *Mortality, 1*(1), 7–25.

Walter, T. (1999). *On bereavement: The culture of grief*. Open University Press.

Worden, J.W. (1983). *Grief counselling and grief therapy*. Routledge.

Resources

Books

Abrams, R. (1992). *When parents die*. Charles Letts.

Forster, M. (2007). *Over*. Chatto & Windus.

Graves, D. (2009). *Talking with bereaved people*. Jessica Kingsley.

Lewis, C.S. (2015). *A grief observed (Reader's Edition)*. Faber and Faber.

Macdonald, H. (2014). *H is for hawk*. Jonathon Cape.

McLoighlin, J. (Ed.). (1994). *On the death of a parent*. Virago.

Porter, M. (2015). *Grief is a thing with feathers*. Faber and Faber.

Rentzenbrink, C. (2017). *Manual for heartache*. Picador.

Riley, D. (2019). *Time lived without its flow*. Picador.

Weller, F. (2015) *The wild edge of sorrow: Rituals of renewal and the sacred work of grief*. North Atlantic Books.

Websites

At a Loss: www.ataloss.org (Signposting website to help bereaved people find support)

Cruse Bereavement Care: www.cruse.org.uk (National organisation providing telephone counselling, on-line support, information about adult and children's grief and a dedicated website for young people)

Grief Encounter: www.griefencounter.org.uk

Health Talk: www.healthtalk.org (Has a section on a wide range of types of bereavement)

Hope Again: www.hopeagain.org.uk ('Young people living after loss')

Hospice UK: www.hospiceuk.org (National organisation for hospice and palliative care. Includes 'Find a Hospice' directory)

National Bereavement Alliance: www.nationalbereavementalliance.org.uk (Aims to support those who work with bereaved people)

Respond: www.respond.org.uk (A trauma informed organisation supporting people with learning disabilities and autism)

Samaritans: www.samaritans.org

Silence of Suicide: www.sossilenceofsuicide.org

Sue Ryder: www.sueryder.org (Palliative, neurological and bereavement support)

The Compassionate Friends: www.tcf.org.uk ('Supporting bereaved parents and their families')

The Dad Project: www.brionycampbell.com/projects/the-dad-project/ (Briony Campbell's photos and film about losing her father to cancer)

The Good Grief Project: www.thegoodgriefproject.co.uk (Dedicated to understanding grief as a creative and active process)

60 Postcards: www.60postcards.com (Rachael Chadwick's project to celebrate and remember her mother)

Podcast

Grief cast. (2018). Cariad Lloyd. ('Funny people talking about death and grief.') https://play.acast.com/s/griefcast

Outside the Box

12 – Death as a teacher

Tongues in trees

Loss is so written into love of any kind that we all belong to this same family of being human. The leaves on the trees soon fall. They too are kindred. Belonging to the earth, they whisper, means greening, dying and seeding again.[1]

Sometimes it just is

I met Mike for the first time seven weeks ago. The day I met Mike was the day that we both started on the same medical trial and the same regime of treatment for the same throat cancer. We were a little bit wary of each other at first, but that changed quickly. Then the checking in, the understanding, the finding humour and the sharing experiences became an important part of the Mondays we spent lying opposite each other having our five hours of chemotherapy and the times when our daily radiotherapy sessions coincided.

But we never got to ring the end-of-treatment bell together.

Mike's immune system took a nosedive. So much so that he would not have been able to cope with chemo. To look after himself, to be as normal as he could be, he went to the pub with his family. He picked up an infection and died the next day.

I've realised how strong the urge is, when something goes wrong, like getting cancer, to find reasons and to apportion blame: why me, why now, why this, what did I do, what did I not do, what should I, you, they have done? Perhaps that's one of the hardest lessons we have to learn, in our Western traditions anyway, when it comes to unavoidable death; we expect there to be a reason, we expect there to be a blame and we expect to understand. We don't expect to have to accept that sometimes, well, it just is.

---

1. From: Ward, T. (2012). *Alternative pastoral prayers: Liturgies and blessings for health and healing, beginnings and endings*. Canterbury Press.

I'm going to live every day

I was diagnosed with terminal cancer at 60 recently and have gone from believing the diagnosis to believing something else is possible. I'm going to live, love, dance, sing and celebrate every day. And celebrate my religion – nature. I've confronted death and am so glad that it is being spoken about more now and celebrated with laughter and tears. I'm not afraid of emotion now and have become less afraid of death.

Seeing you at last

My father was abusive. I always feared his disapproval, his taunts, all the rest. When he died, for the first time in my life I was able to look for a long time into his face without any fear. I saw *him* for the first time. A frightened, weak and damaged man.

Last lesson

My mum died aged 66. She suffered from MS and was a wheelchair user. The very last words she said to me were, 'Are you happy?' I live my life according to these three little words, and if I am not happy, she gives me the courage to make a change.

Buddhist way

As a Buddhist nun, I contemplate daily my own death, which can happen at any time. This contemplation leads me to the realisation that my life is precious, so I must not waste it in meaningless activities. I must make it meaningful by benefitting others.

Am I good enough?

Faith talks about death a lot. Every week when we celebrate the Eucharist, we tell the story of Jesus's death, and it has such potency that we are still doing it 2,000 years after the event. You might think that we would be at ease when our own time came, but of course doctrine and reality are not always aligned. Many people nowadays know that they are dying, and if they have a faith, it's natural to want to have conversations that include that dynamic. There are people who have the most amazing sense of being held by God and their death is for them like giving their life back to their creator.

Much more challenging for me as a pastor is the person who has been taught to be afraid of God. So this is the story of someone I'll call David.

David's wife rang me. She said that David had been told that he was dying and would I go and visit him. We met and I said how sorry I was at his diagnosis, but he wasn't at all concerned about it. He fully accepted that we will all die and that it was simply his turn. Then he began to weep. 'I know I'm not good enough. God will look at me and know that I've been selfish, and unkind and thoughtless. I haven't been a good person.'

David had been going to church for most of his life. His faith was real but powerfully imprinted on his soul was the idea that God was judge, not that God was love. He wasn't afraid of death but he was afraid of God.

The next few weeks were fascinating. Death taught him so much. It taught him that he no longer had the opportunity to run marathons for charity, that he couldn't change the past, that he couldn't even change who he was. So together we made a map of what he might learn. I suggested that he might think about saying sorry, and then listen, really listen to how his family replied and, crucially, believe what they said.

He said sorry. Sorry for all the time he'd spent at work and not with them. Sorry for putting his own needs before theirs. Sorry – a hard one this – for having an affair. Of course, his family were amazing. All they did was tell him how much they loved him – tell him they loved him warts and all, just the way he was. He had imagined they would judge him, and it took his dying to discover how much they loved him.

God was a tougher nut to crack. I think the breakthrough conversation came when we explored baptism. He had been baptised as a young adult and for him it had been all about being washed of his sin. The idea that God might say to him, as he said to Jesus at his baptism, 'You are my beloved son in whom I am well pleased' was mind-blowing. It took him to a new place where it was okay to simply be David and know that he didn't need to earn God's love – he just got it.

David was happier in his dying than he was most of his adult life. Dying had taught him to reorient his faith away from judgement and towards love and acceptance.

Three principles of happiness[2]

If I could turn back the clock, magically deleting my prostate cancer, the surgery I needed and its complications, would I do so? It seems an odd question. But I find it surprisingly hard to answer. It wasn't a lot of fun. But I feel I have learned more about myself and the world around me over the past two months than over the preceding 20 years. The first revelation was the astonishing power of human kindness. The team that treated me, at the Churchill Hospital in Oxford, made me feel I was part, however briefly, of a vast but close family. It was more than just professionalism. It felt like care in every sense. I am convinced that this attention was crucial to my recovery.

At home, I came to think of my bed as an oxytocin tent. The hugs my family gave me seemed to relieve both pain and the symptoms of fever faster than

---

2. Some of this content was originally published in *The Guardian*, 8 May, 2018

any of the drugs I took. The analgesic effect of physical contact, now widely documented, has not been exaggerated.

With this help, I discovered unimagined strengths. You can make resolutions that seem plausible – until they are fully tested. There are three principles that, before I had my surgery, I felt were essential to happiness: imagine how much worse it could be, rather than how much better; change what you can change, accept what you can't, and do not let fear rule your life.

So did they work? They held up remarkably well. By reciting them to myself every day – before the operation, in its aftermath, during the complications and as the tests loomed – I never wavered, never fell prey to anxiety. Knowing I was in the best possible hands, I accepted what every day brought, without worrying about what happens next. I felt not only that these three principles had been vindicated but that they could be assimilated into a broader rule: namely, that the state of being for which we should strive is to be attached to life without being possessive of it. We should seek to love our lives and live fully, but not to extend them indefinitely. We should love our children exuberantly and not cling to them or curtail their freedoms. We should treasure the material world without seeking to own and control it.

Jo

We met in 1966, aged 11, on our first day at boarding school, in a large, austere dorm, wearing oversized, scratchy uniforms, feeling numb with abandonment, as we watched our parents disappear through the swing doors. We became blood sisters through a mutual thumb prick and grew into our teens amidst the rigours of school life, surviving by means of irrepressible giggling, planning rebellion and the spiritual discovery of Joni Mitchell.

We finished school, pursued our careers and contact lessened. She eventually returned to the UK and unexpectedly turned up at my brother's funeral. Shortly after, she emailed to reconnect more fully. The death of her mother, a major car accident, marital separation, serious health issues of a son, impossible financial difficulties, an episode of cancer. None of this particularly fazed her and there was no expectation of sympathy or solutions. We discovered we'd both found nourishment in Buddhist communities and teachings. She cited the three certainties: all things change; we're all going to die; we don't know when.

Her cancer returned with a vengeance, and we grew closer again. In her final two weeks, she took up residence in the local hospice. I helped her write her death plan. I'd been wondering when she would get around to this, slightly anxious that she wouldn't. Eventually she got out an old notebook and dictated her requests, amidst the occasional burst of hoarse giggles crackling through the breathing apparatus. I was witnessing her, as Mary Oliver so beautifully expresses it, 'step through the door full of curiosity, wondering: what is it going to be like, that cottage of darkness?'[3] I wish she were still here to share in the emerging knowledge of our planet's apparent unravelling. I need the comfort of her companionship, bewildered as on that first day at school. I imagine that, at her core, she would remain unfazed. She would channel Thich Nhat Hanh, the Vietnamese monk, and say that we have to accept that the worst can happen; that most of us will die as a species, along with many other species, and that Mother Earth will be capable, after maybe a few million years, to bring us out again, and perhaps this time wiser.

What are your priorities?

Two of the most frequent questions that arise when talking with people of faith about having a humanist philosophy and our approach to death are: 'How can you keep going with no faith?' and: 'Isn't a non-religious funeral ceremony, quite simply, depressing in its hopelessness?'

So, I'd like to tell you about my best friend Alison's death and funeral. I first met Alison when I was eleven. I was a shy and anxious child, and Alison, the most popular girl in the class, put her metaphorical arms around me and infused me with confidence and joy of life. In return, on our final walk together before she died, she told me that I had 'given her depth'. I don't think anyone has ever paid me a bigger compliment.

Alison was diagnosed at the age of 48 with stage 4 bowel cancer, with secondaries, after a year of being told by the doctor that her stomach pain was irritable bowel syndrome. The shock waves that spread through her close community of family and friends were devastating. Of all of us, Alison was the very last person any of us would have imagined would have their life cut short. She infused everything she did with an ebullient life force and radiated good health and positivity.

However, very quickly, Alison led the way. Open to the wonders of life, but not religious, she set about wrapping up her affairs and making sure that each one of us knew how much we were loved and valued, and she also made sure that we were involved as much as we needed to be in her 10-month journey.

She set up a circle of eight women to protect her 11-year-old daughter, Indy, and we met together many times before her death to instil in Indy the sense that she would always have us in her life to support her, however we could.

And about five months in, Alison asked me to take her funeral. We gently set to work on a path that was both pragmatic and deeply personal. About a month before she died, we both curled up on her sofa, wrapped in blankets, and spent the day talking about her life. Humanists don't believe in an afterlife, but we do believe that, crucially, people live on in the hearts and minds of

---

3. Oliver, M. (2017). 'When death comes'. In: *Devotions: The selected poems of Mary Oliver* (p.285). Penguin.

those they have loved and inspired. So we set about distilling Alison's life, her achievements, her passions and her adventures.

The purpose of the exercise was not to prepare her for recommendation to the afterlife; rather, it was an exercise in gratitude and celebration of the life she had lived, and an encapsulation of it so that, on the day, everyone at her funeral, and especially her daughter, would be able to reinforce their connection with it and with her.

We said our final goodbyes to Alison's physical body that day, but we took away a renewed sense of who she had been for us, and who she would always be for us. During the time for reflection, we made silent promises of what we would do differently – or more of – as a result of having known her.

A leap of faith

I lost my partner at the age of 33 to a potentially treatable condition that medics had failed to detect. I stepped past the curtain around her hospital bed and was greeted there with the now indelible image of a hapless nurse ventilating by hand the woman with whom I had expected to spend the rest of my life.

I can't quite describe to you what occurred as I kept an all-night vigil by my partner's bedside. But what came felt like a transmission of pure love – which I can only describe as the filling of a jar that was already hopelessly broken.

The paradox of a love that can enter only when the heart is shattered has enabled me to make sense of death. I have come to see that moment in my life as a gift from a great teacher, who wills me to understand the lesson entitled 'Love transcends death' – which for me is the true message of the resurrection. For many years, this message has sustained me – strong and sure as a safety rope as I scramble up a mountain.

Something in me changed forever that night, 17 years ago. In my moment of greatest darkness, I received a gift of light. It led ultimately to my decision to become a minister and guided me to discover a spiritual path I could follow with all my broken heart. I live daily with the question of how far I am willing to share of its life-giving contents with others, rather than to mend it and render it watertight – and ultimately empty.

Curiosity and longing

My mother died of TB when I was three. By the time I was ordained priest I was 24 and my memories of her were very faint; she rarely crossed my mind.

The first time a newly ordained priest presides at the Eucharist is a very special occasion. As I processed into church to preside, I was stunned to find the place was packed. There was a wonderful atmosphere of loving celebration and the singing almost raised the roof. When it was time for the preparing of the altar with the sacred vessels for Communion, I was suddenly overcome with a feeling of my mum's joy and burst into tears. Mercifully it was a long hymn and I had re-composed myself before it ended. I can't explain how I knew it was her joy. I certainly wasn't thinking about her and hadn't for months. But our understanding of the Eucharist is that time and eternity meet and it is a moment of communion with all who have gone before as well as all who are alive now, caught up in the Mystery of Love and Being we call God. Was this an unlooked for confirmation of Jesus' teaching rather than a pious hope? That experience informed so much of my subsequent ministry, and particularly with people who were bereaved.

Over the years there have been several other such experiences that have confirmed my belief that there is some kind of life in God beyond the grave. What it is like, how it is, I really don't know, but I do know that I have a kind of peace about it, and a gentle curiosity and longing that increasingly draws me as I get older.

Out of a clear sky

Thirty years ago, on a beautiful, clear, mid-August afternoon, I was flying back to White Waltham airfield with a close friend in his two-seater Cessna plane when it fell out of the sky. Against the odds, we both survived. However, although I wasn't physically hurt, I felt as if I had been emotionally flayed alive. Facing death stripped away all my defences and, sitting beside the wreck of the plane, I was forced to confront the mess I was making of life. The word 'sham' came into my head. 'My life is a sham.'

During the following weeks, I experienced a debilitating black depression that made me reassess everything. And I didn't like what I saw. But I also knew I had been given a second chance. If I was to survive and turn my life around, I knew I had to radically change everything. This catapulted me onto a profound healing journey that led me to initially train as a life, death and transition facilitator with the Elisabeth Kübler-Ross Foundation. The training taught me what being Alive really means. It made me admit to how afraid I was, how unconscious unbridled anger underpinned everything that I did, and how my unprocessed childhood conditioning trapped me in a self-destructive vice.

Looking back, I marvel at how the plane crash saved me from myself. It seems as if facing death was the only way the universe could grab my attention so I could create a life that was to be of use and of service. A lot of water has gone under the bridge since then, and I continue to unfold who I am as I explore what it means to be a human being, especially in these challenging times. I am constantly amazed by what life teaches me, and how being engaged with life helps me to make friends with my mortality. I like knowing I am going to die – it keeps me sharp and focused on becoming the best person I can possibly be while I am still alive.

Near-death experience

In 1998, a faulty loft ladder led to a serious accident in my home and my second near-death experience (NDE). There was extensive damage to my lower back, including one broken vertebra and two damaged discs. Open back surgery by a neurosurgery team at the Radcliffe Infirmary followed. I was taken to Intensive Care as my system struggled. I have very clear memories of the doctors, the nurses, the room with all the tubes, machines, beeping etc. I was very sick and weak. And I remember my son Axel arriving; he helped me at the sick bed. He held my hand. Then he went outside.

Next thing I was outside my body, hovering above the wide double-door frame near my bed, looking down at the frantic commotion. I heard the monitor's long beep indicating that there was no pulse, no breathing. I heard the nurse shout, swear; I watched the anaesthetist flying into the room. He swiftly shifted my body from back to the side pulling out the morphine drip that had been set during the surgery. All medications were stopped and CPR performed. Watching all this dispassionately, peacefully, I knew my life had completed; such peace enveloped me. This time I would be allowed to move on. A great satisfaction and joy rose inside while I observed a dissolving of my old self. I felt a veil behind me; all I needed to do was to step through to be on the other side. And then something unfathomable happened. I heard Axel calling me through the ether. It sounded like a distant echo. He said: 'Mum, please stay. Mum, please stay.' There was a pause, silence. I listened. Then Axel again: 'I want you to meet my son.' I was now fully alert, aware of life continuing for my family, and that there was a new generation preparing to join them. An incredible moment of joy and sorrow all at once flooded through me. I could choose. I chose to live. I chose to return to be with my children as a mother and grandmother. I merged with my body again.

My understanding is that CPR was successful because I did not step through that veil. It truly felt like a choice, mine to be made. Axel never said those words, nor did he know I had heard them until exactly four years later, in 2002, when his first son was born in Sydney, Australia. We were both deeply moved, in tears, at the great mystery of life and consciousness. He said: 'Mum, I am so glad that some part of me knew to call out to you.'

I truly consider myself very fortunate to get a third chance at life. The NDEs were a significant awakening to the spiritual path I have been on ever since – a deeply passionate journey for meaning.

One week late

My friend was single, no kids. I was married, three kids, busy life. She kept trying to make a date for a meal. I said I would go out with her to celebrate when she was 40. She died of a brain clot aged 39 and 51 weeks. Can't change things.

Not the body

I have felt for a long time that my body is something I have been given to look after for a few years (86 to date) but it is not me. It is a thing. I am not. I am something like time.

Helping hand

As my father was dying, he, a scientist, not believing in 'ghosts' etc., insisted that he saw his mother and that she said she was helping him. Any doubts we tactfully raised he emphatically rejected, saying he *knew* and that he would help me when he was dead.

Reconnection

Death is not an ending, it is merely a transition on to the next stage. A spiritual shedding of our outer 'overcoat'. For me it is an opportunity to go home to embrace the people who I have lost and to re-connect to the universe and the divine spirit.

Terror of death

When I first found out I had cancer, I was overwhelmed by waves of raw terror. It was as if someone had punched me really hard, my lungs had burst open and I couldn't get enough air. I went from feeling completely healthy and cautiously optimistic about a long future ahead to fearing I might only have months or even weeks to live. This feeling persistently haunted the many days, and especially nights, that followed, as further information came in around the extent of the cancer, the various treatments available and the really tricky choices to be made. I remember sitting on a bed, attempting to breathe, as my wife – bless her – outlined treatments she had researched and their possible efficacy and side effects. I had to keep stopping her so I could suck in enough air to digest each new piece of information, in the knowledge that I was playing dice with death. The dread feeling in my chest, heart, and stomach felt unbearable and inescapable.

A consultant nurse, seeing how frightened I was, asked me what I was frightened of. Through an upsurging swell of tears and fear, I could only find enough air to say one word to her: 'Annihilation.' It wasn't so much the process of dying that terrified me (though that has its own fears), but the ultimate fact of death. I have never drawn any solace from religion with respect to death and find all beliefs in the afterlife, heaven, or reincarnation too incredible to be of any relief. Nor does the fact that atoms from my body will join the great mix and get re-constituted, perhaps as other life in due course, help to any great degree… because it won't be me. My own unfolding pattern of consciousness will be gone; kaput. Others have tried to help by saying they don't share the same fear as me because they know that, if death is final, then they won't be there to contend with any difficult feelings. Sadly, this also doesn't reach me because it is the anticipation of my death, while I am alive, that's the problem.

For many weeks I struggled under the misguided notion that if only I could find some insight, some enlightening new articulation of life, and death, then this might provide a way out of the terror. Then one day I decided that, rather than trying to avoid the terror, I might do just the opposite: invite it in, allow it, love it. I set some time aside, tried to calm myself down and then repeated the questions to myself: Can I just allow this? Can I just let this in? Can I stop fighting the dread and accept that this is how I feel? I focused on the physical sensation of the raw waves of terror flooding through my body and, as I did so, over several minutes, they started, minutely at first, to diminish and my breathing eased. I recognised that what I was labelling 'terror' was actually, more accurately, just a physical feeling, and that I could bear that feeling by not trying to avoid it. This brought a massive sensation of relief. Although I might not be able to make the feeling go away, I had discovered a method for coping with it.

Since then my terror of death, though diminished, has not disappeared. But now, at least, I know that I have a new approach – that of allowing and acknowledging – welcoming even, any fears that arise, rather than battling with them. I no longer aspire to transcend these feelings and I have learnt that it is more compassionate to myself to accept whatever state I am in, rather than try to avoid or transcend it. To the extent that I can love myself, I am modelling a beautifully helpful orientation and I become more available for others. I don't know how much time I have, so there isn't time to waste on not accepting any part of me.

Happiest man

Spike was a miserable sod. He was my loadmaster. When we crashed, Spike was very badly injured. He 'died' in the wreckage. The first responders brought him back. He died again on the operating table. The doctors brought him back. Spike bit his tongue in half so couldn't speak very well but he manged to say, 'I have seen the light. Mike, I have been there twice. I no longer fear death.' Spike was no longer miserable. That was 40 years ago, and Spike is still the happiest man.

Home from home

Vasile taught me to think differently about living and dying. He was 35, Romanian and Roman Catholic. I met him in hospital after he was told there was no further treatment. Because, in Romania, if there's no money, there's no treatment, Vasile was convinced he could live but, because he was poor, he had to die. I was there to assess him, as I managed a homeless hospital discharge service. He was bed-blocking. I can see his face dark, grey, distant with no trust and not a word of English.

Vasile had been trafficked, groomed by someone posing as a Salvation Army worker – told he was coming to work in construction – reality, sex industry. With anal cancer, he was quickly discarded as not fit for purpose. He was sent to our safe house. I was told he had three months. He lived for six. Over those six dying months, I saw Vasile's face become bright. He just wanted to learn and experience life. He wanted to live every day and learn about England.

I saw him manage pain and deep open wounds while learning English from the TV – constant questions and determination. Growing vegetables, playing with my dog, Ringo, and smoking 40 Winstons a day. I took him the to the beach, car boot sale, the river, picnics. I answered constant questions about life in England and what he could do.

I tried to talk to him about his family back in Romania and what he wanted at the end, but he refused to talk about it. After five months, he eventually gave me his wife's number. I was told I could only call her when he was dead. I knew he wanted to be buried in a suit, with red flowers.

Vasile expected nothing. He only demanded when he wanted certain dressings for his wounds. Some nurses thought he should be in a hospice, as he was in so much pain. He took minimal painkillers as they made him sleep and feel sleepy. He wanted to be awake to live what time he had.

He died wearing his favourite T-shirt with his favourite quilt cover on. He looked at peace and full of dignity. I stayed with him until the funeral directors took him away. I wanted to make sure he and that so-damaged body was treated as gently as he deserved .

I made the call to his wife… her reply 'I didn't know he was ill – is there any money?'

I once asked Vasile how he felt about dying in England. He said, 'Madame Claire, since I was a small boy, I have always dreamt of coming to England.' He looked at me, touched my arm and said, 'Be careful what you wish for.'

Sharing Vasile's death was one of the best experiences of my life. I learnt true suffering and true strength. I still talk about him and I still use his death to remember how important learning and living is.

Did he know?

When I was a ward sister in a cardiac/chest ward, I went round and said goodnight to patients at the end of the shift. This one man, who I can still see, was a homeless man with TB. He was fully mobile but in for supervision of medication. He looked me in the eye and said, 'You won't see me tomorrow, Sis, thank you for everything.' I wondered if he was planning to self-discharge. Next morning I came in to hear that he died in the night, quite peacefully and in his sleep. Did he know? I have pondered this regularly. I am convinced he did, and convinced most people do know and, more importantly, are not distressed by knowing.

Soul midwife

I am a soul midwife – a holistic end-of-life practitioner who supports people through the stages of death, much as a birth midwife guides women through labour. When I began my work, I thought I would be 'helping' those at the end of their lives. I now know otherwise. My job is not to help or fix, but rather to serve and support. My job is to be alongside.

In offering my presence at the bedside, I have received too many gifts to count: people have shared their joys, wisdoms and inspiration. But the greatest gift has been the honour of being with people as they unburden their fears, surrender to pain and release themselves to their journey.

With great humility, I now know that my dying friends have actually been 'soul midwiving' me: showing me how to live and teaching me, with great self-compassion, when it's my turn, how to face my journey with courage and love for all that my life has been.

Whisky and oysters

My father died a week before my son was born. Everybody always says, 'How awful' and of course it was. But, and I say this as an agnostic without any firm ideas about souls or whatnot, I always figured he knew he wasn't going to get to see his grandson grow up, so why not meet him in advance? Hang out, tell him some jokes, make sure he knows about whisky and oysters. My son looks a lot like my father.

Life prepares you

I remember, when I was about seven or eight, realising I was going to die and being terrified. My dad sat with me for hours and made me feel better. I've been scared of death ever since, until two years ago, when I became very depressed. Since then, I am not anywhere near as scared. I feel like life prepares you for death and you just need to be patient and honest with yourself.

Fewer regrets

A close friend of ours nearly died four years ago, having a massive heart attack and being in a coma for six weeks. He is now very much alive but that brush with death has made us – his friends – and him appreciate and acknowledge and keep alive our friendship. We make sure we keep in contact much more so that, when one of us dies, we have fewer regrets about what we've not done.

Losing nature

Pretty much everywhere you go in the world, the landscape and its inhabitants bear some impression of human influence, even seemingly pristine wilderness thousands of miles from habitation can be tainted by pollution, from imperceptible particulates in the air to drifts of plastic debris amassed by ocean currents, and the ever-present consequences of man-made climatic changes and sea level rise. Loss of nature and biodiversity should be profoundly worrying for all of us. I strongly feel and understand this ecological grief as I see and record widespread changes happening in the natural world.

Commentary

What death teaches us about life – Liz Rothschild

> ... there is still no remedy
> for mortality
> except mortality (Alice Oswald, 2009)

So, we have come to the chapter where some storytellers take a peek beyond the grave. The human race tends to draw divergent conclusions about what happens after we die, yet allowing mortality to influence how we live seems to lead to very similar conclusions.

What are the themes that emerge from these stories? The need for honesty, the visceral experience of fear, the value of acceptance, the sense of inner knowing, a desire to fully live before we die, the value of life review and re-assessment when faced with death, a commitment to being truthful in the face of irreversible facts and an acceptance of what is. Confrontation with death also sharpens our appreciation of the lives we are still living. And there is the confrontation with the death of the natural world, our habitat, which we increasingly understand we are a part of. These lessons become vividly available both to the person dying and those caring for them.

We imagine death coming at the end of life rather like a cartoon character falling off a cliff edge and suddenly finding air beneath its feet. In fact, all the way through life we are offered the chance to accept change and loss and see what can be learned. When a relationship breaks up, when we move, when we reach menopause and as we begin to age we can either resist or respond and each of these stages is a like a small rehearsal. Every day cells die, never to be replaced. This is the process of life.

Facing death can be very ordinary in the way that is described in *Did He Know?* It is an experience reminiscent of the 'tame death', as described by Philippe Aries in *The Hour of our Death* (1981) – a matter-of-fact acceptance of a knowing in the body, which the person was in touch with but was not recognised by the medical profession. In that moment, he chose to express his gratitude for the care he had received – a response seen commonly, although not universally, in those who are dying. Tony Walter (1996) stringently points out that we tend to romanticise how death was in previous times. There is, however, no denying that, in societies where death is more commonplace and often premature, there can be a more fatalistic acceptance of its presence and more ritualised practice to mitigate its effects on the dying or those around them.

Death does not have to mean anything to the writer of *Sometimes It Just Is*. For them, the hopeless search for some kind of meaning or target for blame feels more painful than the requirement to just accept it and feel the feelings that have arisen from the event, without adding interpretation or story.

Death can strip us bare if we let it, as the storyteller in *Terror of Death* so vividly describes. Similarly, in *Out of a Clear Sky*, the writer is forced to acknowledge the sham of their life and takes the opportunity to review how they are living. Atul Gawande (2014), in his superb book *Being Mortal*, poses this carefully nuanced question, given him by Susan Block, a palliative care specialist: 'If time becomes short, what is most important to you?' It is such a delicate probing that gently takes us to the heart of the matter. The 'if' enables us to hear the question that shortness of time will come to all of us even if we have no warning of it.

In her book, *The Top Five Regrets of the Dying*, Bronnie Ware (2011) lists the key regrets she encounters in the people she works with who are dying:

- I wish I'd had the courage to live a life true to myself, not the life others expected of me.
- I wish I hadn't worked so hard.
- I wish I'd had the courage to express my feelings.
- I wish I had stayed in touch with my friends.
- I wish I had let myself be happier.

She then describes how she tries to mitigate the impact of these bitter and painful regrets. Her focus is on what remains possible in the time that is left to us. She encourages people to see that change and growth can still happen. This is movingly described in Vasile's story in *Home from Home*. Bronnie writes that a carer needs to be one who truly and profoundly listens. In that listening, they encourage people to risk speaking their unadulterated, authentic truth. She encourages people to be gentle with themselves about how they have lived and look to see what changes they might want to make in how they are living. She believes that, until we draw our last breath, we remain in a position to give and receive love. The only impediments to accepting these gifts are pride or lack of self-worth. I wonder which one you sign up to. Mine's an unholy mixture of the two. In allowing this to unfold, old rifts in families can be healed and precious words exchanged. The beauty of a day can be fully appreciated in the midst of suffering, and real connections can be forged between old friends and family and/or complete strangers who become part of people's lives as they come close to death.

For some, this does not happen. In *One Week Late,* the writer concludes that death has closed the chapter and she will have to live with her regrets. There was no second chance of the kind mercifully experienced in *Fewer Regrets*. My own father's death did not unfold as we had hoped. I did not step forward to offer him what he wanted in those final moments, and I have agonised over that many times. Eventually, I realised I would never be able to change that. I could only change my attitude towards it, offer myself some slack and see what good might come of it. It has compelled me to tune more honestly into my feelings and admit more quickly when I need help. This was the final lesson he and death taught me, and it probably led eventually to this book.

Death shines a harsh light into all the places where we are not being truthful with ourselves and others and there is nowhere to hide. In the work I now do with families, I have felt the value of this lesson, of learning to be braver and truer in how I relate to them and not being afraid of the emotions that may emerge or the fact that I cannot make everything better. I am frequently amazed by the raw articulacy of the human heart – of our hearts. Not that of poets and the great philosophers. Us. When we cannot but speak from our feelings, the words flow with a clear, unclichéd truth that we seldom hear in our day-to-day lives – forged by pain and love and reverberating into the listener through tone as well as content.

In the stories in this chapter, we see people really grasping the value of having a human life at all – that extraordinary process of coupling, birthing and surviving that has, for thousands of years, created each one of us. So many possibilities for us not to exist, and yet we do. We are often so preoccupied with our personal story, the wrongs and rights of it, the blame and the shame, that we forget how unlikely it is that we even exist at all. When we suddenly realise that we might not live for ever, it can lead us to consider Mary Oliver's wonderful question in *The Summer Day* (2017): 'What is it you plan to do with your one wild and precious life?' Why wait? We could take a look at those five regrets of the dying and see what might apply to the way we are living now.

Each experience we have shapes the way we view ourselves and the world, and if we are religious, that may also have implications for our life beyond death. From a Hindu perspective, our karma will take us from one life to another and the deeds we commit in this life will influence how we are reborn. Similarly, many Buddhists do not consider this life to be the end; it is just part of the Wheel of Life, which ends only when we truly achieve enlightenment. Indeed, as described in *Buddhist Way* and *Jo* and *Turn Away or Turn Towards,* from Chapter 1, this path actively invites followers to contemplate their death in order to understand the true, transitory nature of existence. From some faith perspectives, our good deeds on earth may influence where we spend eternity – either in a place of love and delight or in one of suffering. This often allows for the possibility of some continuity of being in the afterlife, as suggested by *Curiosity and Longing,* but can also lead to a terrible fear of being judged and found wanting, as in *Am I Good Enough?*. This is another moment of stripping bare, when the subject can no longer conceal his innermost fears about himself and, because he shares his concerns, they are movingly resolved.

The way to influence what happens after we die is, from a religious perspective, to follow the guidelines for best behaviour. At their best, these invite people to examine how they live their lives and aspire to certain altruistic codes. The same applies to humanists, who would also be guided by beliefs that encourage concern for our fellow humans and the planet and awareness of our interdependence. This can see seen in *What are Your Priorities?* Badly applied beliefs can lead to war, division, sectarianism and hypocrisy, but at the heart of all spiritual traditions and benign social philosophies, we find an emphasis on love and community. In *Three Principles of Happiness*, we see the writer discover their own modus vivendi and find that it sustains them. 'Imagine how much worse it could be, rather than how much better; change what you can change, accept what you can't, and do not let fear rule your life.' This got them through, along with the support of family, friends and health professionals. They admit to having learnt more about themselves in the two months of their illness than in the previous 20 years. How many of us wonder how we would react in such circumstances? Few of us take ourselves deliberately to that unblinking edge of truth. Some actively seek it out in war, or extreme sports, or other testing experiences, but most of us stay on safe ground, and our lives can be the blander for it. The final period of life can prove one of the most meaningful, but clearly that cannot always be the case.

Near death experiences (NDEs), as described in *Near-Death Experience* and *Happiest Man*, take us into another territory. There is now quite a substantial body of work recording NDEs (see Resources). While not all NDEs are positive experiences, most of them are, and it is common for people who have survived to report an altered outlook on life, a gratitude for being alive, a desire to do good and a complete lack of fear about what comes after death. Often they become engaged in spiritual quests, when previously they had no such interest. These and similar experiences can come to those who utterly rejected them before, like the scientist in *Helping Hand,* who became convinced that he could see a ghost as he lay dying.

We cannot ever ascertain what causes these experiences but what is clear is that they usually have a very beneficial influence on how people live the rest of their lives. As Atul Gawande (2014) reports, research on the impact of the SARS epidemic in Hong Kong and the 9/11 attacks in New York revealed that, when 'life's fragility is primed', people's goals and motives shift. In fact, he discovers that 'understanding the finitude of one's time could be a gift'. I have had the honour to meet people when ordinary, everyday life has receded and they have to draw on their deepest resources to keep going. Every one of them has been a reminder of how precious and important every single life is – not just the rich, famous and successful ones we are taught to envy and emulate on a daily basis.

We are living in extraordinary, pivotal times. A virus, Covid-19, has had the power to shut down our societies worldwide. As T.S. Eliot wrote in *Burnt Norton* (1968): 'Humankind cannot bear very much reality.' Our refusal to face up to our own fragile existence is a very human response. It is reasonable to fear the obliteration written about here in *Terror of Death*. It implies a healthy attachment to life. Those who experience a daily unease with the business of being alive can be the ones who choose to take their own lives. Or this detachment can demonstrate a profound acceptance of the kind described at the end of *Curiosity and Longing*. The invisibility of death in our society is, I suspect, inextricably linked with our resistance to admitting that we cannot go on living as we are. Just as we don't see death, some of us don't see the poverty in other parts of the world or closer to home, or the disappearing glaciers. Geographical location and financial stability can give us a false sense of immunity. A lot of pain and joy and connection awaits us if we dare to stop turning our faces to the wall. Death teaches us all how to live, if we will only let it.

Advice points

- Consider what you might change about your life if you knew you were dying in a year, six months, four weeks, tomorrow. See what it tells you about your life now.
- Put up a quotation or image that reminds you of your mortality and reflect on your ancestors.
- Go to a death café, festival or other death-related event. Talk to others about what you found out.
- Observe and learn from the daily losses of life, both large and small and practise letting go and accepting the processes we cannot control.
- If the opportunity arises, draw closer rather than withdraw from the experience of someone you know who is dying or bereaved.

References

Aries, P. (1981). *The hour of our death*. Vintage.

Eliot, T.S. (1968). 'Burnt Norton'. In *Four quartets*. Folio Society.

Gawande, A. (2014). *Being mortal*. Profile Books.

Oliver, M. (2017). 'The Summer Day'. In: *Devotions: The selected poems of Mary Oliver*. Penguin.

Oswald, A. (2009). 'Red-veined dock'. In: *Weeds and wildflowers* (p.31). Faber and Faber.

Walter, T. (1996). Facing death without tradition. In: G. Howarth & P.C. Jupp (Eds.), *Contemporary issues in the sociology of death, dying and disposal* (pp. 193–204). Macmillan Press.

Ware, B. (2011). *The top five regrets of the dying*. Hay House.

Resources

Books

Anastasios, A. (2010). *Dying to Know – bringing death to life*. Hardie Grant Publishing.

Bradley, R. (2016). *A matter of life and death*. Jessica Kingsley Publishers.

Coleman, G. & Jinpa T. (Eds.) (G. Dorje Trans.). (2005). *The Tibetan Book of the Dead*. Penguin Classics.

de Hennezel, M. (1997). *Intimate death: How the dying teach us to live*. Vintage Books.

Doughty, C. (2018). *From here to eternity: Travelling the world to find the good death*. Weidenfeld & Nicolson.

Fenwick, P. & Fenwick, E. (2008). *The art of dying*. Continuum Books.

Gross, K. (2015). *Late fragments: Everything I want to tell you (about this magnificent life)*. Harper Collins.

Keleman, S. (1974). *Living your dying*. Random House.

Levine, S. (1986). *Who dies? An investigation into conscious living and conscious dying*. Doubleday.

Levine, S. (2005). *Unattended sorrow: Recovering from loss and reviving the heart*. Melia Publishing Services Ltd.

Murray, S. (2011). *Making an exit*. Picador.

Ostaseski, F. (2017). *The five invitations: What death can teach us about living fully*. Pan Macmillan.

Sacks, O. (2015). *Gratitude*. Picador.

Ward, T. (2012). *Alternative pastoral prayers – liturgies and blessings for health and healing, beginnings and endings*. Canterbury Press.

Websites

Dying Matters: www.dyingmatters.org

The Death Café Movement: https://deathcafe.com

The Transformative Power of Near-Death Experiences: www.drpennysartori.com

Outside the Box

13 – The wider view

Liz Rothschild

Most of us in developed Western countries die slowly now, from non-communicable diseases. Only one in 10 dies suddenly. Most die in hospital, although most of us express the desire to die at home. Infant deaths have plummeted, and we also live longer than our forebears: in 2000, 59% of us died aged over 75, compared with 12% in 1900 (Davies 2015: 21). When we are bereaved in the industrial West, our experience is often not so intimately shared with others. We move away from where we grew up and work away from home, and so our parents and children, even our partners, are not always known to the people we interact with on a daily basis.

If you want to read more widely about social and historical trends associated with death, dying and bereavement, I recommend the works of Philippe Aries, Allan Kellehear, Tony Walter (see Resources) and *The Natural Death Handbook* (Natural Death Centre, 2012). Here I will confine myself to a brief summary of what to me are the key issues.

Walter (1996) offers us three stages through which to view how deaths have been managed over the past centuries: traditional, modern and post-modern. He identifies key differences in the authorities we turn to (from priest to doctor to the self), and the social context (from the community to the hospital and, increasingly, the home). With these shifts come different beliefs and practises as we move from a reliance on tradition to medical expertise and, increasingly nowadays, personal choice.

These stages are not strictly consecutive through time, since different societies, groups and individuals will be turning towards particular aspects of these different approaches or combining them in various unique ways, as Walter explains.

Walter also describes 'a new craft of dying' and counsels against idealising the old ways as much as he does against evangelising for the post-modern way of death. He raises some good questions about whether the current, mostly female-led initiatives, with their focus on emotional expression and sharing, serve everyone equally well. They might even be utterly at odds with some cultural norms. I absolutely concur with that. What matters to me, in my work, is that people are well informed about all the choices available to them. I don't want anyone saying, 'I wish I had known that was possible.'

The traditional death today

The ritualised practices of the traditional death can be deeply reassuring to those they still serve. There is a familiarity and certainty about the religious liturgies and the sequences of events that can hold everyone very safe. For Hindus in Britain, positioning the body on the floor and placing water from the Ganges and a leaf of basil in the mouth ensures safe passage of the soul. Similarly, giving the last rites releases a practising Catholic from sin. Everyone knows what to do and the task of ensuring that the journey from life to death is done well is simplified by having clear pathways that guarantee the person travels to the next stage in their soul's journey without peril, or is enabled to be reborn. That is, unless some aspect of the correct procedure cannot be performed, and then there can be great fear for the impact both on the future lives of the family of the deceased and on the person who is dying or dead.

Practices maintained by families after a death can also offer reassurance. To die knowing that your photograph will be at the centre of your family's next *ofrenda* – the altar for the Mexican *Dia de Muertos* – and that they will be waiting for your spirit to return offers great consolation. One of the greatest fears of dying people is that they will be forgotten; for the bereaved, it is the fear of final, irrevocable separation, and such beliefs and rituals moderate these fears. The significance of the rituals will vary within a family or friendship group and for some these rituals hold no meaning or a diluted or complex one. Holloway (2018) powerfully embraces contemporary ambivalence when he writes: 'When I laid my hands gently on the heads of the dying and prayed the presence of a loving God into their minds, in that moment the truth or untruth of my action did not matter. The act contained its own meaning.'

The postmodern death

The postmodern death, where there is only a guiding personal ethic, not a religious framework, is now many people's experience in the UK, and it nearly always intersects with the modern medicalised death. We no longer await death with the fatalism common in societies with little access to medical treatment; we are grateful for the alleviation of symptoms that modern palliative medicine can offer us, but there is also now some push-back against what can seem like an unquestioning attempt to keep the body alive at all costs. With the hospice movement came the return of the notion that is really embedded in the traditional death: Cicely Saunders' belief that the dying person needs more than medical care; they are a whole human being, with emotional, spiritual, social and physical needs. Gawande (2014, p.249) succinctly sums up the drawbacks of the modern death where we leave all to the skill of the doctor, who may not have been trained in subtle palliative understanding and communication:

> Technological society has forgotten what scholars call the 'dying role' and its importance to people as life approaches its end. People want to share memories, pass on wisdoms and keepsakes, settle relationships, establish their legacies, make peace with God, and ensure that those who are left behind will be okay. They want to end their stories on their own terms.

Dr Rachel Clarke (2020, p.80) explores the tension between how doctors are trained and what is required of them when interacting with patients, and points to the paucity of content about death in medical training. I have encountered very creative approaches in some medical schools, but death and dying are still mainly relegated to a few optional hours rather than considered core content. Clarke writes:

> The challenge, then, for every doctor was to acquire sufficient detachment to be useful, while maintaining one's essential humanity… How had nobody taught me through my years of medical school the sheer power of small acts of kindness, and of simple human touch to transcend primal fear?

In the past, some of these needs have been met by family, friends or a religious leader. Now others are stepping forward – art and music therapists, massage and aromatherapists, death dualas and soul midwives – to offer comfort and connection when other support is not sufficient. Many of these approaches are more easily accessed in a hospice. When someone dies elsewhere, there can be a lack of this rounded, holistic support. It can be a threadbare death.

In the 20th and 21st centuries, the diminishing role of the religious leader has been supplemented by an increase in humanist celebrants, inter-faith ministers and others of a less clear-cut position as regards their spiritual or non-spiritual values. The word 'celebrant' is in common usage now but is frequently not really understood. Some celebrants are humanists, others occupy the nuanced territory between organised religion and humanism. When working as a celebrant, I see my role as exploring the core beliefs of both the person who died and those left behind (since they are not always the same) and how to reflect them in the funeral we develop together. My presence at the funeral may be minimal or quite central, according to their needs, resources and preferences. In some rare cases, in the end, I may not take part at all. Each funeral will be personally tailored, although many share features, such as using music and/ or poetry and a description of the life of the person who has died. This might be written and spoken by me, or by several family members and friends, or it may largely comprise a sequence of music or improvised contributions in the moment and a slab of the person's favourite cake to tickle the taste buds and the memories into life.

I am very aware that most of the families I work with choose the familiar and resist invitations to step too far outside the box. This is sometimes caused by fear of offending certain family members or a wider concern about what people in general will think. In the face of so much that is unknown and unfamiliar, people reach for the shelter of the recognisable. As is noted in *The Natural Death Handbook* (Natural Death Centre, 2012), although only 12% of the population say they belong to a faith group, 75% of all funerals are still religious, in form at least. I suspect that proportion will have shifted somewhat since 2012, but the point still stands, and increasingly funerals will need to accommodate several traditions: for example, the one a person was born into and the one(s) they adopted later in life. Some families take the whole proceedings into their own hands.

Changes in conventional funeral practice are becoming increasingly evident too. Church services often include significant contributions from friends and family and the bearers are also drawn from people who knew the deceased. Families and friends routinely bear and lower at our burial ground and report how rewarding they find it to be able to offer this final act of love. However, only recently we encountered a funeral director who said he never allowed families to be involved in this way. This paternalistic response reveals a battle for control over funerals and, I suspect, fear – whether of an accident or loss of dignity (a key word in the funeral industry). This attitude perpetuates because these funeral directors never witness how moving it is to watch a family supporting one another to do this and how well they can do it without any previous training. It also explodes the convenient myth that this task can only really be done by professionals.

Burial and cremation

Until the 19th century, disposal of the body in the industrialised West was always by burial on land or at sea. The UK was the first country to change this. The Cremation Society announced in their founding declaration (1874) that:

> We, the undersigned, disapprove the present custom of burying the dead, and we desire to substitute some mode which shall rapidly resolve the body into its component elements, by a process which cannot offend the living, and shall render the remains perfectly innocuous. Until some better method is devised we desire to adopt that usually known as cremation.

Concern about the pollution of groundwater, overcrowding of grave spaces and the many scandals concerning the theft and sale of corpses made this seem, to some, the rational, modern approach. Dr William Price, a Welshman and archdruid, was, at his own request, burnt in an iron casket on a pyre of two tonnes of coal on 31st January, 1893. Thousands came to witness the sight, and many considered it blasphemous. Strong opposition to cremation remained within the Christian community. It was only in 1963, for example, that the Catholic church passed ecclesiastical legislation in support of it, and only on condition that the cremated remains were kept together and placed in a religious location. In China, some elders took their own lives in order to pre-empt its 2014 Cremation Act, because they believed that, unless they could be buried, they would not be able to gain the status of an ancestor in their families (Walter, 1996). Of course, for other faith traditions, such as Hindu, cremation has always been the only acceptable option.

Today, 72% of the British public now choose cremation. This sharp rise can be attributed to a decline in religious objections and religiosity, and the ongoing concerns about the lack of burial spaces, particularly in urban areas. It is also true that ashes allow people considerable flexibility about final disposal. They can even be carried around with us, as gloriously fictionalised in Graham Greene's novel, *Travels with my Aunt* (1969).

However, opposition has been building from another quarter – environmental. Crematoria consume huge amounts of energy to generate the necessary heat and few repurpose it well. On average, cremating a body at 1100 degrees celsius takes 285 kilowatt hours of gas, roughly equivalent to one person's home consumption for a month. Pollution is still emitted from the chimneys from our mercury fillings, the veneers and plastic fittings on the coffins and other items put into them. Abatement measures have improved but not solved the problem.

Space does remain a problem, and a variety of creative solutions are needed to handle the increase in our population and the growing need for burial spaces. One solution is to have vertical burials, but few burial grounds have the appropriate equipment to do this, and it doesn't have much popular appeal.

In 1993, Ken West came up with a new approach, which he trialled in Carlisle council cemetery. In response to requests from families for somewhere a little wilder and more relaxed in feel, he created a section with more trees and without gravel paths, and called it 'green burial'. It was such a success that it began a movement that has now spread to the US, Australia, New Zealand, Holland, Ireland and, more recently, France. There are at least 100 green burial grounds in the UK that adhere to the full environmental rules of the movement, and up to 200 more offering hybrid or diluted versions of the original idea. The sites available range from small fields grazed with sheep and no facilities, sites equipped with their own funeral directors and full facilities, and corners of existing church or council burial grounds. They offer a very appealing solution to those wishing to have a low impact on the environment and they repurpose areas of land of little or no value for agriculture or horticulture. In one case, it has led to the creation of an orchard, and I once heard of a sailing club considering using the land around their lake, although I don't believe they pursued it.

The majority of green burial grounds in Britain pursuing the original vision are members of the Association of Natural Burial Grounds, run by the Natural Death Centre (a pioneering charity begun by Nicolas Albery and Josefine Spyer in 1991). The aim is to reduce the environmental impact by requiring the use of biodegradable coffins and liners and not using large, imported stone headstones. You are unlikely to see tarmac paths, and management of the sites is often organic and aimed at encouraging the emergence of native wildflowers and trees.

In the UK, bodies are not embalmed unless they have to be returned from abroad. This is to avoid the leaching of chemicals into the ground, as well as the needless interference with the body. If you want to know more about embalming, read Jessica Mitford's funny and furious book, *The American Way of Death* (1978, 1998), or, for a more contemporary take, Caitlin Doughty's *Smoke Gets in your Eyes* (2015). In Western cultures, for centuries, the need for rapid burial of bodies meant minimal preservation with alcohol or charcoal was used, or none. However, during the American Civil War a new method of embalming was introduced to ensure soldiers could be brought home from the battlefield, giving families more chance for closure. When President Lincoln was assassinated, his body was embalmed and taken across the country on a slow train back to Washington and put on view to the public. Embalming then became fashionable and routine practice and this began to have an influence in the UK. The viewing period was extended in both countries, requiring artificial means to keep the body in an acceptable state and, in the US, open-casket funerals became common. In some US states today there is even drive-through viewing!

Embalming is totally unnecessary today, with our modern refrigeration systems, unless a body has to be transported between countries. It simply arrests the natural processes of decay for cosmetic purposes, to give the impression the person is sleeping rather than dead. Often families are unaware it is being done as it is usually termed 'hygienic services', making it sound like a public health requirement.

Planning for death

There is no doubt that developers should also be making proper provision for burial areas when building town and village expansions. Just as there is increasing and not always well-planned pressure on local schools and medical services from housing developments, no one is properly planning for the dead. Researchers at the Bath Centre for Death and Society have created the

Future Cemetery Design Competition to stimulate discussion and creative responses.

You can bury someone in your back garden – up to three people, in fact, so long as you put a letter with your deeds explaining this and noting the location(s). But this will not guarantee you access if you sell the house, and the body could be exhumed, at great expense to the new owner or you, if you did not give them the right paperwork. I know of a publican who was buried in the back garden of his pub and is still occasionally stood a pint by some of his regulars. But, as the story *Unfuneral* (Chapter 11) illustrates, even burying ashes in the garden can lead to emotional complications that should be taken into account.

What might the future look like?

Alkaline hydrolysis is already in use in the US and is likely to arrive here soon. There has been concern about the effect on the groundwater, but the process is much less energy intensive and results in a powder that is finer than the current cremains (who thought of that term?). A freeze-drying technique has also been developed in Sweden, using liquid nitrogen to freeze the body and then break it down into a fine powder, but it has not proved viable to date. In development stage in the US is the idea of composting human bodies. Recompose, in Seattle, US, claims to be able to produce a cubic metre of fertile soil after 30 days of composting in their specially designed containers. Nothing remains of the body and it is then available for use as soil improver. Given the way our soil is degrading, this could be a small contribution to resolving the problem. However, this technology is not about to become available soon anywhere near you. Although, if you live in the Netherlands, you can now have a coffin made of mycelium, designed to speed up the decomposition of your body in your final resting place.

Then there are the futuristic versions that aim to preserve rather than dispose of the body. Known as cryogenics, these are reserved for the very wealthy . There are three facilities in the US and one in Russia. The largest is the US corporation Alcor Life Extension Foundation. For a price tag of $200,000, your blood can be replaced with antifreeze and your body stored at a temperature of -190° centigrade to await your second coming. Or, if you want a cheaper version, your brain and head can be preserved so it can be attached to a prosthetic body.

Others hope to augment their bodies gradually with more and more technical improvements and replacements and ultimately reach the point where their brain (possibly also enhanced) is alive in a totally rebuilt artificial body. I find myself utterly at odds with anyone reaching for this kind of future. Our planet is already alarmingly overcrowded. For the sake of future generations, we cannot stick around indefinitely. Let's hear Philip Gould, writing about living with an incurable cancer in *When I Die* (Gould, 2013, p.127):

> We are in one big paradox here. It is death that gives intensity to life. All of us know this, all of us living in the Death Zone.

Why should we be more immortal than a daisy, kingfisher or a wasp? Many of the supporters of cryogenics are very successful, wealthy innovators from the information technology and artificial intelligence industries. They have a burning curiosity about what comes next and believe in an ever-improving future. I am with Bill Drummond, interviewed in *The Natural Death Handbook* (Natural Death Centre, 2012, p.13):

> It seems to me like another way for the marketplace to try and edge its way into making big bucks from the illusion that death can be cheated.

New opportunities and challenges

Death dualas and soul midwives

Just as there has been a resurgence in home births, so there is a steady, if minority commitment to home deaths. There simply are not enough hospice places, hospice-at-home teams or wider resources to support this choice, but, as with all outliers, its proponents are influencing the centre ground. However, the recent growth of the home funeral movement in the UK and the training of soul midwives and death dualas (both, interestingly, taking their names from the world of natural birthing) broaden our choices. These people will sit with the dying and support those around them. Some are former nurses who want to bring another dimension to the support they offer; others are from a wide array of occupations – painters, storytellers, musicians, massage therapists and more. They offer these skills along with an understanding of the dying process and an ability to listen profoundly to the needs of the dying person. They are there to complement, not replace, the medical and healthcare staff who may be involved. They can then guide families in how to care for the body after death and advise them on how to keep it at home until the time of burial, if that is what they want. (Chapter 9 has more information about this.)

However, there is a danger that we create very high expectations of ourselves about how our death, or that of someone close, will unfold. Death, like birth, is unpredictable. Duncan Forbes (quoted in Stevens et al, 2009), former CEO of the Shakespeare Hospice in Stratford-on-Avon, wisely warns us against 'the tyranny of the perfect death'.

Community involvement

It used to be routine for people to come to the house to view the dead and for friends and neighbours to bear the body. This is still within the living memory of many people I meet as I tour the country with my *Outside the Box* show, and is still common practice in parts of Scotland and Ireland.

The people supporting the dying and helping with funerals were also part of the community and they all had other jobs, apart from the doctor and priest. The cabinet-maker made the coffins, the coalman swept down his cart and moved the coffin if there was no communal village bier; the midwife laid out the bodies.

Interestingly, there has been a recent move to reclaim coffin-making from the funeral industry. It was begun in 2010 in Rotorua, New Zealand, by Katie Williams, a 77-year-old retired palliative care nurse, working out of her garage. She invited other people to join her in assembling and decorating their own coffins. In *The Coffin Club* (Fitzgerald, 2020), Cathy Fitzgerald's delightful BBC World Service documentary, the women describe their coffins. One has Elvis under her lid so 'he will be lying on top of me for eternity'; another covers hers in Maori designs, reflecting her ancestry, and one woman lines her coffin with letters between her and her husband, who predeceased her. In the documentary, they are laughing, crying and supporting one another, practically and emotionally, and they now offer their service to others in their community. The idea has since spread to the UK (see Resources).

Social (and other) media

Due to Covid-19, we have all heard recently of NHS and care staff using phones and tablets to enable isolated patients to communicate with family and friends. People have been able to virtually attend funerals live-streamed from crematoria. So how can new forms of communication help us when we are dying and bereaved? *The Comfort of People* by Daniel Miller (2017) explores this. Miller interviewed patients and staff connected to one hospice to see how they interacted with different forms of media. There was a wide range of responses, reflecting individual preferences. In one family, the son set his mum up with a Facebook account on the day of her diagnosis. She was a very social person and it enabled her to continue to feel part of her social group when she couldn't receive lots of visitors. One friend simply posted beautiful photographs of nature, enabling him to engage with her even though he felt he had nothing he could say. She was even contacted by old friends with whom she had lost touch, so her social circle expanded.

Some of Miller's interviewees joined online forums where they could discuss concerns with others facing the same health challenges and offer one another moral support. Older patients tended to find social media intrusive and hard to understand and relied on the telephone. But others of the same age were delighted by the opportunities it opened up, such as being able to see photographs of events almost as they were happening, chat to geographically scattered grandchildren, and even feel a part of their family's everyday life, with the computer left permanently on for them to talk when they felt like it. Sometimes people felt that social media and telephone contact replaced what might have been a face-to-face visit (this was in pre-Covid days), but on the whole interviewees felt it augmented rather than reduced the amount of contact they had with family and friends.

Some of Miller's interviewees used social media to blog about their illness and felt they were able to give something back by sharing their journey and bringing the process into the open. There have been many well publicised examples of this. Jade Goody (Channel 4, 2019), for example, was able to talk openly about her cancer, invaluably raising awareness of cervical cancer among her age group; Dr Kate Granger's blogs (2016) influenced how patients are treated, when she was diagnosed with a rare cancer and began to write about her experience of the health service as a user, not a doctor, and Alice Byron (2016) blogged about the experience of a younger person living with a terminal diagnosis.

Sometimes opening a WhatsApp message or a text was all Miller's interviewees could manage but these brought a bit of humour or a lovely image into their confined world, even if they were not feeling well enough to respond. We all learnt the benefits of this during the Covid-19 lockdown in 2020. There is also the advantage of being able to send multiple messages to a wide group, so avoiding the exhaustion of multiple calls and being able to be more selective about who you actually speak to. And, commonly, younger patients preferred sharing their feelings via digital media.

Some patients in Miller's research also found social media a better way to contact medical staff, as they felt it was less demanding and intrusive and sometimes found they even got a quicker response via email. Many medical staff wished there was a more efficient way of information-sharing using the internet, reducing the amount of paper record-keeping and speeding up communication, but some had confidentiality concerns. During the Covid-19 lockdown in 2020, some routine bureaucratic practices were digitalised, such as the Green Form certificate of burial, although the paper one was still required as well.

But social media has its limitations. Alice Maloney (2020), despite being an illustrator and creative strategist at Google, found she preferred to send pictures and postcards to her father when he was dying – physical objects for him to hold – or to talk to him directly. She found it hard to convey tone and intention or modulate with social media. There is 'an emotional black hole in technology', she said. She also found it impossible to fully communicate what she described as 'negative emotions'. I think this way of describing them reveals why they are less catered for. Our rejection of a whole range of emotional responses as a society makes them much harder to experience and admit to and so we seek to avoid them if we can, and our social media reflect this. Perhaps, in fact, the essential interconnectedness of rain and sun is reflected in our emotions too. Growth requires both: 'Pain, it turns out, moves through the same inner networks as rapture. When one moves, so can the other. This is the victory of brokenness,' writes Rebecca Loncraine (2018, p.84).

After someone has died, huge comfort can be got from being sent pictures you have never seen and hearing from people you may never have met who knew the person. Some parents, for example, find that maintaining their dead child's Facebook account enables them to feel connected to them and their community. Others want to shut the account down and move forward in other ways. Online obituary services now offer people the facility to create forums for pictures and memories, although we can, of course, create them ourselves. One man sampled his father's voice and built a programme that enabled him to ask his father questions and get computer-generated replies that sounded like his father in tone and content. Eventually, he realised he had to let this go. Each one of us has to find a way that allows us to healthily stay connected to the person who has died while at the same time accepting that they are no longer alive.

Dementia

There is little material written to date on dementia and dying and bereavement and yet, as Hazel May discusses in her commentary in Chapter 6, it is an increasingly common challenge and requires creative and well-funded responses. It also brings with it the unique experience of bereavement before a death takes place. The loss of the person they knew, at the same time that their care needs are making increasing demands on time and resources, can take spouses, partners and family caring for someone with dementia to the very edge, both financially and emotionally. More work and more awareness are needed on this subject.

Prolonged coma and CPR

Never before has medicine been so skilful at maintaining life, and all of us benefit from that in numerous ways, but it has also thrown up deep ethical problems, such as those relating to prolonged coma. These problems take us to the heart of what it means to be alive or dead. The definition of being dead has become increasingly blurred as we come to understand better how the physical body shuts down. There is brain death, organ death, cell death and molecular death. Death used to be the cessation of breathing and heartbeat but these can now be artificially maintained, so there are other factors to consider. The law does not permit the wishes of the person in a coma to override the duty of the medical team to maintain life, leaving families in an agonising position of powerlessness. The Kitzinger family have lived with this since Polly Kitzinger was injured in a car crash in 2009. As a result of their experiences, they have been campaigning to bring this issue to public attention (see Commission on the Value of Death, listed in Resources). How do we mourn someone who is physically, alive thanks to mechanical assistance, yet apparently totally unconscious and unaware?

A special initiative bringing together Macmillan nurses and paramedics in the South West Ambulance Service has led to an impressive review of practice and enhancement of professional skills. One of their stories is included in this book (see Chapter 8, p.143). The aim of this inspiring project was to reduce the amount of futile CPR and hospital admissions when a person with cancer is clearly in the final stages of dying. CPR is usually unsuccessful and often leaves patients with broken ribs or damaged brain function, but is frequently passionately requested by those around them. Clarke (2020, p.100) writes:

> Modern CPR is a brutal, undignified process that was never intended to be performed on patients who are dying from an irreversible condition… Sometimes our heart stops because it is time for us to go.

Assisted dying

Assisted dying continues to be a topic of heated debate. For some, the inclusion here of two stories about assisted dying will be offensive; for others, it will be a relief. According to the campaign group Dignity in Dying (2020), 84% of the public support assisted suicide for terminally ill adults and 54% of GPs are supportive or neutral to a change in the law to enable this in the UK. This choice was not available anywhere in the world until Dignitas opened its doors in Switzerland in 1998. Since then, Holland, Canada, Belgium and some states in the US have changed their legislation to permit assisted dying, each with their own, slightly differing terms and conditions. Before that, and still now in the UK, the opportunity to die by choice was only available if you ended your own life. Depending on your physical state, this could implicate friends and family and leave them open to prosecution. This is still theoretically possible if you accompany someone to Switzerland from the UK, but no one has ever been prosecuted for doing so.

I know that many staff who work in hospices find this option unthinkable. They passionately believe that everyone could and should be offered a reasonable death, if not a good one. Some people have religious objections. There is also concern about pressure from family or friends for financial or other gain. So far, no substantial evidence of this happening has emerged in countries where assisted dying is allowed. Many people rely on the grey area where doctors enable the dying process to unfold by not intervening or by simply providing increasing doses of pain relief. This is a lottery, however, as it depends on the attitude of the GP and what is physically possible. Doctors have also become more cautious about doing it, after the GP Harold Shipman was found to have murdered some 250 of his older patients by this method.

I find it very interesting that the numbers of people who apply to Dignitas and those who actually use its service are dramatically different. Of those who register, few use the service. This is the same in Oregon, US. There, in 20 years, 15,000 people acquired the medication needed to end their life but only

900 took it. This tells me that having a sense of agency gives most people the resilience they need to endure life up until its natural end. Personally I would like the right to choose but I also believe we all have to take responsibility as we age for considering at what point we refuse further medical intervention, as exemplified in *Home Death* (Chapter 9, p.166).

There is a mistrust of playing God when it comes to taking a life, but we don't hesitate to play God when we maintain life. Fitting a pacemaker into a person in their mid-90s is not necessarily the right decision, or subjecting them to yet another punishing round of chemotherapy and radiotherapy. It is so hard to know when to say no, but I hope I can remain in touch with this question if faced with these choices. Doctors have to work to maintain life. Perhaps our job, as patients, is to decide when to relieve them of that responsibility and avoid a dwindling quality of life. Never before have we lived so long but this longevity can feel undesirable to some, especially when living with an incurable, progressive illness.

Death chic and the overlooked

Death has always had a following and it is definitely in fashion at the moment. It is seen by some as glamorous, edgy and transgressive. I think it is both more ordinary and more extraordinary than that. When attending certain conferences, I find myself surrounded by flocks of gorgeous, lively, younger women, with extravagant tattoos, exotic hair and a taste for skulls and crossbones. I love it. It has the feel of a glamorous, anarchic cult. Death, I suspect, has always drawn this kind of response from the young. As mainstream society pushes it away, so the fringes and alternative sub-cultures embrace it. You don't like this stuff? Okay, we definitely do then. And from these fringes have come some of the most original, articulate and creative voices. They include Carla Valentine, pathologist and technical curator at Barts Pathology Museum, who brought death to life via her blog, *thechickandthedead.com*, and book, *Past Mortems* (2017), and John Crow and Katy Kaos, who created a shrine at Cross Bones burial ground in Southwark to celebrate the outcast dead – the prostitutes buried beyond the sanctuary of the churchyard. They and many others have done so much to open up the conversation and have a huge and varied following.

The work of honouring those who have been marginalised or overlooked is reflected in many different ways. The queer people who died from AIDS were initially at best ignored and at worst vilified in the mainstream media because of their sexual orientation. The creation of the AIDS remembrance quilt (*www.aidsmemorial.org/interactive-aids-quilt*), which grew from 1,920 panels in 1987 to some 48,000, the sheer scale of the project and its ambitious public display finally brought the enormity of those losses to public attention with great beauty and creativity. Other absences remain unnoticed in plain sight, and I applaud Amy Padnani (2019) for retrospectively celebrating the unsung stories of many women and men of colour since taking up her position as an obituary writer at the *New York Times*. How we die and are remembered is all about how we live in our society and our community.

Having the conversation

Dr Rachel Clarke (2020) compares preparing for end of life to doing our tax return, clearing out the garage or thinking about damage to the environment. We put it off until we are forced to do it, or we never get around to it. She regards it not so much as taboo as something we just don't want to face. I feel the taboo still holds in our culture. I encounter so many people who think that talking about death will bring it closer – that it will jinx them. If you don't name it, you will stay safe. It is often easier to approach the subject with people you are not close to. This may seem unlikely. Why talk to strangers? But those closest to us are also those most emotionally affected by hearing us talk about our death, and it can be a very valuable rehearsal to approach the subject with strangers on more neutral ground. More and more initiatives exist to try to kickstart these conversations we all dread and tend to avoid, and the revelation is they are often fun, surprising and touching. The Death Café movement, brought to England by Jon Underwood, has spread worldwide and you can find out where they are happening by visiting the website (see Resources). The Church of England has produced a useful set of cards called Grave Talk (see Resources) that can also be used to stimulate conversation. Using the categories Life, Death, Society, Funerals and Grief, the cards pose a series of questions of which only two out of 50 have any overt religious connotations. For example, they ask: Have you seen a dead body? What are the reasons for a funeral? How would you like to be remembered? You do not have to answer the questions. You can just use them as a litmus test to find out what you are ready to talk about.

All these groups are facilitated by people who can ensure that confidentiality is observed and that everyone gets a chance to speak if they wish to and is properly heard without interruption. Sometimes, gatherings have an overt focus on more practical tasks. The Men's Shed movement was set up to encourage men to come together to work on tasks such as mending or making household and other items and has proved to be a place where they also support one another emotionally. Working alongside someone at a lathe or making a timely cup of tea can be equally valuable in supporting a person as they grieve.

A basket-maker friend teaches coffin-weaving courses, and reports that extraordinary conversations arise from this, unlike those on any of her other courses. The simple act of speaking and listening should never be underestimated. Traditionally, the priest would have responded to some of the fears and doubts around death among his congregation, and, as Walter rightly observes (1996), the therapist has, to some extent, taken on this role. It has never been the official remit of doctors, although many are privy to people's profoundest concerns and are usually better able to treat them as a consequence. For those living alone, without close family nearby, these may be their only opportunities.

Our community at the burial ground revolves around wellies and cups of tea. Often people working side by side, planting trees, have found they have much in common and have exchanged phone numbers and forged friendships. Not everyone wants to talk, of course. However, it is my experience that most people who come to me professionally or personally take up that opportunity when it is offered to them. I hope this book can help facilitate a few more such conversations.

References

Byron, A. (2016). *Alice Byron: Talking as much normal lifestyle as possible whilst learning to live with MDS.* alicebyron.com

Channel 4. (2019, 7 August). *Jade: The reality star who changed Britain.* www.channel4.com/programmes/jade-the-reality-star-who-changed-britain/on-demand/68301-003

Clarke, R. (2020). *Dear life: A doctor's story of love and loss.* Little, Brown.

Cremation Society. (1874). *Declaration.* www.cremation.org.uk/history-of-cremation-in-the-united-kingdom#declaration

Davies, D. (2015). *Mors Britannica: Lifestyle and deathstyle in Britain today.* Oxford University Press.

Dignity in Dying. (2020). *Assisted dying: The case for change.* Dignity in Dying.

Doughty, C. (2015). *Smoke gets in your eyes and other lessons from the crematorium.* Canongate.

Fitzgerald, C. (Presenter). (2020, January 19). *The coffin club.* BBC World Service. www.bbc.co.uk/programmes/w3ct047r

Gawande, A. (2014). *On being mortal.* Profile Books.

Gould, P. (2013). *When I die: Lessons from the death zone.* Abacus.

Granger, K. (2016). *Hello, my name is...* http://hellomynameis.org.uk/home and http://drkategranger.wordpress.com

Greene, G. (1969). *Travels with my aunt.* Penguin.

Holloway, R. (2018). *Waiting for the last bus: Reflections on life and death.* Canongate.

Loncraine, R. (2018). *Skybound.* Picador.

Maloney, A. (2020, February 1). *Digital sadness.* Four Thought. BBC Radio 4. www.bbc.co.uk/programmes/m000dqfl

Miller, D. (2017). *The comfort of people*. Polity Press.

Mitford, J. (1978). *The American way of death*. Simon & Schuster.

Mitford, J. (1998). *The American way of death revisited*. Alfred A. Knopf.

The Natural Death Centre. (2012). *The natural death handbook* (5th ed.). The Natural Death Centre.

Padnani, A. (2019, June). *How we're honoring people overlooked by history.* TEDtalk. www.ted.com/talks/amy_padnani_how_we_re_honoring_people_overlooked_by_history

Stevens, E., Jackson, S. & Milligan, S. (Eds.). (2009). *Palliative nursing: across the spectrum of care*. Wiley.

Valentine, C. (2017). *Post-mortems: Life and death behind mortuary doors*. Sphere.

Walter, T. (1996). Facing death without tradition. In: Howarth, G. & Jupp, P.C . (Eds.). *Contemporary issues in the sociology of death, dying and disposal* (pp. 193–204). Macmillan.

Resources

Books

Anastasios, A. (2010). *Dying to know: Bringing death to life*. Hardie Grant Publishing.

Aries, P. (1982). *The hour of our death: The classic history of western attitudes toward death over the last one thousand years*. Vintage.

Doughty, C. (2015). *Smoke gets in your eyes and other lessons from the crematorium*. Canongate.

Kellehear, A. (2007). *A social history of dying*. Cambridge University Press.

Mitford, J. (1963, 2000). *The American way of death revisited*. Vintage Books.

Rentzenbrink, C. (2015). *The last act of love: The story of my brother and his sister*. Picador.

Walter, T. (2017). *What death means now: Thinking critically about dying and grieving*. Policy Press.

West, K. (2010). *A guide to natural burial*. Sweet & Maxwell.

Other resources

Davies, B. (2015). *Grave Talk Cards: A cafe space to talk about death, dying and funerals*. Church House Publishing. www.chpublishing.co.uk/features/grave-talk

Websites

Association for the Study of Death & Society: www.deathandsociety.org

Centre for Death and Society, Bath University: www.bath.ac.uk/research-centres/centre-for-death-society

Coffin Club: www.coffinclub.co.uk ('A safe space to plan and cost your perfect send-off')

Coma and Disorders of Consciousness Research Centre: https://cdoc.org.uk

Commission on the Value of Death: https://commissiononthevalueofdeath.wordpress.com (An independent commission set up to review the medicalisation of death and grieving, advanced directives, assisted suicide, palliative care, the concept of a good death, and the pursuit of immortality)

Compassion in Dying: https://compassionindying.org.uk (Supports people to use their existing rights within the law)

Compassionate Communities UK: www.compassionate-communitiesuk.co.uk

Death Café Movement: www.deathcafe.com

Death Reference Desk: www.deathreferencedesk.org (Online reference library for 'all things death: the bizarre, the batty and the beautiful, from interesting blogs and recommended books to commentary and analysis of death in the news')

Dignity in Dying: www.dignityindying.org.uk Centre for Death and Life Studies, University of Durham: www.dur.ac.uk/cdals

Hospice Biographers: www.thehospicebiographers.com (Nationwide charity that trains and mentors specialist volunteers to record the life stories of patients in UK hospices)

Living Well Dying Well: www.livingwelldyingwell.net (Training for death dualas)

Natural Death Centre: www.naturaldeath.org.uk

OMEGA – Journal of Death and Dying: https://journals.sagepub.com/home/ome

Soul Midwives: www.soulmidwives.co.uk

The Future Cemetery: www.futurecemetery.org (Provides the space for high quality research, innovation and creative exploration into the social, cultural and technological aspects of end of life, death and remembrance)

Films / Talks

How to Die: Simon's Choice (2016). Rowan Deacon (Dir.). Minnow Films production.

Sir Terry Pratchett: Shaking Hands with Death (2010). The Richard Dimbleby Lecture. BBC One.

Outside the Box

Postscript: Covid-19

Books will be written about Covid-19, but (as I put the final touches to this collection in early September 2020) it has felt too soon to seek stories of those affected closely by the pandemic. I include these two, which were given to me and which speak to certain aspects of the experience.

Who will hold my hand?
We had long ago divorced, and were all-but strangers, except that we would always be tied by the two golden threads of our relationship… our children.

The years sped by, too fast, until we both slipped into that uncomfortable realisation that we were getting old. Sometimes there would be conversations with my son and daughter that 'Things aren't so good with his Parkinson's… He's had a fall… I've had to go down again… We're getting in some extra care…' All this before the cloud of Covid dropped its bombshell on us all.

I could only be there for my son and daughter, but when the lockdown took place, none of us could be anywhere for anyone in the way we normally would. Our arms, so anxious to enfold those we loved, hung useless, and the hands with which we would tenderly touch another's were grappling with Skype or Zoom or a mobile phone, in our attempts to somehow keep in touch. It wasn't just the feeling of deep frustration that surfaced then but also an overwhelming sense of guilt.

Their father fell again and was hospitalised, but it was soon clear he could not cope at home, and a place was found for him in a local care home, in the middle of the pandemic. Only a few days later, he started showing signs of the virus.

My daughter spent time talking with me about the agonies she felt around all that was going on without her and her brother being able to be involved, and the stress was leaving everyone exhausted. In the end, she was able to visit him under very strict guidance, with personal protective equipment in place. That was a great comfort, but two days later he slipped away, and she felt guilty that she had not gone back for those final hours.

Lockdown was easing a little by the time of the funeral, but it was a strange experience as there were just four of us there for the saddest of send-offs. We emerged into bright sunlight, feeling only an emptiness and sadness that we had not been able to fulfil even this basic rite of sharing his life with all his friends and sending him off well.

All this happened in May 2020. It is now August, bringing the worries of a second wave. Sometimes I wonder if this will be my experience. Who will hold my hand? And I pray that I will find strength to face it, whatever the answer to that question.

What if?

Sometimes I wonder if my mother's death would have been different had it not happened during the Covid lockdown. Maybe if she'd been able to see the doctor face to face, he might have realised how ill she was earlier on. Maybe if her friends had been able to visit her, she might have found reserves of energy to keep going. Or if she had still been able to go out to concerts and plays and restaurants – would that have made a difference?

None of that really matters now. The things that do matter, at least to me, are that her last days were spent at home, with her family around her. Whatever Covid regulations were or weren't in place at the time didn't matter anymore – we were a 'bubble', supporting my mother through the final stages of her journey and that was the most important thing for all of us.

How do you know when a person is dying? Sometimes you can tell. I remember when I worked in a care home, watching an old lady, Alice, slowly dying from the feet up, the life literally draining from her body over the course of a day, until finally she stopped breathing and lay there, peaceful and serene. But that's the exception. Death is a messy, unpredictable affair that keeps you guessing right up until the end.

I thought Mum was nearing the end, so wasn't surprised when the doctor said that her blood tests indicated 'something sinister, probably cancer', though the weeks to months that he suggested she had left actually turned out to be a matter of a few days. Mum knew. On that Thursday (the day after my conversation with her doctor), with the rain pouring down outside, she wanted her three children there with her, so she could say goodbye. And so we gathered, like in a Chekov play, and there was laughter and tears and reminiscing. And then we waited. But real life isn't a play. Things don't happen as they should. People don't just say their farewells and then roll over and breathe their last.

It's awkward – waiting for someone to die. You don't want to admit that's what you are doing, even if it is for the best. Such a tangle of emotions. And so it was with my mum. Over the next 48 hours, she became steadily weaker, the days punctuated by visits from the district nurses administering drugs to keep her as comfortable as possible. Until, on Sunday morning, after several hours of restlessness, when all I could do was to wipe her face with a cooling flannel and hope that the nurse turned up soon to give another dose of drugs, she took a few last gulps of air and relaxed into death. I know it's a cliché, but she did look so beautiful and peaceful lying there, it really was as though she had drifted off into the deepest sleep imaginable, from which she could wake refreshed and completely renewed.

Would it have made a difference if there had been no such thing as the Covid virus, throwing all our lives up the air at once? I don't think it would have altered the timescales or the outcome: my mum would still have died when she did. But what it did do was to somehow clear away a lot of the 'clutter' of our lives and give us a chance to focus on what was really important – my mother, how special she was, and how much she meant to each one of us.

And that theme was carried through to her funeral too, a beautiful woodland burial, with the sun shining and the skylarks singing. Because of Covid, the number of attendees was limited to 20, just enough for immediate family and a couple of close friends. And it offered the opportunity for a real intimacy, giving everyone a chance to share their memories as part of the celebration, and people opened up in a way that was touching and memorable. And now my mum is resting in the earth, beside my dad, where she always wanted to be. And there is a peace, for all of us.

Commentary – *Liz Rothschild*

It will require a longer view to understand the full impact of the virus on many aspects of our lives, so this will be brief. The many inequalities in our society, particularly around poverty and race, were brutally revealed, as was our level of trust in government and each other. We discovered that employers could , after all, be flexible about working patterns. Thousands of people stepped forward to support each other and their local community. Death moved straight up everyone's agenda, and with it emerged a lot of the fear that I believe is always part of our daily lives but often suppressed. It emerged in the face of the very real possibility of dying, and even when the risk was less immediate. Attendance at online death cafés and requests for therapeutic and other forms of support rocketed. What was forced upon both those ill and dying and the bereaved was an isolation that runs contrary to everything that current work around death and dying has been promoting. Efforts were made to bridge gaps with technology, overstretched staff did what they could, but humans usually need the comfort of those they know at these times, and the reassurance of touch – forbidden to the families of the elderly in their care homes and the dying in hospitals, due to Covid precautions.

The bereaved could not attend funerals where Covid-19 was involved, and only limited numbers could be present at other funerals. In some countries, the only way to handle the speed of deaths was to create mass graves. The epidemic will, I suspect, leave many people with trauma arising out of these lonely deaths and the lonely bereavements that followed.

It was noticeable that, when government guidelines were drawn up around social gatherings, weddings were covered, but not funerals, despite them being all-too relevant. It was months before the guidelines included the instruction that people should wear masks when visiting a funeral director. I do not think these omissions were accidental. I think it is another manifestation of the squeamishness about bringing death openly into our lives.

For many people around the world, life always feels fragile and unpredictable; now the more affluent West has been exposed to new levels of uncertainty and feels in the grip of forces beyond its control. The truth is that this is in many ways always true, wherever you live.

Outside the Box

The storytellers

Gail Abbott
Jenny Allen
Claire Anagnostopulos
Susie Armsden
Yaa Asare
Razia Aziz
Sarah Baurez
Sophie Bishops Lynham
Kate Boddy
Jo Bousfield
Margaret Bradshaw
Rebecca Brain
Sue Brayne
Jane Broom
Eleanor Brown
Mhari Brown
Bev Bulmer
Anna Butcher
Calypso
Lizzie Cambray
Gillian Cameron
Jamie Carr
Rachael Chadwick
Jo Clarke
Mary Ann Clements
Mary Colwell
Jane Coutanche
Lindsey Cuthill
Ruby Debonnaire
Gordon Dowell
Jane Duncan Rogers
Lynn Dunne

Mary Dunsford
Ann Durnell
Jimmy Edmonds
Joy Elliott
Judith Emmanuel
Vivienne Ettinghausen
Alison Farmer
Kathy Fawcett
Duncan Forbes
Laura Forman
Oliver Fox
Kathy Freeman
Deborah Glass-Woodin
Zoe Goodman
Janet Green
Wendy Halford
Rosie Harper
Martin Hawes
Abigail Hehir
Gabrielle Hock
Ruth Holland
Jayne Howard
Rachel Hughes
Ebinehita Iyere
Lucy James
Louise Jenkins
Pat Johnson
Joe and Norah Kennedy
Sylvia Lancaster
Anita Luby
Rosanne Mackenzie
Mary Maltby

Anne Margetts
Dr Louella Matsunaga
Hazel May
Uschi May
Laura McCormack-Long
George Monbiot
Dani Morgan
Adele Moss
Figen Murray
Nam
Louise Nuttall
Rose-Anne O'Hare
Sarah Oliver
Phoenix Rising group
Jan Power
Mandy Preece
Claire Preston
Fiona Quinn
Katie Reynolds
Liz Rider
Terry Rigby
Katie Roberts
Liz Rothschild
Isabel Russo
Natalie Santana
Anne Schilizzi
Bob Shaw
Jackie Singer
Sue Smart
Yuli Sømme
Alison Sorlie
Claire Stagg
Wyon Stansfeld
Barton Stephen
Brother Stuart
Hilary Sturgeon
Charlotte Swarbrick
Ann Tandy-Treiber
Rachel Thompson
Cathy Turbinskyj
Karen Turner
Susan Turner

Karen and Sjoerd Vogt
Marguerite Wallis
Pete Wallis
Tess Ward
Jane Watkins
Lindsay Wheatley
Bob Whorton
Trish Wickstead and Gill Palmer
Lucy Wilkinson-Moore
Judith Williams
Thomas Williams
Sue Wilson
Georgia Wingfield-Hayes
Nicho Wooding
Jacqueline Woodward Smith
Annabelle Zinovieff

The artists

Jake Attree
Born in York in 1950, Attree attended the art school there in the late 1960s, going on to Liverpool College of Art on what was then the Diploma in Art & Design (DipAD) course, and later to the Royal Academy Schools to do post-graduate studies. In 1987, he and his wife returned to Yorkshire, moving to the world heritage village of Saltaire. He has a studio in Dean Clough, Halifax, and exhibits regularly, both nationally and internationally. His work is held by numerous private and public collections in Britain and abroad. Drawing is fundamental to his practice; it is, he has said 'how I explain the world to myself, wordlessly'. Attree is currently engaged on a collaborative project for Fine Press Poetry with the poet Michael Symmons Roberts. He is represented internationally by Messum's of Cork Street. The pictures are pen and ink drawings.

Julia Ball
Trained as a printmaker at Reading Art School, Julia has lived in Cambridge since the 1960s, where she also taught painting at Anglia Ruskin College. Her longstanding concern is to use the colour she finds in the East Anglian landscape to explore light, water, the seasons and particular times of day. Her aim is to balance the visual with her own sensation of a particular moment. The surface of the canvas, its proportion, is crucial to the form of each painting, as is the translucency of the oil paint for the colour to express both her internal and external experience. Alongside her paintings, she has always made prints and drawings, frequently of plants. *www.juliaball.org*

Meg Buick
Meg has lived in Rome, Leeds and London and is currently based in Bristol. Since completing her postgraduate degree at the Royal Drawing School, she has specialised in painting and printmaking, with drawing always at the core of her practice. Meg has won various travel scholarships. She spent two months drawing in Madrid as an artist in residence at the Museo del Prado and was the recipient of an RBA scholarship that enabled her to spend a month in Rome. She co-founded the printmaking studio Cato Press, where she also teaches. *www.megbuick.co.uk*

Halima Cassell
Halima was born in 1975 in Pakistan, brought up in Lancashire and now lives in Shropshire. She works mainly in clay and her varied, multi-cultural background is tangibly present in her work, which is always sculptural. A natural creativity presented itself at an early age and was nurtured through an art-based education, an undergraduate degree in 1997 and an MA in 2002. Fusing her Asian roots with a fascination for African pattern work and her deep passion for architectural geometry, Cassell's work is intense yet playful, structured yet creative and invariably compelling in its originality. Her work uses definite lines and dramatic angles to try to manifest the universal language of numbers and create an unsettling sense of movement. Her simple forms maximise the impact of the complex surface patterns in combination with heavily contrasting contours. *info@halimacassell.com | www.halimacassell.com*

Hugh Cowling
Hugh Cowling (b.1990, Lincoln UK) is an illustrator, composer and animation director based in Bristol. Hugh's work often deals with sensitive and difficult subject matter through use of metaphor, texture and subtlety. There are two pieces of his work in this book. The first, 'Gestalt', is made entirely from scraps and off-cuts found in the print room at his studio in Bristol. The second, 'Skeleton Leaf', which closes the book, is a monoprint. *www.hughcowling.co.uk*

Clare Davis
Recapturing a dream of youth, Clare has become an exploratory artist in later life, working mainly in ink, wire and textile. She is founder of the Pop-Up Arts Collective, a diverse community of painters, sculptors, photographers, wordsmiths, makers and mixed-media artists who have made a connection through family, friendship and creativity. They share a commitment to their artistic journeys, equality and access and come together for workshops, creative conversations, residencies and exhibitions. Clare is a facilitator, mentor and tutor and works creatively with individuals and groups to encourage the creative flow, often working towards exhibition and communicating a story with a broad and dynamic approach to what art is and who artists are. *www.popupartscollective.co.uk*

Louis Debonnaire Ward
Louis is four years old and lives with his mum, dad and baby sister in Easton, Bristol. Life is good for Louis; his best friends live in the house next door; it's handy having neighbours who are also your godparents. Louis likes to eat a lot of food but is still always hungry. In his garden he has a hammock, an apple tree and a Wendy house, which he was once found redecorating with an entire tub of white emulsion paint. He likes to get stuck in with these sorts of tasks…

Louis wouldn't call himself an artist, but is pleased as punch to have his picture displayed in Lizzie's book.

Jemma Gunning
Jemma's practice researches into industrial decline, exploring abandoned spaces that have been left to fall into disrepair. Jemma's work asks us to slow down and consider the buildings that too many of us just walk straight past and ignore. Each location she documents deserves to be remembered, with all their underlying social heritage and cultural history. Drawing underpins her practice and she specialises in etching and stone lithography, using an enforced decay, whereby acids erode metal and physically alter the surface of a limestone, echoing with the natural decay of the architectural forms she draws. She is a technical instructor at UWE, a printmaking fellow at the City and Guilds School of Art in London and a founder member of the Bristol Print Collective, who deliver pop-up workshops in galleries, festivals and community spaces, aiming to keep the traditions of printmaking alive by offering accessible and engaging workshops for all. *@jemma_gunning_printmaker* | *www.jemmagunning.com*

Carol Honess
Carol is an artist and printmaker living and working in the beautiful Cotswold countryside of the Stroud Valleys. She is a member of the Gloucestershire Printmaking Co-Operative and has her studio at Pegasus Art Shop. She works from here and from her home, Fern Cottage. Her work is inspired always by the intricacies and patterns of the natural world, its rhythms and seasons. She specialises in ink drawing, and her detailed drawings – usually of birds, trees and insects – are sometimes realistic, sometimes imaginative. Many of these are then handprinted by the artist to make unique and affordable editioned prints, some of which are then also hand coloured. The featured image, 'Fallen nest', is typical of this, showing the beautiful but fragile constructions made by nature. *carolhoness@gmail.com* | Instagram: *fern_cottage_studio* | Etsy: *Fern Cottage Studio*

Wren Hughes
Wren is a sculptor and creative arts therapist. She originally trained as a sculptor in the studios of Sally Arnup and John Skeaping RA and went on to study sculpture at the City and Guilds School of Art in London. Her work has been exhibited internationally over the last 40 years. The materials she uses vary from drawing, painting and printmaking to sculpture in paper, welded steel, wax and bronze. Her themes of death, transition and rebirth are an ongoing inquiry into the void and its significance in the creative process. Wren's retreats and contemplative art groups offer a combination of silence and creative expression, an invitation to live in the moment and trust what comes, moving beyond the

world of known and expectation into the world of the unknown and unlimited potential. *www.wrenhughes.co.uk*

Kate Lynch
Kate takes rural Somerset as her subject matter – the wetland landscape, its people and its traditions. She paints with a low-key palette or makes drawings with charcoal made from locally grown Somerset willow – enjoying its velvety blacks and atmospheric tones. Kate mixes her own art with teaching, community projects and local history and has produced several books of paintings and drawings of Somerset farming life, which include reminiscences from her subjects. She is a founder member of a local troupe of actors, The Langport Mummers, who perform a reinvigorated ancient play in pubs and Wassails at the turn of the year, and occasionally this features in her artwork. The winter starling murmurations at dusk above the reed beds nearby are also sometimes the inspiration for drawings. Kate is married to artist James Lynch and they live on a hill overlooking the Somerset Levels. *www.katelynch.co.uk*

Cathy Turbinskyj
Cathy dropped in and out of three art degree courses, eventually discovering gardening as a means of earning a living while bringing the dog to work with her. Making and tending a garden is like painting/sculpting in at least four dimensions, co-creating with natural processes, none all in her control. Thirty years of gardening; more than 30 years of keeping a journal. Poems come out too. Sometimes she sings/performs them. Drawings appear in these journals too. Not so much recently.

Rowan Twine
Rowan is a behavioural insights researcher and part-time creator. Having explored cultures across two continents and three countries, she is currently based in Manchester, UK, where she is completing a Master's in visual anthropology. People are at the centre of her work and she is passionate about understanding their relationships both to each other and their environments. Conducting research through art and creating art through research, she works across a range of mediums, returning most frequently to photography.

Thomas Williams
Thomas is an artist living and working in Wales. He uses, amongst other things, printmaking, writing and performance, drawing, sewing and knitting.

Sarah Woolfenden
Sarah trained at The Slade School of Fine Art in the 70s, then as an art teacher. She lives in North Devon and draws trees and woods on a large scale with fine artist's